WHAT ELCA PASTORS ARE SAYING:

A wonderful tool for the mission of the church written from a biblical, missional, theological, Lutheran, and contextual perspective.

Khader El-Yateem
Salam Arabic Lutheran Church, Brooklyn, NY

The discussion in this book comes at a crucial time. . . . Lutherans want to remain faithful to a God-centered approach to evangelizing, and [this book's] presentation of the proclamation of the gospel is an emblem of this.

James M. Capers
Mission Develop, Indianapolis, IN

This is the most refreshing and reenergizing book I have ever read on becoming an evangelizing church. A new fire burns in my heart to see the church live out the true vision and mission of this message.

Walt Kallastad
Senior Pastor, Community Church of Joy, Glendale, Arizona

Indispensable for everyone interested in the organic growth of the church.

Rayford J. Grady
Pastor, Lutheran Church of the Holy Spirit, Chicago, IL

WHAT ELCA BISHOPS ARE SAYING:

The ELCA Evangelism Task Force longed to provoke our best thinkers to engage the issue of evangelical witness for our church. This book rises to that challenge.

Jon V. Anderson
Bishop, Southwestern Minnesota Synod, Evangelical Lutheran Church in America

I have been praying that we as a denomination would reflect deeply about a Lutheran theology and practice of evangelizing. I thank God for this important contribution to the conversation about mission in the Lutheran Church.

Gary Wollersheim
Bishop, Northern Illinois Synod, Evangelical Luthe

WHAT PRESIDENTS OF ELCA SEM

This book is a strong and reforming proposal f
for its mission. It is a must read for seminary fac
the baptized.

Philip D. Krey
President, Lutheran Theological Seminary at Philadelphia

These authors call for *the resurrection of the evangelizing church.* This *Lutheran* re-claiming of the Gospel's mission imperative is just what we—and the world—need.

Duane H. Larson
President, Wartburg Theological Seminary

WHAT ELCA THEOLOGICAL PROFESSORS ARE SAYING:

This carefully crafted and a welcoming book will generate enthusiasm not only among Lutherans but all those who cherish the Protestant heritage. . . . A sought-after volume at a time when the ELCA is engaging in an Evangelism Strategy.

H.S. Wilson
Professor of Mission and Cultures, Lutheran Theological Seminary at Philadelphia

This timely and practical volume builds on the thesis that Lutherans have a critical contribution to make, but only if the church heeds the call of its own Confessions to become an evangelizing church.

William O. Avery
Professor of Stewardship and Parish Ministry, Lutheran Theological Seminary at Gettysburg

Is there any unique contribution Lutheran theology can bring to an understanding of God's call on the church in North America? Grounded in a Lutheran understanding of God's action in Word and Sacrament, the authors answer "yes!"

Phillip Baker
Associate Professor of Missiology and Evangelism, Lutheran Theological Southern Seminary

The Evangelizing Church offers a thorough analysis of obstacles which Lutherans face in proclaiming and witnessing to the Gospel. It also presents helpful theological insights into the creation of an evangelizing church.

Mark Thomsen
Visiting Professor of Mission, Lutheran School of Theology at Chicago

Serious scholars of mission theology analyze contemporary Lutheran practices in light of Lutheran theology. They offer clear guidance for re-rooting Lutheran practice in the fertile soil of a Lutheran confessional understanding.

Tim Huffman
Professor of Christian Mission, Trinity Lutheran Seminary, Columbus, Ohio

If you: (a) couldn't care less about reading another book on evangelism—tricks, trends, and techniques; (b) are interested in being evangelical without doing evangelism; and (c) believe that Lutherans have something to offer to this conversation; then look no farther than this book.

Nathan C. P. Frambach
Professor of Youth, Culture & Mission, Wartburg Theological Seminary

This book offers an interesting variety of perspectives on Lutheran missionary and evangelistic approaches. It opens up a much-needed discussion.

Frieder Ludwig
Assoc. Professor of Mission & World Christianity, Luther Seminary

This book issues a two-fold challenge: to recognize the essential evangelizing identity of the church that is grounded in the gospel of Jesus Christ; and to actually practice evangelizing in our pluralistic world in light of the confessional foundations in the Lutheran heritage.

Winston D. Persaud
Professor of Systematic Theology, Wartburg Theological Seminary

This book calls for "the death of evangelism" and "the resurrection of an evangelizing church culture." To my knowledge no other group of Lutheran church leaders have provided such a candid analysis and rich agenda.

Patrick Keifert
Professor of Systematic Theology, Luther Seminary

It is not easy to develop a dialectic between the evangelizing vocation of the church and the theology of the cross. This book makes a uniquely Lutheran contribution to the evangelical vocation and challenge for the church.

Charles Amjad-Ali
Professor of Justice and Christian Community & Christian-Muslim Relations, Luther Seminary

WHAT ELCA CHURCHWIDE STAFF ARE SAYING:

As Lutherans, we so often fail to grasp the rich and practical meaning of the word *Evangelical*. This book helps us recapture and resurrect our imagination, vision, and truth-speaking about the *Good News*.

Y. Franklin Ishida
Director for Leadership Development, ELCA Division for Global Mission

Can Lutherans be evangelical? This book uses [justification by grace through faith] to substantiate the claim that evangelism as a program must die so that the priesthood of all believers can flourish through an evangelizing people.

Richard Magnus
Executive Director, Division for Outreach, Evangelical Lutheran Church in America

Working as a community of leaders these scholars have written about a key question for Lutherans: "How do we go about the work of being evangelical?" Anyone in whom that question burns will want to read this book.

Dave Daubert
Executive for Renewal of Congregations, ELCA Division for Outreach

In this book we are called to a resurrection life, and it propels us to be a witnessing church—to be about the task of transforming, releasing, healing, and inspiring.

Kathryn Bradley-Love
Associate Director for Evangelism, Division for Congregation Ministries ELCA

This provocative and challenging contribution offers fresh insights, valuable motivation, and new practices for communities of faith. This is a must read for seminary students, parish pastors, and congregational leaders.

Brent Dahlseng
Director for Evangelism & Prayer Ministries, Division for Congregational Ministries, ELCA

One of my homiletics teachers taught that many good sermons tread the edge of heresy to let the gospel get through. Perhaps the same is true of good books. This book is observational theology, not abstract theory. I think the ideas will preach.

Stanley N. Olson
Executive Director, Division for Ministry, Evangelical Lutheran Church in America

Many American Protestant leaders have observed that Lutheranism could make important contributions to the church if Lutherans would only tap their tradition's theological resources and find their voice. This book sets that agenda.

Mark Wilhelm
Director for Ministry Leadership—Planning, Division for Ministry, ELCA

Are evangelizing passion and wisdom something Lutheran congregations must simply import or outsource? These authors respond with a clear, unanimous "No" and invite readers into identifying the mission resources—and imperatives!—in central Lutheran themes.

Jonathan Strandjord
Director for Theological Education, Division for Ministry, ELCA

WHAT THE GOSPEL AND OUR CULTURE NETWORK (GOCN) PARTICIPANTS ARE SAYING:

Finally, a book that tasks seriously both a church's *confessional* heritage and its *missional* identity! These authors take a hard and honest look at their Lutheran heritage and discover rich resources for "the resurrection of an evangelizing church culture."

George Hunsberger
Professor of Congregational Mission, Western Theological Seminary, Holland, MI

Cruising along with my own biases, I would not have sought out Lutherans for a word on evangelizing. I was not prepared for this invigorating encounter. These authors serve those of us who long for churches that see the world through God's eyes in seeking to participate in the Holy Spirit's ongoing missional initiatives.

Mark Lau Branson
Associate Professor of Practical Theology, Fuller Theological Seminary

An excellent example of how missional church theology can be embraced from within a particular ecclesial tradition. The authors delve into historic confessions and Scripture to connect evangelizing with Word and Sacrament, as well as with a Christian community. May other church traditions follow their example!

Lois Barrett
Director, Great Plains Extension, Associated Mennonite Biblical Seminary

THE EVANGELIZING CHURCH

A LUTHERAN CONTRIBUTION

Editors

Richard H. Bliese
Craig Van Gelder

Contributing Authors
Richard H. Bliese
M. Wyvetta Bullock
Kelly A. Fryer
Craig L. Nessan
J. Paul Rajashekar
Craig Van Gelder

Foreword by Mark S. Hanson

Augsburg Fortress
MINNEAPOLIS

THE EVANGELIZING CHURCH
A Lutheran Contribution

Cover image: © Corbis
Cover design: Lauri Ingram
Book design: James Korsmo

Library of Congress Cataloging-in-Publication Data

The evangelizing church : a Lutheran contribution / editors, Richard H. Bliese,
Craig Van Gelder.
    p. cm.
 Includes bibliographical references and index.
 ISBN 0-8066-5109-1 (alk. paper)
 1. Evangelistic work. 2. Lutheran Church—Doctrines. I. Bliese, Richard H.,
1956- II. Van Gelder, Craig.

 BV3793.E93 2005
 266'.41—dc22

                                                                    2004030681

The paper used in this publication meets the minimum requirements of
American National Standard for Information Sciences — Permanence of Paper
for Printed Library Materials, ANSI Z329.48-1984.

Manufactured in the U.S.A.

09   08   07   06   3   4   5   6   7   8   9   10

CONTENTS

Foreword, *Mark S. Hanson*   ix
Preface, *David L. Tiede*   xi
Project Team Members   xiii

1. A LUTHERAN CONFESSION   1

2. THE GIFT IS A CALL   11

3. ADDRESSING CAPTIVES IN BABYLON   32

4. FOR THE SAKE OF THE WORLD   51

5. CALLED OUT OF OUR COMFORT ZONE   71

6. NAVIGATING DIFFICULT QUESTIONS   92

7. AFTER THE DEATH OF EVANGELISM—THE RESURRECTION
   OF AN EVANGELIZING CHURCH   113

EPILOGUE: A LUTHERAN CONTRIBUTION TO
   AN EVANGELIZING CHURCH   133

Study Guide   138
Annotated Bibliography   148
Notes   154
Index of Topics   170
Index of Names   175

FOREWORD

I am tempted to say from the outset, "Read this book at your own risk," because it challenges us to be the church we all claim to be—evangelical and Lutheran—in more than name only.

Often we seem to act as if those two words are almost in opposition to one another. That is, to be evangelical one cannot be Lutheran, or to be Lutheran one cannot be evangelical. Yet, just as Bonhoeffer challenged the Christian church in his day to hear the call to discipleship and answer it, each of the contributing writers challenges us to recognize that in fact *Lutheran* and *evangelical* are inseparable. To be Lutheran is to be an evangelizing church! To be a baptized believer is to be justified by grace through faith *and* "to proclaim the good news of God in Christ through word and deed." That is our declaration when we affirm our intentions to live in God's baptismal covenant of grace.

This is not a how-to manual for evangelism committees. It goes much deeper than that—to the heart of our identity and purpose as Lutheran Christians. It is not about evangelism at all, but about being an evangelizing church. How wonderfully these writers remind us that we have within the theological gifts of the Lutheran Reformation all we need to be an evangelizing church. Now we need to pray for the power of the Holy Spirit to confront the obstacles that get in our way and to find the courage to live out that call.

It may seem attractive, in the midst of our conflicted world and an increasingly diverse society, to withdraw and live in the security of our faith and our congregations—our Lutheran comfort zones. After we have read this book, this will no longer be an option. By the end, we will all join the Samaritan woman who left her encounter with Jesus at the well running to invite her friends to "come and see this Jesus."

Read, discuss, absorb, and share the book with others—it's not for Lutherans only. Thanks be to God for the witness of these writers and for the joy of proclaiming God's love in Christ for the sake of the world.

Mark S. Hanson
Presiding Bishop
Evangelical Lutheran Church in America

PREFACE

This project had its beginnings in September of 1987, when 550 pastors wrote to the new president at Luther Seminary declaring, in the words of one of them, "Quit preparing your graduates for a church that no longer exists." All of the ELCA seminaries became publicly engaged together in this effort in 1995, when the ELCA churchwide assembly adopted *The Study of Theological Education*. Again the message was clear: "This church needs more and better prepared leaders for a time of mission."

In 1999, the Lilly Endowment awarded Luther Seminary a grant for the purpose of helping to develop such leadership, which was entitled Learning Congregational Leadership in Context. Dr. Craig Van Gelder agreed to direct the implementation of a writing project for the grant to support this initiative, working in coordination with Luther Seminary's strategic plan for 2000–2005, entitled *Serving the Promise of Our Mission*. At the same time, funds from the contextual leadership grant were used in 2000 and 2001 to convene conversations among missiologists from all the ELCA seminaries, and staff from several churchwide agencies, to share what was being learned about leadership development. Dr. Richard Bliese, at the time from the Lutheran School of Theology at Chicago, agreed to host these conversations.

At the third annual gathering of this group in 2002, the missiologists were invited to offer a critique of the emerging work of the ELCA Evangelism Task Force. The lack of attention in this work to theological foundations for evangelism led Craig Van Gelder and Richard Bliese to gather the writing team that pursued this present project. This team was intentionally formed to represent the broader network of institutions within the ELCA, including faculty from four seminaries, a staff member of a churchwide agency, and a local pastor.

The challenge of these essays lies in their conviction that our Lutheran confessional tradition finds its fruition in its *missional* engagement. Historically identified in European Christendom as "evangelical" in contrast to the "Catholic" church, the focal calling of this tradition is no longer its conservation of pure doctrine in the wars of Christendom, but our public confession of the Christian faith in a world of many cultures and religions.

The promise of this work extends far beyond the academic origins of these essays. This is theology for Christian ministry, even confessional theology in service of public witness. Here theological teachers of the church seek to set the tradition free from cautions and constraints that have impeded the church's apostolic calling. Nothing less is intended than a renewal of the commission to make disciples of all nations, calling all people to faith in Jesus Christ and sending the faithful to the work God gives them in the world.

God only knows where this effort will lead. But if the church's theological faculties can be converted in service of the mission of the Triune God, this project is a sign that God is up to something in the renewal of this confessional church to its evangelical calling.

David L. Tiede
President and Professor of New Testament
Luther Seminary

PROJECT TEAM MEMBERS

RICHARD H. BLIESE is professor of mission and academic dean of Luther Seminary in St. Paul, Minnesota. Before coming to Luther Seminary, Richard Bliese was the Augustana Heritage Professor of Mission and Evangelism at the Lutheran School of Theology at Chicago. In addition to teaching at LSTC, he served for thirteen years as pastor of St. Andrews Lutheran Church in Glenwood, Illinois. He is a graduate of Christ Seminary-Seminex in St. Louis and finished his doctoral studies in the theology of Dietrich Bonhoeffer at LSTC. He is the author, with Steve Bevans, of the English edition of the *Dictionary of Mission*. Richard is the primary author of chapter three, "Addressing Captives in Babylon," and coauthor of chapter one, "A Lutheran Confession."

M. WYVETTA BULLOCK is executive director of the Division for Congregational Ministries in the Evangelical Lutheran Church in America. She has served on ELCA churchwide staff since 1987. Prior to that, she served for six years in the Division for Parish Services of the Lutheran Church in America. Her graduate degrees include a Master of Divinity and Doctor of Ministry in preaching from the Lutheran School of Theology at Chicago. She has an honorary Doctor of Humane Letters from Grand View College in Des Moines, Iowa, and in 2003 received the Distinguished Alumni Award from the Lutheran School of Theology at Chicago. She is ordained in the ELCA and has served as pastoral associate at Bethel Lutheran Church in Chicago for the past fifteen years. Wyvetta is the primary author of chapter five, "Called Out of Our Comfort Zone."

KELLY A. FRYER is assistant professor of congregational leadership at Luther Seminary in St. Paul, Minnesota. She was ordained as a pastor in the Evangelical Lutheran Church in America in 1989. Her first call was to a congregation in rural northern Illinois. She served as pastor to a redeveloping mission congregation in the Chicago area from 1992 to 2003. Kelly has been a member of the Transformational Ministries Team of the ELCA (Division for Outreach) since 1999 and was a member of the ELCA's Task Force on Evangelism. She has authored three books published by Augsburg Fortress: *No Experience Necessary: On-the-Job Training for a Life of Faith*; *Dancing down the Hallway: Spiritual Reflections for the Everyday*; and *Reclaiming the "L" Word: Renewing the Church from Its Lutheran Core*. She has also served as contributing editor for *A Story Worth Sharing: Engaging Evangelism*. Kelly is the primary author of chapter two, "The Gift Is a Call."

CRAIG L. NESSAN is professor of contextual theology and academic dean at Wartburg Theological Seminary in Dubuque, Iowa. Ordained in 1978, his ministry experience includes pastorates at Trinity Evangelical Lutheran Church in Philadelphia, Pennsylvania, and St. Mark Lutheran Church in Cape Girardeau, Missouri. His graduate degrees include a master of divinity and master of sacred theology from Wartburg Theological Seminary and a doctorate in systematic theology from the University of Munich. He is the author of *Beyond Maintenance to Mission: A Theology of the Congregation*; *Give Us This Day: A Lutheran Proposal for Ending World Hunger*; and *Many Members, Yet One Body: Committed to Same-Gender Relationships and the Mission of the Church*. Craig is the primary author of chapter seven, "After the Death of Evangelism—The Resurrection of an Evangelizing Church Culture" and "Epilogue: A Lutheran Contribution to an Evangelizing Church."

J. PAUL RAJASHEKAR is Luther D. Reed Professor of Systematic Theology and academic dean at the Lutheran Theological Seminary at Philadelphia. Prior to joining the seminary faculty at LTSP in 1991, he served the Lutheran World Federation as executive secretary for "Church and People of Other Faiths" in the Department of Studies. Originally from India, he received his seminary education at the United Theological College, Bangalore, and Concordia Seminary-Seminex. He holds a doctorate of philosophy from the University of Iowa and has served pastorates in India and in Iowa. He is the editor of *Religious Pluralism and Lutheran Theology*; *New Religious Movements and the Churches*; *Islam in Asia*; and *Asian Ministry: Which Way*. Paul is the primary author of chapter six, "Navigating Difficult Questions."

CRAIG VAN GELDER is professor of congregational mission at Luther Seminary in St. Paul, Minnesota. He came to this position in 1998 after teaching for ten years as professor of domestic missiology at Calvin Theological Seminary. Ordained in the Presbyterian Church (USA) in 1984, he now serves as an ordained minister in the Christian Reformed Church. His ministry background includes ten years of campus ministry and ten years of serving as a church consultant and on a presbytery staff. His graduate degrees include a master of divinity from Reformed Theological Seminary, a doctor of philosophy in mission from Southwestern Baptist Theological Seminary, and a doctor of philosophy in administration in urban affairs from the University of Texas at Arlington. He is coeditor with George R. Hunsberger of *The Church between Gospel and Culture*, editor of *Confident Witness—Changing World*, and author of *The Essence of the Church*. Craig is the primary author of chapter four, "For the Sake of the World," and coauthor of chapter one, "A Lutheran Confession."

KRISTINE M. STACHE is a doctoral student (ABD) at Luther Seminary in St. Paul, Minnesota, in congregational mission and leadership. Presently she serves as Director of Partnership for Missional Church with Church Innovations Institute. She has three years' experience serving as a missionary in Japan. She also worked for eleven years in congregations, developing ministries for children, youth, and family, and most recently served as Director of Congregational Ministry Development at Shepherd of the Hills in Shoreview, Minnesota. She received her master of arts in congregational lay ministry from Luther Seminary in 2002. Kris served as administrative assistant for all aspects of this writing project, compiled the bibliography, and authored the annotated bibliographies for the study guide.

CHAPTER 1

A LUTHERAN CONFESSION

Mark Noll, in a recent article entitled "American Lutherans Yesterday and Today," raised an important question about a Lutheran contribution to Christian ministry in our contemporary twenty-first-century postmodern context. He puts the issue this way: "Whether Lutherans are in a position to offer [any contribution] from their own tradition to Americans more generally would seem to depend on two matters: on how much genuine Lutheranism is left in American Lutherans, and on whether Lutherans can bring this Lutheranism to bear."[1] This challenge certainly relates to the issue of evangelizing, because evangelizing is a ministry area about which Lutherans are often conflicted or ambivalent.

Lutherans have a confession to make. As is readily apparent, this statement has a double meaning that stands at the heart of this book. The authors believe that in relationship to evangelizing there is much that Lutherans have not done, or have not done well—Lutherans have a confession to make. But we also believe that, in relationship to evangelizing, Lutherans have an incredible theological heritage upon which to draw, especially when viewed from a missional perspective—Lutherans have a confession to make.

Lutherans Have a Confession to Make: What We Have Not Done or Have Not Done Well

There are at least three different positions various Lutherans take when it comes to evangelizing. A position taken by some is the tendency to be *skeptical*—to approach the whole issue of evangelizing from the perspective of plausible deniability. In this approach, Lutherans frame the issue of evangelizing in a variety of ways, such as the following:

1

- Evangelizing is proselytizing and, as such, should be avoided.
- Evangelizing is part of the whole colonial era of missions about which the church needs to repent.
- Evangelizing is out of step with the present reality of religious pluralism, and we need to respect the faith traditions of other people.

These perspectives take the approach of canceling out the necessity of evangelizing on the grounds of its negative consequences, whether perceived or real. The skeptical view seems to believe that the establishment of a negative assertion removes the requirement of having to address any constructive argument for the necessity of evangelizing.

Other Lutherans take a position that tends to be very *pragmatic*—to approach evangelizing in a programmatic way. Often in reaction to the skeptical position, these Lutherans stress the necessity of a congregation having an explicit evangelistic program. Unfortunately, Lutherans are better borrowers than creators of such approaches and have often ended up doing cut-and-paste versions of programs such as:

- Evangelism Explosion
- Four Spiritual Laws
- Church Growth
- Alpha

These programs can certainly contribute something toward a Lutheran understanding of evangelizing. But they usually carry within them untested assumptions about such matters as decision theology and sanctification that do not fit very well within a Lutheran confessional understanding.

Still other Lutherans tend to *romanticize* evangelizing—to understand everything the church does as an expression of evangelizing. In this approach, evangelizing ends up being understood to include such things as:

- living a good Christian moral life as a witness to the world;
- providing a clothes closet or food pantry for those in need;
- speaking up against an injustice in the community; and
- being concerned about the ecological stewardship of the earth.

All these activities can certainly be associated with the concept of evangelizing. But they fall short, even collectively, of getting at the heart of an evangelical understanding of the gospel that proclaims salvation by grace through faith that results in the forgiveness of our sins.

Many who tend to romanticize evangelizing are ready to criticize the pragmatists for what they perceive as a selling out of the gospel to evangelical theology. Many on the pragmatic side criticize their romanticizing colleagues for what they perceive as a lack of any clear evangelical center to the gospel they claim to profess.

And both of these groups criticize the skeptics for having compromised the clarity of the Lutheran confessional tradition.

Lutherans Have a Confession to Make by Rereading the Confessional Heritage through a Missional Lens

In contrast to the skeptics, the pragmatists, and those who want to romanticize evangelizing, this book offers an alternative way of engaging in evangelizing from a Lutheran perspective. It is a conception that draws deeply on the Lutheran confessional heritage but does so by rereading this heritage from a missional perspective. In this rereading, the church's identity and ministry are centered in the gospel and are thoroughly grounded in the twin realities of mission and confession. These are essential dimensions for the formation of the evangelizing church.

Evangelizing tends to be a controversial topic among almost all Lutherans.[2] But it is really an odd family quarrel for a church that centers itself on *confession* to be constantly debating about how to give away the faith. This is the *missional* itch that Lutherans are constantly trying to scratch with the fingers of their Reformation tradition, but the itch seems to keep on spreading. The puzzle Lutherans must solve in the twenty-first century is how to marry the concepts of mission and confession in our ministry context of the United States. They need to do this while simultaneously escaping the traps of a skeptical dismissal of evangelizing, a narrow evangelistic pragmatism, and a generalized romanticizing of evangelizing.

Lutherans are a church family united by a common gospel confession that is centered on justification. Yet they tend to be uncomfortable with evangelism—its language, its grammar, its methodology, and its programs. The irony of this mission/confession dilemma is striking. Its history is one that is long and convoluted, and goes back to those famous nineteenth-century Pennsylvanian confrontations that took place between Samuel S. Schmucker and Charles Porterfield Krauth. The aim of the American Lutherans led by Schmucker was to adapt language, historical confessions, and liturgical practices of the German Lutheran Church to meet the changed cultural conditions being experienced in the newly formed United States. Although Krauth was deeply committed to being Lutheran and missionary, he led the "Evangelical Lutheran Church in America" into conservative patterns regarding the orthodox theology, confessions, and the "Old Lutheran" traditions of the Reformation.[3] True Lutheranism should not be the servant of any nationality, language, or cultural entity.

Amazingly, these mission/confession confrontations of the early nineteenth century remain entrenched within much of Lutheranism at the beginning of the twenty-first century. This is certainly true in the Evangelical Lutheran Church in America (ELCA). But the task of addressing evangelizing is now gaining more clarity as the primary audience being served continues to shift. The decline of Lutheran immigrants from Europe during this past century, sometimes referred to as the *boats and babies* strategy, has left many Lutheran congregations in plateau or decline. In place of Lutheran European immigrants, many of these congregations now have immigrants of color from around the world moving into their neighborhoods. Some of these new immigrants are coming as professing Christians, but many of these immigrants profess religious faiths quite different from Christianity. In addition, the larger cultural context has become increasingly secular. In facing these changes, Lutherans are being required to reread their tradition in a way that lifts up both mission and confession. It is a rereading that must not allow these central loci to be either separated or played off against one another. And it is a rereading that can never again allow the gospel to be reduced to the homogeneous-unit principle of congregations serving only their own ethnic communities.

The theology of the gospel as salvation by grace through faith is central to the Lutheran tradition. It serves as a key referent for every decision concerning the praxis of the church. The Lutheran church is not a Johnny-come-lately to this business of proclaiming the gospel of Christ as the power of salvation. Our style, however, has been primarily churchly and sacramental, rather than that of a religious crusade. We have tended not to pursue organized programs or high-powered campaigns to encourage individuals to make decisions for Christ. These theologically foreign methods have worked well for many Baptists, Methodists, Evangelicals, and Pentecostals within the American context. They have even worked for some Lutherans. But should we always be just adapting ourselves to whatever works?

For Lutherans who wonder about how their tradition fits into the missional landscape, there are some elements that can be very helpfully borrowed from other theological traditions. This is possible and also viable because Lutherans are ecumenical in character. But ecumenical borrowing will only work when Lutherans have claimed their own center—their evangelical center. The driving question behind this book, therefore, is not, "What is a uniquely Lutheran evangelistic approach?" Rather, the pressing question is, "What are key Lutheran perspectives that help create an evangelizing church in our context?" Our conviction is that by framing these perspectives, Lutherans will likewise rediscover their own evangelical identity and reclaim a Lutheran understanding of the church.

FRAMING THE ARGUMENT

This argument for an evangelizing church has as its primary subject the Evangelical Lutheran Church in America, although we believe that it relates directly to other Lutheran churches, and also has relevance for the broader church. This argument for an evangelizing church has as its central focus the ministry context of the United States. This context is a regular referent for constructing points within this discussion, because the authors seek to provide theological foundations for helping the ELCA engage this context as an evangelizing church. The authors do not attempt a thorough critique of the current ministry challenges in the context of the United States. Although such a critique would be quite helpful, it would require another book for it to be sufficiently made.

Today we are encountering an important fork in the road in the unfolding story of our church, the Evangelical Lutheran Church in America. Different ecclesiologies are vying to be the heart of Christian mission in our present ministry context. Lutherans are standing at the crossroads trying to decide which way to go. The authors of this book believe that evangelizing lies at the heart of this decision because we believe that it lies at the heart of all mission theology.

If we are correct in our assessment, it means that Lutherans face a double opportunity in our context. First, we have the opportunity to rediscover the missional roots of the Reformation tradition. Second, we have the opportunity to assist fellow Christians to develop a fresh understanding of mission and evangelizing. We believe that this understanding needs to be faithful to the key insights of the Reformation but also crafted for contextually relevant ministry within our world of many cultures and religions.

Since the Reformation, Lutherans have challenged the church with an evangelical proposal for doing theology and ministry. Admittedly, this challenge has remained relatively mute among Lutherans within missiological circles over the past fifty years.[4] But the authors of this volume are convinced that Lutherans are in a strategic position to once again build upon the Reformation's insights regarding human nature and God's grace to address mission and evangelizing. Among the most important elements of historical Lutheranism are Luther's conceptions of human nature and the divine grace that comes to us through the cross of Christ.

Regarding human nature, American confidence regarding our perceived ability to shape a political future and to master human motivations has grown over the past two centuries. In this context, American revivalists have tended to invert spiritual ends and means and have thus gutted Luther's insights about sin and grace. The result has been that American Protestants have lost an important dynamic in evangelizing: an understanding of the depths of human sin and evil in the world and, just as important, the majestic power of God's grace in Christ.

Regarding divine grace, we find that a related casualty has been the Reformation conviction about the nature of salvation. With the perennial confidence that Americans have in human agency and powers, it has been difficult to retain a biblical emphasis on God's work in salvation. Church life in America has a tendency to underscore the importance of spiritual practices: worship, preaching, Bible reading, prayer, spiritual disciplines, and Christian fellowship. These activities have often been defined merely as occasions for human action. That *God calls* people to faith, that *God saves* in the waters of baptism, that *God gives* God's self in bread and wine, that *God announces* God's word through the voice of regular Christians, that *God is the best interpreter* of God's written word—these foundational affirmations of God's saving activity, which no one articulated better than Luther, have been consistently eclipsed by our obsession as Americans with human ability and action.[5]

Do these Reformation insights still work in our context? Yes! Nevertheless, simply handing down Luther's insights packaged within his sixteenth-century worldview and vocabulary will prove insufficient for Christians doing mission today. Lutherans must dig deep within their tradition, but they also must engage their present context to search for a way that mission and confession can connect and ignite a new imagination for ministry in our twenty-first century. This is hard work. It is also risky work. The great challenge of trying to write this book was to discover language for today that informs and motivates for mission and evangelizing while remaining rooted in the Lutheran tradition.

Although the authors choose, in light of Lutheran theological perspectives, to use the concept of evangelizing rather than evangelism, their argument does follow the same basic distinction between mission and evangelism that is found in ecumenical discussions, especially those of the Commission on World Mission and Evangelism of the World Council of Churches. This means that the authors are committed to an understanding of the gospel that is about both belief and a view of redemption that engages all of life.[6] The primary intent of this book is to think theologically about evangelizing within this larger framework of mission, in seeking to inspire the formation of a Lutheran evangelizing church in the world in the twenty-first century.

We want to acknowledge that Dietrich Bonhoeffer's writings have greatly influenced the writing of this book, both in content and tone.[7] Bonhoeffer used risky language throughout his short career. His intent was evangelical in nature. The German church needed to be awakened to rediscover discipleship. When Bonhoeffer spoke of "cheap grace," his critics first thought that he had departed from his Reformation tradition. The opposite was true. "Cheap grace" was creative language that reaffirmed and proclaimed the doctrine of justification in Bonhoeffer's day. This was risky language, but it was the language needed to evangelize the church context.

In Luther's primary Reformation writings, a rich abundance of hints and suggestions about mission and evangelizing is available. However, at first glance, the authoritative Lutheran confessions appear to make no explicit statements about mission theology or the practice of evangelizing. Thus in the late nineteenth century when Christendom started to crack, when overseas missions expanded, and as revivalism emerged at home and abroad, controversy arose among Lutherans regarding how to define mission and evangelizing.[8] Our vocabulary failed us in that context, and controversy over how to talk about evangelism continues to the present time.

In the broader church today, there is much talk about evangelism in terms such as *outreach, church growth, church effectiveness,* or *church planting.* Many voices are advocates of such strategies for evangelism, while others offer a sharp critique of these strategies as overly pragmatic, or being insufficient to convey the substance of the historic Christian faith. This conversation creates dissonance for many Lutherans, because Lutherans often have difficulty clarifying their own position and finding their own voice regarding such strategies.

A shared conviction of the authors of this book is that the Lutheran position and voice can be found only by returning to the basics of the Lutheran tradition. The center of this tradition involves the way that Jesus comes to people in their lives—by grace through faith through the means of Word, Sacrament, and Christian community. An acid test of this project will be whether our language is faithful to the tradition while being effective in communicating these truths to a twenty-first-century audience of church leaders, pastors, seminary students, and seminary faculty who do not share a common vocabulary about evangelizing.

Perhaps most interestingly, Christianity in our context tends to go its own way without the benefit of the Lutheran gift of dialectic, what might be called a gift for *ambiguity*.[9] Many Protestants more easily follow the Calvinist tendency to seek cultural transformation according to a vision of what they believe the kingdom should look like. Other Protestants have moved in the opposite direction, turning their backs on the world in an effort to block out cultural influences they perceive as corrupting the church.

The main point is the following: rarely have Christians in our context utilized Luther's dialectical understanding of how to relate to context and culture. Luther was deeply committed to understanding Christian activity within a specific cultural context, but he always brought to that understanding deep reservations regarding human ability. This is expressed well in the variety of paradoxes found within Lutheranism—simultaneously saint and sinner (*simul justus et peccator*), two kingdoms, law and gospel, and the hidden and revealed character of the theology of the cross. But these have not tended to flourish in our context.

This is where we need to return to the question asked by Mark Noll: "Whether Lutherans are in a position to offer [any contribution] from their own tradition to Americans more generally would seem to depend on two matters: on how much genuine Lutheranism is left in American Lutherans, and on whether Lutherans can bring this Lutheranism to bear."[10] Interestingly, recent missiological writings have essentially dismissed the contributions of the Reformation, especially the Lutheran wing of the Reformation.[11] The authors of this book accept Noll's challenge and in this work frame an argument for understanding mission and evangelizing from a Lutheran perspective.

THE SPECIFICS OF THE ARGUMENT

As noted in the preface, this writing project was funded as part of a grant from the Lilly Endowment to Luther Seminary for *Learning Congregational Leadership in Context*. The six authors of the writing team met seven times over a period of two years to engage this task. The purpose of these meetings was about much more than writing a book on evangelizing. Mutual formation and re-formation of our personal and shared viewpoints was intentionally pursued as a desired outcome. To accomplish this, we engaged in extensive reading of the existing literature on evangelism, focusing especially on Lutheran sources. We engaged in Bible study and reflected deeply on biblical themes related to evangelism. We engaged in extended conversation in seeking to develop shared understandings and a common argument. And often, we engaged in spirited debate in exploring and clarifying our differences, some of which remain among members of the team on various theological points.

What we discovered, however, is that in wrestling for two years with the concept of evangelizing, all the authors were themselves evangelized in significant ways. We are grateful for the process, the marvelous conversations, and the shared outcome. Each author took primary responsibility for writing one chapter, but each chapter was carefully reviewed and critiqued at least twice by the entire team. This means that the overall argument of this book is a shared perspective among all of the authors.

This introduction was coauthored by the editors of this book, Richard Bliese and Craig Van Gelder, and is intended to set up the argument. Chapters two through four are organized around laying down some key theological foundations for evangelizing. Chapters five through seven build on these foundations in reference to congregational practices, navigating the tough questions, and forming an evangelizing church culture in the Lutheran church.

The primary author of chapter two is Kelly Fryer. In this chapter, the argument for the necessity of reconceiving evangelizing is presented around the concept that the gift of the gospel we receive from God always represents a call on our lives.

The primary author of chapter three is Richard Bliese. The argument here is that the classic formulation of a Lutheran understanding of ministry around Word and Sacrament needs to be revisited in order to open up the missional dimension within its confessional formulation. The captivities resulting from a lack of such understanding need to be named and addressed, while the fuller reality of Word and Sacrament in relation to the Christian community needs to be developed.

The primary author of chapter four is Craig Van Gelder. Working from a biblical-theological perspective, an argument is made that the good news of the gospel is always about being for the sake of the world. This biblical-theological understanding is then used to reread the Lutheran confessional tradition from the perspective of a missional hermeneutic.

The primary author of chapter five is Wyvetta Bullock. This chapter argues that a missional understanding of the gospel as being for the sake of the world has profound implications for shaping congregational life and practices. It is God's mission that needs to shape the mission of a congregation. God's mission always leads a congregation into deeper internal growth, even as it gives its life away for the sake of the world.

The primary author of chapter six is Paul Rajashekar. Clearly there are important questions that must be answered in order to have a fully developed theology of evangelizing. This chapter critically and constructively explores how to navigate difficult questions by use of the *simuls* and *solas* in the Lutheran theological tradition. Also covered in this chapter are how to evangelize from the perspective of the theology of the cross and how to evangelize within a postmodern context.

The primary author of chapter seven is Craig Nessan. While evangelizing for Lutherans must be deeply informed by a Lutheran perspective, there are other perspectives that can help shape and inform our practice. This chapter explores the contributions Lutherans should consider accepting both from other Christians and from other religions. The trinitarian foundations that underlie evangelizing are then used to help develop an evangelizing church culture.

In the epilogue, primary author Craig Nessan provides a summary of the foundational commitments that the writing team developed concerning a Lutheran perspective on evangelizing. The twelve commitments outlined provide a framework for congregations to both understand and practice evangelizing.

Fresh Lenses

The writing team's goal was to approach evangelizing with fresh lenses informed by a rereading of the Lutheran confessional heritage from a missional perspective and to do so primarily in relation to our context in the United States. The audiences that will likely profit most from this book are pastors and congregation leaders who want to engage in evangelizing that is grounded theologically and theological students and professors who want to understand how to engage in evangelizing from a Lutheran perspective. The language of each chapter is meant to be orthodox yet fresh; traditional yet contextually relevant; and theological in content yet evangelizing in nature.

Finally, our deep desire is to initiate a fresh dialogue about how the Lutheran Reformation tradition can serve as a catalyst for thinking missionally in our context. Each chapter tries to reengage key topics within the framework of evangelizing, topics such as justification, Word and Sacrament, ecclesiology, and Lutheran hermeneutics. New terms being used include *the gift is the call*; *word, sacrament, and the Christian community*; *simuls* and *solas*; and *evangelizing*. Our intent is to reengage the whole evangelistic discussion. The reader will have to judge whether our efforts have succeeded in stimulating your imagination and strengthening your courage for evangelizing.

Two terms hold particular meaning throughout the book. These are *evangelizing* and *word, sacrament, and the Christian community*. First, we chose to use the term *evangelizing* to replace the word *evangelism*. This was done primarily because evangelism has come to be associated primarily with particular outreach programs of a congregation or specialized activities for which the church is responsible.

Evangelism as a Christian term is of fairly recent origin, being a historical construct that emerged during the modern missions movement of the nineteenth century. This understanding of evangelism as being primarily programmatic or a specialized activity continues to be perpetuated by many Lutheran congregations, synods, and even churchwide agencies. We believe that evangelism from this perspective tends to be reductionistic in respect to understanding the fullness of the gospel as being good news. A church committed to evangelism tends to have a program to which only a few laity are committed. In contrast, an evangelizing church puts an evangelical imagination at the center of all its activities. Thus, the gospel witness becomes core to the entire life of the congregation and does not just function as a peripheral or programmatic activity.

The phrase *word, sacrament, and the Christian community* is used throughout this book to replace the more familiar *Word and Sacrament* language that is normally employed by Lutherans. This revised language is being used to bring out the fuller significance of the Lutheran affirmation that Christ is present for the world—in the word and through the sacraments but also in relation to the Christian community. This is clear in Article VII of the Augsburg Confession, but we do not believe that the connection of the presence of Christ in the Christian community is sufficiently captured in the phrase *Word and Sacrament*. Luther made this connection explicit through his adding "*mutual conversation and consolation of the brothers and sisters*" (Smalcald Articles, Part III, Article 4) to Word and Sacrament as something the gospel gives to us. The gospel comes to us as Word and Sacrament within Christian communities. There is always a social reality to the church in relation to the ministry of Word and Sacrament. While not arguing for an institutional understanding of the church as a means of grace, the authors of this book are taking the position that the presence of Christ is also available to all—available in, with, and through the social reality of the Christian community that lives its life in relation to the world.[12] In this sense, the church is also a means of grace, of being the presence of Christ in the world, an evangelizing presence that is for the sake of the world. In other words, Word and Sacrament create evangelizing communities. Thus, Christ comes to the world in an embodied way where words and rituals take on life and meaning within relational communities.

CONCLUSION

The authors believe that, finally, what is at stake in this book is the question about the church's identity. The key issue is, "What does it mean to be the church, an evangelical church that lives for the sake of the world?" For Lutherans, this question can be exciting, because it is best answered by reaching deep within our heritage. It is a foundational question. It challenges, probes, invites; kills and makes alive. It simply won't leave us Lutherans alone. Our prayer for you as the reader is that, as you read this book, God will engage your imagination for mission in the same way that *the resurrection of the evangelizing church* has engaged ours. After the *death of evangelism* in your congregation, may you experience new life through the marvelous gift of Jesus Christ in becoming an evangelizing community. The gift is a call! It's a free gift! It's a tremendous call! They cannot be separated!

CHAPTER 2

THE GIFT IS A CALL

Frank Abagnale Jr.: *I don't want to lie to you anymore, alright. I'm not a doctor.*
I never went to medical school. I'm not a lawyer, or a Harvard Graduate, or a Lutheran.
I ran away from home a year and a half ago when I was fifteen.

Brenda Strong: *Frank? You're not a Lutheran?*

—*From the 2002 box office hit* Catch Me If You Can,
starring Leonardo DiCaprio and Tom Hanks

For those of us who are Lutheran, it was a bit startling to see ourselves, bigger than life, represented by the Strong family in the box office hit *Catch Me If You Can*. We aren't used to having people notice that we're here. We smiled, of course, along with the rest of the audience, at the absurdity that this would be the single lie that would upset Frank Abagnale's future in-laws the most. They didn't seem to care that Frank wasn't a real doctor or lawyer, but they were horrified to discover that he wasn't really a *Lutheran*! The truth is, though, that this unexpected and unusual big screen moment made us feel sort of exposed, as if everyone was *looking* at us. We're simply not used to this. And, if we're really honest, it made us feel just a little uncomfortable.

As Christians, we have been given something precious, something the world needs as much today as it ever has. We have the gospel message, the good news of a God who comes down here to call us out of an old life of darkness and death and into a new life of purpose and hope and uncontainable joy. But, for some reason, we Lutherans are often very shy about sharing this gift with others. And it is about time we get over it. The gift is a call.

As Lutherans, we know that there is absolutely nothing we could ever do or say or be that could make God love us more. We know that God comes down! God comes down in the word and in the meal and in the water of baptism and within the Christian community. God shows up whenever and wherever we are at worship or at work. God came down, most astonishingly of all, in Jesus. God comes

11

down to save us and to set us free, and there is nothing we could ever do to make our way up to God. Our salvation is a gift from God through Jesus Christ. We can recite this from memory, right? *We are saved by grace through faith in Jesus Christ and not by any work of the law.* This is the article upon which, as Martin Luther said, our church stands or falls. This is most certainly true. But, given the strange new world we find ourselves in and the way in which our church is floundering in the midst of it, we must dare to ask ourselves some hard questions. And the hardest of all is *this* question about our most cherished doctrine: "*So what?*"

For too long, Lutherans in the United States and throughout the West have allowed this article—and the assurance of this most wonderful gift—to lull us to sleep. We have burrowed down into our comfortable dens, surrounded by all the familiar trappings of ethnic and cultural heritage, and allowed our faith to slip into hibernation. We have taken the gift for granted. And, in the meantime, there is a world that lies just outside our door, groaning in pain, hungry for anything that will fill it up and make it whole, wrecked by sin and longing to become everything it was created to be. This is *God's* world. And it is a world that God deeply loves, a world Christ died to save. This world needs what we have been given, although at this point most people would never even think to look to us for help or answers.

A lot of people gave up on us long ago. Others come looking for something and quickly leave unsatisfied. Even as the population grows, every year the number of people who worship in our churches declines. As the American public diversifies, our membership remains as homogenous as ever. There are sociological labels, now, for multiple generations of people under the age of forty (Gen Xers, busters, millennials, etc.) who couldn't think of a single good reason to show up at one of our worship services on a Sunday morning. We know that in order to turn this situation around, we will have to make big changes in the way we live and worship and learn and work together.

We know that, unless we do this, our churches will continue to dwindle and, perhaps, eventually even die. We invent programs to address these problems and craft inspired slogans to stir the troops to action. But nothing, it seems, can move us—really move us—to take the kind of action or be the kind of church that makes a difference to the legions of people in our communities who believe that we are irrelevant. Even some of *us* are wondering whether we have anything worth sharing. We are hard pressed to say what it is that makes our faith something other people might need. We, too, have bought into the popular notion that faith is a private thing and a matter of personal preference; that any story is as good as the gospel Story; that truth is relative.

Somewhere along the way, we lost track of what the gift we have been given really is; we only remember that it is a gift. We assume, therefore, that it is ours to do with as we please, which includes doing nothing at all. We have forgotten that the gift we have been given is Christ himself. And Christ comes with a call. *Christ comes with a call!* Christ comes down here, busting through our comfortable complacency, to call us out of ourselves. He loves this world so much that he will not leave it without witnesses to the love and the hope and the power of God. And he loves *us* so much that he will not leave us where we are, snoozing away in the sanctuary of shallow spirituality and false security, dead to the world. Christ wants more for us than that. He wants *life* for us! And so Christ comes down here and, through no merit of our own, calls us to follow him.

He calls us out of the hollow emptiness of our sleepy lives and sets us free for a life that means something, a life of witness and service and self-giving love, a life that gives itself away for the sake of the world. Christ has given us a most wonderful gift. *So what?* So that we can really live! The gift Christ gives is not a blanket of forgiveness that we can wrap around us to keep us warm and dry. The gift Christ gives is a wake-up call! It is a call to a new life. To reject this call is to reject the gift. To ignore this call is to ignore the gift. *The two cannot be separated.*

This may come as quite a shock to those of us who are used to thinking that because our salvation is a gift, we don't have to *do* anything. Some of us want to stay in hiding, tucked safely away in the burrow of our quiet churches. We are perfectly content knowing that Hollywood has bought our Lake Wobegon image of humble, harmless Lutheranism enough to feature us in its latest blockbuster movies. But God has other plans for us. Through us, God wants to bless the world.

A Confession

Those of us who count ourselves as theological descendants of those sixteenth-century Reformers have inherited a powerful message. Living as we do, in an age of elusive and *expensive* happiness, the words of Martin Luther are as clear and compelling today as they were five hundred years ago: "One thing, and only one thing, is necessary for Christian life, righteousness, and freedom. That one thing is the most holy Word of God . . ."[1]

Furthermore, this word is not just any word. It is, Luther explained, "the gospel of God concerning his Son, who was made flesh, suffered, rose from the dead, and was glorified through the Spirit who sanctifies."[2] Those who hear this word—and believe it—find that it feeds the soul, makes it righteous, sets it free, and saves it. The message for today is simply this: We can, finally, stop looking. Through no merit of our own, God comes down here to set things right, to save us from ourselves, and to set us free from whatever would kill us. God comes down here with love and mercy to deliver us from evil and death and into unexpectedly abundant life. God comes down most powerfully of all in Christ Jesus, of course, and makes all things new.

This gospel message had gotten lost in Luther's day, as it has in our own. It had, in fact, vanished from the landscape. Although virtually everyone understood themselves to be Christian, very few were familiar with the Bible or knew what Christianity was all about. Indulgences (the way people tried to buy their way to happiness back then!) and other good works were understood to lead to salvation, rather than the cross of Christ. People lived in fear of a wrathful God. There was no peace on earth and precious little hope for it in the life to come. And so it was that in Luther's time, as in ours, the people who most needed to hear the gospel were living right next door. They were his neighbors, his friends. They were the priests in the local parishes and the prince in his own territory.

Having heard and believed this gospel message himself, Luther, like a man obsessed by the dire urgency of his mission, set about awakening the Christian faith in the people of his time. His life became a frenzy of traveling, preaching, teaching, translating, and writing. He was committed to the idea that the gospel would transform each and every life it touched, forming a *priesthood of all believers* in which each person would have his or her own faith, understand service and witness to be a part of his or her vocation, and be educated and equipped for ministry.[3] It is not surprising that, whatever valid critiques there might be of Luther's thought and work, he has been credited "with being the father of genuine church-centered evangelical mission work based on the gospel."[4] The news he heard as he encountered the gospel of Christ in Scripture was too good, too powerful, not to share.

So, what in the world happened? By the middle of the twentieth century, Lutheranism in the northern hemisphere had lost virtually all evidence of the evangelical fervor that characterized its founders and was marked instead by a palpable "reticence, hesitation, and loss of nerve." Late twentieth-century Lutheranism especially found itself in a crisis of "fundamental conviction and motivation, undermining belief in the urgency and validity of the Christian mission."[5] Any practical questions about "how" to do mission were replaced by the basic question of "why?" And, here, at the beginning of this new century, we find the question still largely unanswered, leading Mark Hanson, bishop of the Evangelical Lutheran Church in America, to quip:

> It's been said that the average Lutheran invites someone to worship once every twenty-three years. If that's not bad enough, research also shows that it takes three invitations before the people invited come. That makes for sixty-nine years—and most of us don't have that much time![6]

Whether this statistic is correct is hard to say. However, the majority of Lutherans in the United States today remain stubbornly resistant to the evangelizing mission. When asked if they would share their faith *with someone they know*, a little more than twenty percent of those who belong to the Evangelical Lutheran Church in America (ELCA), for example, say they would do it "reluctantly." Thirty-three percent say they're not sure whether they would do it or not. And almost forty percent say they would actually refuse.[7] This is the case, unhappily, after a decade-long emphasis on evangelism in the ELCA. Furthermore, these numbers show a marked *decrease* in those who said they would be willing to share their faith compared to twenty years ago. The steady decline in the number of ELCA congregations, members, and people attending worship each week must be seen as one of the consequences of our evangelical diffidence.

Lutherans possess a powerful message about a God who comes down, even though we do not deserve it and could never possibly earn it, to save us and set us free. We are the product of what was arguably one of the most powerful evangelical movements in history, perhaps second only to the initial outpouring from Jerusalem. We are the theological descendants of people who gave everything they had to give to get the word out. But today we have to confess that we just are not doing this very well. And so it is that we begin a conversation about evangelizing with repentance, *metanoia*, a turning around, at Jesus' invitation, to see what God is up to.

The Mission of God

Among the very first words Jesus spoke once his public ministry began was an invitation to turn around because "the kingdom of heaven has come near" (Matt. 4:17). Then he spent the whole rest of his life showing us what he meant by that invitation and invited us to be a part of it. With mixed results, to be sure, Jesus nevertheless extended this offer to any and all: "Come, follow me" (Matt. 19:21). Come, be a part of the adventure on which my Father has sent me, the loving purpose of which is nothing less than the salvation of the whole world (John 3:16-17). Every single thing we do as Christians, including evangelizing, happens within this context. *Our* mission happens within the framework of God's mission (*missio Dei*)[8]; this is the starting point in conversations about mission across nearly every Christian tradition today.

Now, it must be said, of course, that Jesus is at the center of this mission to save the world. But, from the very beginning, the gospel Story has been about a world full of people who insist on going their own way and a God who relentlessly pursues them. "Again and again," the psalmist sang, "[the LORD] delivered them, but they continued to rebel against him" (Ps. 106:43). God would have had every reason, time after time, to forsake this world and all the people in it. "Even so, he pitied them in their distress and listened to their cries. He remembered his covenant with them and relented because of his unfailing love" (Ps. 106:44-45). This is how the Story goes. As soon as there is bad news, of our own making or not, God steps in to save the day:

"Come here, Adam," God said. "Try on this new set of clothes before you go." (Gen. 3:21)

"Hey, Sarah, I'm *serious*," God smiled. (Gen. 18:12)

"Jeremiah, have you bought that land yet?" God asked. "You know, one day, it'll be worth something." (Jer. 32:6-8)

"Hang on, Martha," Jesus whispered to her through both their tears. "Help is on the way." (John 11:32-35)

From the very beginning, God has had good news to share. And, all along the way, God has sent someone to share it. We see this most clearly in the trinitarian nature of God. The Father sent the Son (John 8:16). The Father and the Son sent the Spirit (John 15:26). And we are sent (John 17:18) in, with, and by the power of the Spirit, to be witnesses in a world that desperately needs our help to see what we have seen (Acts 1:8). God is on a mission! And although God may choose methods—and messengers—that seem to us at times to be strange and even ineffective, God is relentless in the effort. Our God will not rest until all creation—and everyone in it—is home again, safe and sound (2 Cor. 5:18-20).

It is this eschatological vision, of a world reconciled and whole, that stands at the very center of the Story, driving the action and propelling us toward the promised, brilliant conclusion. Part of being human, and being made in the *image* of God, is the ability to *imagine* this future.[9] We believe, in some primal place deep within ourselves, that one day all things will be made new. We know, at the very core of our being, that a time will come when there will be no more mourning and no more pain and no more death (Rev. 21:1-4). We trust that one day God will restore us and all creation to everything we were meant to be. "And all of the other good news along the way—the possibility of forgiveness, the gift of the Spirit to change us, the breaking down of human barriers, the guidance of Scripture, the sustenance of worship, and a thousand others—will finally reach its climax in a huge, ultimate, literally cosmic celebration of God's goodness, when human creation and natural creation will party together."[10] This is where we are headed, together. And although we may not always have words for it or, even if we did, may not dare to speak it out loud, we know that it is true. Or, at least, with everything we are, we hope that it is.

It is human nature to imagine a new future. This is how God made us. And God has promised it (Isa. 2:1-5)! But those of us who are God's people *through Christ* know that, in a very real way, the promise of this new day has already arrived. When Jesus came along, something radically different happened. Everything changed because the future, which God had been promising all along, suddenly began. The kingdom of heaven drew near! Luther states it formally in the Large Catechism when he answers the question "What is the kingdom of God?" with a proclamation, not of some future reality, but with a word about Christ:

> Answer: Simply what we have learned in the Creed, namely, that God sent his Son, Christ our Lord, into the world to redeem and deliver us from the power of the devil and to bring us to himself and rule us as a king of righteousness, life, and salvation against sin, death, and an evil conscience.[11]

Since Jesus, there is no turning back. God has opened the curtain on the final, glorious act. The future is coming! And it is already here. It is not yet. But it is also very much now. The blind see and the deaf hear (Luke 7:18-22). The barriers that separated Jew from Gentile, men from women, and slave from free have been obliterated (Gal. 3:28). Ordinary and uneducated women and men suddenly find themselves with power enough to turn the world upside down (Acts 17:6-7). Satan falls like lightning from his perch of power (Luke 10:18). And people everywhere find new hearts beating within them (Luke 19:8). All things look somehow possible! *The reign of God has begun!*

It was the reality of this in-breaking kingdom—the arrival of this new day— that fired the imaginations and enflamed the passions of those early Christians.[12] This was the reality about which John and Peter could not help but speak (Acts 4:20). This was the hope for which Stephen died (Acts 7:55-56). This was the good news that Mary gathered up her robes and ran to share (Matt. 28:8-10). This was the surprise that opened up a whole new world of possibilities for Priscilla and her husband, and for everyone who said yes to their invitation to join them in a new kind of community (Rom. 16:3-5). This radical message about what God had inaugurated with the life, death, and resurrection of Jesus could not be contained. The very stones would have cried out if those first followers had not (Luke 19:40). No one needed to tell them more than once what to do. "You will be my witnesses," Jesus said, more as a statement of fact than a command (Acts 1:8). "You WILL be my witnesses!" because, really, how could you not?

With Jesus, something happened that had never happened before, and God will not be finished until what was begun in Christ is done (Phil. 1:6). God will see it through. This will happen with or without us! Luther explained this is why we pray:

> *Your kingdom come* [italics added], not because human faith and prayer make the kingdom come—for God's kingdom comes of itself without our prayer—but that it may be realized in us and that God's name may be praised through his word and our holy lives.[13]

We do not participate in mission simply because Jesus tells us to but, rather, because we can't help but get caught up in what God has already done and is doing. The kingdom of God, which is here among us and is yet to come, is the basis of all our hope and the vision that drives us forward in mission. It is the very thing for which we give God thanks and praise, and it makes us "sigh for more. Living in the tension of such a posture, we cannot be religious dropouts with an idle faith and a passive hope. The call of the kingdom is an invitation to work while it is day, to be active in love, to sow the seeds of the word and spread the flame of the Spirit."[14]

THE HURDLES

Through Christ, God calls us to be a part of this great adventure. We have already confessed that we have not always answered this call very faithfully or very well. In fact, there have been seasons in the life of this church when we have seemingly been unable even to hear the call. We are, arguably, in the middle of just such a season. What will be required for us to retool for a new century and begin, finally, to live into our name as an *evangelical* church? Well, the problem is not primarily one of methodology. For the most part, even in this strange new world, we know *what* to do. And, as challenging as our context is here in the United States—increasingly postmodern, post-Christendom, religiously diverse, wireless—the biggest challenges we face are not *out there* somewhere, either. They are right here, within us. There are, in fact, at least four major hurdles we face in becoming the evangelical church we claim and have been called to be.

EXPERIENTIAL HURDLE. This one may be the easiest to identify and understand. The terrible truth is that many people in our congregations have been victims of an unpleasant *evangelism* experience. As a whole, even the word makes us uncomfortable. Partly, this is due to a problem that is uniquely American. Evangelizing has been divorced from the church.

> [Instead] the evangelistic enterprise has been carried by big-name evangelists—Finney, Moody, Graham, and the latter-day TV evangelists. Its overall effect has been reductionist, individualistic, emotionalistic, revivalistic, and manipulative. Its engagement with the deeper issues of contemporary culture has been superficial.[15]

People in our congregations are suspicious enough of the evangelical project to warrant asking the question, "Do We HATE Evangelism?"[16] At best, our experiences leave us feeling ambiguous about it.

CULTURAL/ETHNIC/CLASS HURDLE. This hurdle is, perhaps, the one that will be hardest to talk about or even admit. The reality is, however, that our doctrinal positions, liturgical life, and ecclesiastical behaviors are often held captive to our northern European ethnic traditions and to our middle-class values. We cling tightly to the way we have *always done it*. Most of our congregations simply are not hospitable to people who are *different*. They have a bland homogeneity that comes with being a closed system. Consider that forty percent of Lutherans have been members of their present congregations for more than twenty years and sixty-three percent have been members of the same congregation for more than ten years. In a typical Lutheran congregation, three of every four members have been raised from childhood as Lutherans. Another fifteen percent became Lutherans as a result of a marriage relationship.[17] Is it any wonder that our congregations simply do not exhibit the kind of diversity that characterizes the culture within which we live?

PHILOSOPHICAL HURDLE. We face a powerful hurdle that emerged out of the Enlightenment. Christians in the northern hemisphere have been created and "nurtured in the assumptions of liberalism; that the individual is the sovereign unit of society; that there are certain universally experienced values inherent in all people everywhere; that there is no truth other than that truth which is self-derived; that it is possible to find some neutral philosophical ground whereby conflicts between points of view can be resolved."[18] For many people today, even those who are members of our congregations, the gospel is *good advice* but not necessarily good news. The Bible is one source among many; there are stories, not a Story. And what *I* think matters most of all. There is no such thing, really, as sin; we just make mistakes. In fact, there is believed to be a clear continuity between the gospel and the best human thought. Jesus, in other words, came to affirm and, maybe, improve us; but he did not come to transform us. In the larger culture, the church may have a voice at the table, but it is no longer our table. And many have come to think that, if the Christian story fits neatly into the cultural story, if there really isn't anything transforming about it, if it simply affirms what I already believe, then why bother?

THEOLOGICAL HURDLE. Arguably, the biggest hurdle we must overcome to be the evangelical people we say we are is, of all things, a theological hurdle.[19] This is, admittedly, a harsh word for Lutherans. We pride ourselves on having *good theology*. All the great battles within Lutheranism have been fought over right doctrine; over the clear distinction between law and gospel/promise; over faith alone (*sola fide*), grace alone (*sola gratia*), Scripture alone (*sola scriptura*)! Heroic stands have been taken, friendships have been lost, and churches have been split over the theological positions we have defended or fought. But, here's the thing: for all of our theological intensity, we Lutherans have a hard time explaining why we should *do anything*, much less the really hard and scary work of evangelizing. When you come right down to it, "Lutherans seem to lack one essential requirement for fulfilling their missionary task. They lack a compulsive reason for sharing the good news of God's kingdom in Jesus Christ with others."[20] In other words, we don't have an answer to the question, "Why?" This explains, in large part, our evangelical indifference and our reluctance to engage in the missional task. And the problem lies right at the heart of how our most cherished theological doctrine—justification by grace through faith—has commonly been interpreted and understood.

Justification by grace through faith is the article upon which, as Luther said, the church stands or falls. It is the tenacity with which Lutherans cling to this article that sets them apart as a church of the Reformation. Lutherans will resist with all their might any attempt to suggest that human beings are able, by their own effort or will, to achieve their salvation or win God's saving favor. This is the powerful message we have to share with a world that futilely searches for its own happiness and fulfillment. But, throughout the history of Lutheranism, this strong emphasis on *God's* activity has made it difficult to know exactly how to talk about *ours*.

One controversy after another broke out in the immediate aftermath of the Reformation between groups who disagreed about how to connect the gift of salvation and the call to new obedience. Some tried to clarify and strengthen the teaching of the Augsburg Confession that good works should and must be done. Others, afraid that what they believed was a trend toward making too many concessions to Catholics on the one hand and Calvinists on the other, argued for a clearer stance against the role of good works, at least as they relate to salvation. Those in this camp, who defended the most radical position, held enough political power to send those who disagreed to prison and into exile. At least one preacher, Jon Funck, was beheaded in 1566 by those on a fanatical quest for *pure doctrine*. In the heat of this conflict, some Lutheran theologians made increasingly extreme declarations. "Good works are harmful for salvation!" represents perhaps the most provocative and unhelpful.[21]

We have not been helped, in contemporary Lutheranism, by the ongoing nature of this controversy. Too many of the people in our pews, unknowingly captive to the philosophical liberalism that permeates our culture, are questioning whether or not they have a Story worth sharing. At the same time, many of our theological and ecclesiastical leaders, afraid of talking about good works, are not convinced we would *need* to share the Story even if we had one. Our people, many of them anyway, are ho-hum about their faith. And our pastors, afraid of getting it wrong, do not know how to talk about discipleship or conversion or sanctification or growth (personal or congregational). They lack urgency, conviction, and passion in their preaching. They offer forgiveness from sin but not freedom to serve. They share the gift of Christ without the call to follow him. In our well-intentioned effort to preserve right doctrine and protect God's prerogative in the act of salvation, we have risked giving people the impression that no good thing is expected from them at all.

A friend, who is a lifelong Lutheran, tells a story from her childhood that illustrates only too well how distorted our understanding of what it means to be a Christian can become. She was in the locker room after gym class toward the middle of her eighth-grade year in school. Two girls, who also happened to be members of her confirmation class, were on the other end of the bench. One of them, in the course of their laughter and early adolescent banter, issued an earthy curse. In other words, she swore. Her friend, startled, said, "Hey! Watch your language!" To which the first friend said, "What's the problem? I'm saved by grace, aren't I?" Our friend, listening in astonishment, thought to herself (not for the last time), "There is something wrong here." And, indeed, there is. There *is* something wrong when the awesome gift of salvation through Christ is separated from the call to follow Christ. There is something terribly wrong when the sacrifice of our Lord Jesus becomes an excuse for indolence or apathy.

This great divide between the gift of salvation and the call to discipleship leads to individual lethargy. But it has implications for our life together, too. Without a clear call to discipleship, there is no mission. There is no call to the church to *do* anything at all. We end up using our confessions to define the church, woodenly, as an "assembly of saints in which the gospel is taught purely and the sacraments are administered rightly" (Augsburg Confession, Article VII), and that is where it ends. We lose the creative, life-giving, sending power of the Holy Spirit, which "is given" through the Word and Sacraments, "as through instruments" to effect "faith where and when it pleases God in those who hear the gospel" (Augsburg Confession, Article V). We stifle the "new obedience" and the good works "that this faith is bound to yield" in the lives of Christians who have been put to work in the world (Augsburg Confession, Article VI).

Instead, once the connection between salvation and discipleship is severed, Word and Sacrament become something that is just *for us*, and the focal point of our life together becomes what happens within our buildings, presided over by professional ministers. We quibble over what setting of the liturgy to use and who has the power to say the "magic words" at communion. We debate the merits of multimedia technology and resist opening up our facilities to the neighborhood because strangers might not keep things as clean as we would like them to be. We reduce church to its role as a distributor of grace and, therefore, promote ordained pastors rather than the universal priesthood as the apex of ministry. We turn inward, hanging on for dear life to language and customs that do not have currency in the world today, in spite of our heritage as a church that understands its need to be *always reforming* so that the gospel gets out to everyone. We replace evangelizing with ecumenism. We fight about the *form* of worship instead of wondering about the *fruits* of worship. We let the budget decide. We are afraid to change pretty much anything.

We should clarify, at this point, that we are speaking here specifically of the theological hurdle facing the Lutheran church in the United States. This may also be an issue in Western European Lutheranism, but we cannot speak of this from our experience. It certainly is *not* an issue in Lutheranism as it is spreading throughout the southern hemisphere. In fact, the experience of Lutherans in the south challenges us to renewal and reform. This is why, for example, the Lutheran World Federation, deeply influenced by our brothers and sisters around the world, can declare unapologetically: "God's gracious justification is not only justification *from* but also *for*, namely for participation in God's mission."[22] But, here in the United States, too few Lutherans would think to ground our call to discipleship in the gift of salvation that is ours through Christ Jesus. And too few of our congregations seem driven into mission by their encounter with a God who comes down, above all in Christ, but now also in Word and Sacrament, to set them free *from* sin and death *for* witness and service. Until we can overcome this theological hurdle by connecting these two—salvation by grace and the call to discipleship—in the hearts and minds of North American Lutherans, our church will continue to flounder in the middle of this strange new world and we will remain decidedly *un*-evangelical.

THE REFORMATION IMPULSE

The temptation to separate the call to discipleship from the gift of salvation is not, of course, a uniquely Lutheran problem.[23] It is a serious issue for us, and it has always been so. But throughout the history of Lutheranism there has been a powerful urge to break the gospel free from whatever has held it captive; there has been a reformation impulse that has, at every turn, rediscovered the true nature of the gospel and let it explode into the culture in a new and powerful way. Martin Luther himself addressed this issue in a variety of places, most notably perhaps in *The Freedom of a Christian*.

Luther and the Nature of Christian Freedom

Luther, of course, was not a systematic theologian. He was a reformer, a transla-tor, a pastor, a teacher, and a leader. He responded to the theological needs of the church and the people of his day. When he wrote, he did so to address a specific situation or to answer a key question or to respond to an angry critic. And, when he addressed ecclesiological topics or issues related to Christian discipleship, he did so in the same way, in a variety of documents addressed to specific situations and localized issues. In the absence of a formal theology, we are left having to syn-thesize Luther's writings in trying to discern his views. We have been left, if you will, reading between the lines and in the margins of Luther's works.[24]

That being said, this little document issues a call to discipleship so clear that we can hear it ringing out across the centuries. *The Freedom of a Christian* is one of the few documents that Luther wrote in a "conciliatory spirit. Yet it contained a positive and unequivocal statement of Luther's evangelical theology as applied to Christian life."[25] It was, in many ways, Luther's defining statement of what it means to be a Christian. It was written to "make the way smoother for the unlearned,"[26] to outline in the clearest possible terms what it means to live a justified life. And here Luther declares in a way that could not be more direct: "A Christian is a per-fectly free lord of all, subject to none. A Christian is a perfectly dutiful servant of all, subject to all."[27]

Luther knew, from personal experience, that something happens to us when we are met by Christ, in the word. There is, in fact, "no greater mercy than when [God] sends forth his Word, as we read in Psalm 107:20: 'He sent forth his word, and healed them, and delivered them from destruction.'" Transformed by this word, which sets us free from death and sin and the devil (and every other thing that would kill us if it could), the Christian goes into action. But this action is not a burden. Good works are done "out of spontaneous love in obedience to God."[28] The word of grace is proclaimed and forgiveness offered.[29] The needy are cared for and those who are burdened are relieved.[30] "From faith thus flow forth love and joy in the Lord, and from love a joyful, willing, and free mind that serves one's neighbor . . . not distinguish[ing] between friends and enemies."[31] In fact, "any work that is not done solely for the purpose of keeping body under control or of serving one's neighbor, as long as he asks nothing contrary to God, is not good or Christian."[32] Grace and discipleship belong together, so much so that Luther could "conclude, therefore, that a Christian lives not in himself, but in Christ and in his neighbor. Otherwise he is not a Christian."[33]

The Pietists vs. Orthodoxy

Luther himself had no problem connecting the gift of salvation through Christ with the call to follow Christ. But the reality is that not even the very next gen-eration of Lutherans showed any evidence that they had caught Luther's pas-sion for sharing the gospel with those who did not know it. Critics would say that this paralysis in regard to evangelism was essentially institutionalized when the Lutheran Reformers defined the church in their confessional documents according to the "correctness of teaching and sacraments" rather than around the concept of mission.[34] Those who followed Luther were left with a church "defined in terms of what happens inside its four walls, not in terms of its calling in the world."[35] Indeed, the seventeenth century in Germany saw the emergence of theological orthodoxy, whose theologians taught that the apostles had already fulfilled the Great Commission. Non-Christians already "had their chance," in a sense. And, besides, it was believed that pagans were impervious to the gospel. Orthodox theologians rejected any responsibility for mission, claiming that this responsibility belonged to God alone and even then, only within the boundaries established by the state.[36]

This hostility toward the concept of mission grew, in part, out of a radically theocentric theological bias—it's all about God. This bias was one of the consequences of that seventeenth-century orthodox perversion of Luther's teaching about salvation by grace through faith. A distorted view of orthodoxy in the century that followed the Reformation tilted toward the idea that no works *at all* were necessary, good, or helpful. Some have suggested, therefore, that it is no wonder seventeenth-century Germany was characterized by what has been described as moral depravity. "People were content and certain of their salvation simply because they had been baptized and part of the church system."[37]

A brief but powerful evangelical surge occurred in Germany in reaction to seventeenth-century orthodox theology and the moral laziness it produced. This movement became known as Pietism. Leaders like Philipp Jakob Spener (1635–1705) and August Hermann Franke (1663–1727) taught that the gospel is only effective if people are actually using the Scriptures! They challenged Lutherans to radically live out the priesthood of all believers, arguing that the laity needed to be reactivated for service to others. They wanted to see love at the center of community and practice before knowledge, pastors who are true believers, and church reform that would begin with individual transformation.[38] Franke, especially, "affirmed most clearly that the salvation won by Christ is for the whole world. His understanding was that God wants all to be saved, and so he sends his call to repentance to all people. . . . Such a general 'gracious call' from God places the responsibility for response squarely at the feet of every individual."[39]

The Pietists, full of evangelical passion, continue to have heirs within Lutheranism into the present day. Certainly they were behind at least some of the enthusiasm for taking the gospel into new lands during the nineteenth-century missionary ventures. It cannot be overlooked that Lutherans were the first Protestant missionaries! The fact that Lutheran congregations, over a hundred years old, dot the landscape of the United States—and that Lutheranism, like every other Christian sect, planted in previous centuries, is growing like crazy around the world[40] and even helping the northern churches recover their missional essence—is a testimony to the evangelical fervor of the Pietist movement. But, for the most part, the Pietists have become a footnote in Lutheranism, often accused even by their fans of replacing Luther's gospel-centered action with law.[41]

Kierkegaard's Wake-Up Call

With the Pietists marginalized and persecuted by the orthodox majority, Lutheranism across Europe slipped deeper into quietism and passivity. This is what was behind the scathing critique issued by the Danish philosopher Søren Kierkegaard against the church in his day, in his land, two hundred years ago. Today, in Denmark, an estimated two percent of the population attends worship on a Sunday morning, and only one-half percent of the people in Copenhagen bother.[42] The grand old churches scattered across this traditionally Lutheran nation are empty. And Kierkegaard saw it coming. He believed then that *the moment* had arrived, a "new thing that does not lie in circumstances" but is "the stroke of eternity and the gift of heaven." Eternity, Kierkegaard believed, "was striking into time in judgment over the church"[43] because the church was sick. He called this sickness "Christendom." And, although there were many ways to describe this sickness, he believed the *reason* for this sickness was a lost sense of mission: "[W]e have completely forgotten," he said, "that to be a Christian means essentially to be a missionary. . . . Christianity in repose, stagnant Christianity, creates an obstruction, and this formidable obstruction is the sickness of Christendom."[44] In even more graphic terms, Kierkegaard described the problem this way:

> The sickness has come about by obstructing the mission. Christianity is always restless; Christendom is like constipation after a surfeit of food.[45]

True Christianity, Kierkegaard knew, is always in action. Christendom, on the other hand, is nothing more than constipated Christianity. It has taken in everything it can while refusing to get up and *do* anything.

Part of the reason for this sickness, Kierkegaard argued, was a perversion of Reformation thinking. He explains that the church of the Middle Ages made works the *only* thing. What Martin Luther and the sixteenth-century Protestant reformers did was to respond as helpfully as they could to what had become this gross exaggeration. But "the turn that Luther made," he said, "[can] all too easily become a wrong road as soon as there is no Luther whose life makes the true turn the truth."[46] Luther witnessed to the truth with his life and "voluntarily exposed himself there to dangers enough (yet without deluding himself that this was meritorious)."[47] But the next generation made a mockery of Luther, turning his words into doctrine and ignoring the reality of the life he led. Luther's own life, in other words, bears witness that he never intended Christianity to lose all enthusiasm for *action*. Nevertheless, over the centuries, his words have been used to justify exactly that:

> Luther's emphasis is a corrective—but a corrective made into the normative, into the sum total, is *eo ipso* confusing in another generation (where that for which it was a corrective does not exist). And with every generation that goes by in this way, it must become worse, until the end result is that this corrective, which has independently established itself, produces characteristics exactly the opposite of the original.[48]

There was, Kierkegaard believed, a need in his time for a rediscovery of Christianity, a rethinking of what it means to be Christian, a reimagining of what God was calling the church to be and to do. This was especially the case, he knew, in those places where Lutheranism had been perverted. Kierkegaard's occasionally shrill voice was meant to be an alarm clock. He believed that people had been lulled into thinking they were Christians. And, because of this illusion, people were allowed to live self-centered and decidedly un-Christian lives. It was Kierkegaard's driving purpose to bring Christians back to a place "where the message of salvation would be a life-belt and not a pillow to them."[49]

True Christianity, Kierkegaard declared, will always be moving, always acting, always awake. "Faith is a restless thing," he said.[50] It is always looking for the next new, creative, courageous, generous thing it can do. Kierkegaard noted, "Just as Christianity detests adultery, murder, theft, and everything else that can defile a person, it knows yet another defilement—cowardly sagacity and flabby sensibleness, despicable thralldom in probability."[51] In other words, there is nothing true Christianity can stand less than doing nothing. And it was Kierkegaard's view that what his generation needed "was not an opiate but a stimulant."[52] Unfortunately, Kierkegaard was ostracized and ridiculed in his time.[53] He would certainly not be surprised, therefore, to find Christianity all but dead in his homeland today. And he would be saddened, but not startled, to find Lutheranism in such trouble here in our land. He saw it coming two hundred years ago.

Bonhoeffer's Challenge

In many ways, the German pastor-theologian Dietrich Bonhoeffer saw the same thing in his own day. Writing to the church in Germany, in the middle of the twentieth century, Bonhoeffer warned that the doctrine of justification by grace through faith had been utterly divorced from the call to discipleship. The result, of course, would be a church that stood idly by while the most notorious regime in modern history took power, wreaking horror and devastation upon millions of people. Bonhoeffer, along with other members of the confessing church in Germany, did everything he could to try to lead his church in a different direction. His words still ring out across the decades:

> Because we cannot deny that we no longer stand in true discipleship to Christ, while being members of a true-believing church with a pure doctrine of grace, but no longer members of a church which follows Christ, we therefore simply have to try to understand grace and discipleship again in correct relationship to each other. We can no longer avoid this.[54]

Having good theology isn't enough, in other words, unless it leads to a life of action.

Bonhoeffer, of course, described this perversion of justification as "cheap grace" and declared: "[This] is the mortal enemy of our church. Our struggle today is for costly grace."[55] He described cheap grace in graphic terms. It is "preaching forgiveness without repentance; it is baptism without the discipline of community; it is the Lord's Supper without confession of sin; it is absolution without personal confession. Cheap grace is grace without discipleship, grace without the cross, grace without the living incarnate Jesus Christ."[56] Costly grace, on the other hand, "is the hidden treasure in the field, for the sake of which people go and sell with joy everything they have. It is the costly pearl, for whose price the merchant sells all that he has; it is Christ's sovereignty, for the sake of which you tear out an eye if it causes you to stumble. It is the call of Jesus Christ which causes a disciple to leave his nets and follow him."[57] Costly grace is costly because it calls people to leave everything behind to follow Christ in a life of witness and service. It is grace because it calls people to follow *Jesus Christ,* the only source of real life.

Somehow, Bonhoeffer said, the gift of grace and the call to discipleship had been wrenched apart. And he challenged the Christian church in his day, sanctimonious and self-satisfied by the all too easy assurance of salvation, to hear the call to discipleship and answer it. One does not come without the other.

Rediscovering the Gospel for Today

There has always been, throughout the history of Lutheranism, a powerful impulse to break free of whatever has held the gospel captive. There have always been, in every generation, those voices proclaiming the fullness of the gospel message and calling the church to mission. Perhaps it is time, right now, for this generation to reclaim our heritage as an *Evangelical* Lutheran Church in America. It is time, perhaps, for a reformation. Some might even say it is time for a resurrection. God has called us to be an evangelizing church. We have something the world desperately needs.

Our Context

Whether or not we realize it, Christians in the United States find ourselves surrounded on every side by lost and lonely people. We have witnessed, in recent years, "an acceleration of the deterioration of life on this continent. Faltering social structures and failing social values are driving people to search for personal identity and for a larger meaning for life in ever-new ways, as the proliferation of Christian and non-Christian sects reveals."[58] Interestingly, surveys consistently show that

> the level of importance assigned by people to their religious faith in North America is very high. Two-thirds say their faith is very important to them. More than four out of five people pray during the week. Bible reading is on the increase. Half of all adults claim to have a devotional or quiet time at least once during a typical week.[59]

There is, by all accounts, a growing spiritual hunger deep within the U.S. population. People are looking for something to fill up the emptiness of life in a culture that promises happiness if only you are rich enough to afford it. And, yet, less than forty percent of people in the United States are at worship on a typical weekend, and the numbers, even in this post–September 11 world, continue to decline.

Frankly, living as we do in a post-Christendom, pre-Christian culture, the church can no longer be taken for granted. The local congregation, in any setting, is no longer at the center of community life. The Christian community and its leaders provide the punch line for jokes told by the derelict kids in *South Park*; and the adults in town are atheists. Postmodernism challenges the very idea that there can even be a sure "starting point in giving an account of the things we hold to be true. . . .What you say is your take on things, your opinion, your interpretation, and it has no more claim on the truth than anyone else's."[60] In the United States, as in the rest of the nations in the West, Christendom is dead.[61] In fact, it is being argued that the United States is or is quickly becoming the third or fourth largest mission field in the world.[62] Everywhere we turn, we are surrounded by lost and lonely people *whom God deeply loves*. And God *does* love them. In fact, there is nothing our God wouldn't do in order to save them.

> For this is what the sovereign LORD says: I myself will search and find my sheep. I will be like a shepherd looking for his scattered flock. I will find my sheep and rescue them from all the places to which they were scattered on that dark and cloudy day. I will bring them back home. (Ezek. 34:11-13 NLT)

There is what seems to be an increasing number of Christians, among them Lutherans in the United States, who are beginning to pay attention to the reality of this new mission field and who are being moved to love the world God loves. Mission, outreach, and evangelizing are hot topics in our seminaries and in our congregations, in our publications and in our prayers. There are a variety of voices—some new and some that have been around for a while—calling this church to be who it says it is, the *Evangelical* Lutheran Church in America.[63] These voices each have their own way of talking about the evangelical task. It is hard to find agreement for a single definition of evangelizing. There is a reluctance to use any words that convey the worst aspects of previous evangelism efforts.

While some may lament this strange new world, it has in fact opened up new opportunities for Christians courageous enough to begin asking the really important questions: *What in the world is God up to? And what does that mean for us? What does that mean for* me? More and more, as these questions are wrestled over, there is the sense that to be a Christian means to answer the call to follow Christ into a life of witness and service; and that to be the church means to be in mission. There is, in fact,

> no doubt that mission is an issue today, and it is precisely mission to their own countries which is beginning to take a prominent role in the Lutheran churches of the Western world. Mission is no longer simply giving donations for someone to go

and work among peoples which have not known the Christian faith. Rather, mission is in "six continents" and Lutherans in the West are being told that every Christian is a missionary and that every congregation is a missionary congregation.[64]

There is a growing conviction that, for too long, ecclesiology has been understood apart from mission and that this is "a legacy of the Christendom mentality" that has to be corrected.[65] The bottom line is "a church without mission and a mission without the church are both contradictions."[66]

In some ways, this strange new world is offering Christians and their communities of faith an opportunity to reimagine who and what they are and to redefine themselves on the basis of God's saving mission in the world. This is a moment for the church to "be reconceived within the horizon of the eschatological mission of God in world history."[67] It is a rare and wonderful moment. But, in order to seize it, Lutherans in this day have to deal with that age-old theological hurdle. In other words, in order to do the hard work of evangelism, we Lutherans are going to need a really good reason for doing it. We need, today, some way to understand the connection between the gift of salvation through Christ and the call to follow Christ.

The Gift Is a Call

First, let's be clear. There is nothing we have to do—or even can do—to deserve the call to follow Christ. It is a gift. But let us also be clear: the gift we are given in Christ is a call.

The apostle Paul[68] believed that, in Christ, we are saved and set free "from the law of sin and of death" (Rom. 8:2). He knew that "nothing in all creation" will ever be able to take this away from us; nothing will ever be able to "separate us from the love of God in Christ Jesus our Lord" (Rom. 8:31-39). "As a widow is set free by the law to be joined to another husband, so the road to that other life, where there is no duplicity, no ambiguity, is thrown open to us."[69] We are set free for a life, in other words, that opens up to eternity, righteousness, and a whole new existence with Christ. But this freedom that comes with our salvation cannot be for us "an opportunity for self-indulgence" (Gal. 5:13). "What then?" Paul asks rhetorically. "Should we sin because we are not under law but under grace? By no means!" (Rom. 6:15). When we are freed from the rulers of this age, we receive a new Lord, Jesus Christ. There is no *lord-less* option. We will either be slaves to the law and to sin, which lead to death (Rom. 6:16), or we will "belong to another, to him who has been raised from the dead" (Rom. 7:4). It is "for that Other we have been unfettered and set at liberty."[70] We, Paul says, "belong to Christ" (1 Cor. 3:21).

Furthermore, Christ saves us and sets us free to follow him for a reason: "in order that we may bear fruit for God" (Rom. 7:4). "Christian freedom is thus not the absence of restraints but rather life under a new Lord. Freedom is not the ability and opportunity to determine one's life for oneself."[71] Christian freedom is life lived under Christ, in service to others. For this reason, Paul calls us, through love, to become "slaves to one another" (Gal. 5:13). "Am I not free [from the law]?" he asks (1 Cor. 9:1), knowing full well the answer is yes. But freedom from the law is not freedom at the expense of others. "Though I am free with respect to all," he explains, "I have made myself a slave to all" (1 Cor. 9:19). A Christian, freed from the law to serve Christ, will do what is "beneficial" to others, that which "builds up." We will seek, not our own advantage, "but that of the other" (1 Cor. 10:23). Those who have been saved and set free by Christ will bear the fruit of "love, joy, peace, patience, kindness, generosity, faithfulness, gentleness, and self-control" (Gal. 5:22-23). Christian freedom is "the voluntary slavery of love."[72]

It was Paul's own experience of salvation—and his understanding of the freedom God had in store for the world—that propelled him into mission. "The love of Christ urges us on," he proclaims, "because we are convinced that one has died for all; therefore all have died. And he died for all, so that those who live might live no longer for themselves, but for him who died and was raised for them" (2 Cor. 5:14-15). Saved and set free by Christ, Paul could no longer live for himself. Rather, his life was consumed by a passion for sharing the gospel of freedom with others who had not heard or believed it:

> "Everyone who calls on the name of the Lord shall be saved." But how are they to call on one in whom they have not believed? And how are they to believe in one of whom they have never heard? And how are they to hear without someone to proclaim him? And how are they to proclaim him unless they are sent? As it is written, "How beautiful are the feet of those who bring good news!" (Rom. 10:13-15)

"Once Paul became convinced that God was offering salvation to all people through the death and resurrection of Jesus, and that this message was his to proclaim, then the apostle felt a driving compulsion to preach."[73] He knew that he was free from any "legal" obligation to do this work. But he was "obligated," nevertheless, by Christ. "Woe to me," he said, "if I do not proclaim the gospel!" (1 Cor. 9:16).

For Paul, the gift of salvation was a call to freedom, freedom *from* whatever leads to darkness and death, *for* a life spent following Christ. Surely his understanding of salvation was influenced by his engagement with the Hebrew Scriptures and, perhaps especially, the words of Isaiah.[74] This is what the LORD says, according to the prophet:

> In the time of my favor I will answer you, and in the day of salvation I will help you; I will keep you and will make you to be a covenant for the people, to restore the land and to reassign its desolate inheritances, to say to the captives, "Come out," and to those in darkness, "Be free!" (Isa. 49:8-9)

The gift of salvation is a call to freedom, freedom to be a people chosen to carry God's good news to the nations, freedom to call others out of darkness and into new life, freedom to give ourselves away in witness and service, freedom to follow.

It is hard, really, to understand how we could so consistently get it wrong. Nothing in Scripture can justify splitting the gift from the call. Isaiah doesn't do it. Paul doesn't do it. And neither does Jesus. Look at Peter! "Twice the call went out to [him]: Follow me! It was Jesus' first and last word to his disciple (Mark 1:17; John 21:22). His whole life lies between these two calls."[75] Notice what Jesus did *not* say when he met Peter on the beach that first day. Jesus did *not* say, "Hey, Peter. You are *so* forgiven! I love you, man!" Peter, the rough-and-tumble fisherman, would likely not have responded to such a greeting very well! Rather, Jesus said this: "Hey, Peter. Come follow me. Come follow me into a life of witness and service. Leave your nets behind and all of your worldly plans, and follow me into a life that really means something, a life that makes a difference." When Peter looked into Jesus' eyes, he must have been awestruck. "But Jesus, you know me! You know everything about me. Why in the world would you want *me*?" There was no question that Jesus' call to Peter was a gift. Peter did not deserve it! And he knew it. But that gift was a call.

In Peter's life, as in our own, "grace and discipleship belong inseparably together."[76] The gift Jesus gave to Peter was unearned and undeserved. Peter didn't even ask for it! It was a *gift* of unconditional grace! But the gift was a *call*, a call to follow Christ.[77] So inextricably bound are these two things—the gift and the call—we even dare to ask: If someone does not accept or answer the call, have they received the gift at all? In some Lutheran circles, this question may border on heresy! In former times, a beheading might have been in order. But in an age when so many of our congregations have turned in on themselves, where witness and service to those outside the walls is weak or absent, we ask this question precisely because it is so provocative.

The Gift Is a Call!

This call comes to each of us. And, in spite of ourselves, we answer it, turning away from an old life of sin and death, toward the only one in whom true life can be found. We go, because we know it is the only way we will ever find what we are really looking for. We give ourselves away because, in the end, this is the only hope we have of gaining everything that truly matters. There is no other source of light and life, purpose and hope, freedom and everlasting joy. And so, when Christ calls, we follow. We answer his call, which comes to us as a gift of grace, and leave our nets and give ourselves away. This is the hardest thing we will ever do. It will mean putting the needs of a broken world ahead of our own. It will mean loving our neighbors more, even, than we love our church. It will mean setting aside our own agendas, our own fears, our own prejudices, our own needs. It will mean risking everything, trying anything, doing whatever it takes to share the good news with others. This is a costly call. But we answer it because, when all is said and done, there is no other choice that makes any sense at all.

Summary

We Lutherans are not too sure we like the idea of people noticing that we are here. But it is way past time for us to get over it. This strange new world of ours needs the good news that we know by heart: Through no merit of our own, God comes down to save us and to set us free! And, besides, sharing this good news is at the very heart of what it means to be church. We have been sent by a sending God for this very purpose. In fact, a church that is not caught up in God's mission in the world is no church at all. We need to stop acting as though the gift of salvation can be split apart from the call to discipleship. We will be an evangelical church only when we rediscover the true meaning of being *saved by grace*.

The gift we are given by grace is the gift of Christ himself. And Jesus calls us to follow him. Therefore, we dare to say quite boldly that we believe: *The gift is a call!* It is a call to leave behind that old life of sin and death, and turn toward new life. It is a call to freedom! It is a call to follow. Make no mistake: answering this call will be costly. For those of us used to the comfort of our doctrinal pillows, lulled to sleep by the seductive sound of cheap grace, waking up to Jesus' voice calling us to leave everything behind will be quite a shock. But we will go, anyway. We will go, at the sound of Christ's call, to witness and to serve and to give ourselves away, because we know that our lives—and our congregations—will finally be all that they are meant to be only when we answer it.

CHAPTER 3

ADDRESSING CAPTIVES
IN BABYLON

Pastor Gunter Rahner was, in many ways, a typical Lutheran pastor in Westphalia, West Germany, in the 1980s. Pastor Rahner was a fifty-year-old congregational leader of one of the most prestigious churches in his region of Germany. He was respected in the wider community and recognized by his colleagues as a strong theologian and a caring pastor. The problem was, in Rahner's own words, "my ministry was failing." Fifty people attended two regular worship services conducted in one of the most brilliantly renovated church buildings in the city. Easter services were no better (although the pews were packed on Christmas Eve). One midweek Bible study for women was sporadically attended. Youth, after confirmation, were nowhere to be found within the life of the parish. The depressing statistics about Rahner's congregation seemed never ending, but they also served to define the status quo for many attending the pastoral leadership conference sponsored by our congregation. Rahner related his story to our group of forty-five pastors. Many nodded in agreement; they understood his situation all too well. Yet, as Rahner himself confessed, "I have the resources to do anything I want in my congregation. Now, what do I want to do? I don't know. Maybe evangelism will work."

What made Pastor Rahner so intriguing to the whole group was both his honesty about his dilemma and his willingness to be challenged by a conference on evangelizing. Few German pastors risked this kind of theological adventure in the 80s. Rahner knew that his congregational life wasn't in sync with biblical descriptions of Christian community. He came to our conference at St. Stephanus Kirche in order to discover a new way to do church.

St. Stephanus Church was a unique German congregation in the heart of the industrial area of the Ruhr region. Pastor Bernd Schlottoff, a remarkable preacher and musician, had led the renewal of this community of coal miners and industrial workers for almost fifteen years before I arrived in the congregation. The congregation was alive, vibrant, and growing. Pastors all around Europe wanted to visit the community to discover why. Sunday services were packed with worshipers. One

hundred and fifty high school youth came every Saturday night to sing contemporary Christian music and hear one another preach. Fifty adult groups met every
week to read the Bible together and pray. Service projects abounded. Youth work,
music, worship, small-group ministries, social activism, and evangelism formed the
core of the congregation's competencies.

Pastors from all over Europe had come to St. Stephanus for a four-day conference on how to start an evangelism program in their congregations. What
came as a surprise to many of them during the conference were two basic discov-
eries: (1) evangelizing still might work in Germany and (2) St. Stephanus's laity
were ready and able to equip them, the most thoroughly trained theologians in
the world, for how to share the gospel. No pastor at that conference failed to miss
the significance, or the irony, of this situation.

My job during the conference was to teach the theory of evangelizing before
these pastors made actual home visits. I will never forget what happened on that
first morning during my inaugural presentation. The pastors tore me to shreds—
theologically. After having taught evangelizing to Lutherans in the United States
for many years, nothing had prepared me to withstand the firestorm of fundamental objections that came at me like machine gun fire from all corners of the room.
These pastors, who actually came to learn about evangelism were, at the same
time, extremely skeptical about evangelizing. Some were even hostile to the whole
concept. They complained: "Isn't all evangelizing decision theology?" "Lutherans
don't do evangelizing, we do catechesis!" "Your method is too Calvinistic, maybe
even Wesleyan." "Show me your theological roots in the Lutheran confessional
writings." "Your program is too sales-oriented and too tied to American culture."
"Your message is too simple for our complex world." "What is the relationship
between your gospel and German culture?" "What is your theology of conversion?" "Where does baptism play a role in these gospel presentations?" "Can justification be reconciled with any evangelism program?"

After my three-hour theology debacle, I felt emotionally shell-shocked. No
one left that room thinking that their Lutheran objections to evangelizing had
been met. They were, of course, correct. I had done a horrible job. Fortunately, a
miracle happened that night. Our laity took these pastors out in groups of three
on home visits. The visits were electrifying! The conference pastors, after seeing
the power of the gospel presentations in action with real people, opened up. When
they witnessed firsthand simple coal miners sharing the straightforward message
of Jesus with perfect strangers, they were converted. The results were stunning. The
pastors returned to the conference the next morning, with few exceptions, wanting
to equip their laity to share the gospel "just like your people did last night." Praxis
won the day over bald theory. These pastors reported numerous stories of people
whom they visited being transformed by the story of Jesus. Unfortunately, our
laity didn't hear these powerful testimonials. Our people, of course, were back at
their respective workplaces.

The question about how Lutheran theology informed this program now
became of huge importance. Rahner spoke more eloquently and honestly than the

rest, summing up the feelings of many in the room. "I want to be able to share the gospel in my congregation the way that your laity did last night. So, do I want my laity to learn this program? Yes, of course I do. But I want to go first. I'm not going to leave this conference until you show me how to evangelize as a Lutheran."

Identifying the Critical Question

Since this initial German parish experience, I have repeatedly asked myself the question: "Who are the real evangelists in the local congregation?" This can be a trickier question than first appears. Are the clergy the evangelists by ecclesiastical design since they are given the privilege of using the pulpit and altar every week? Or are all the baptized the evangelists because they reach people with the word of God in their daily lives?

In a clergy-centered church, it is often argued, the pastors must take the lead in transforming the whole church into an organization focused on evangelism. This activity is an integral part of their call! On the other hand, many church members maintain that no cultural change toward mission in the Lutheran church can take root until all the baptized embrace evangelizing as a core value within our *evangelical* Lutheran church. The baptized have always been our church's most effective evangelists.

As an ordained pastor myself, I need to approach this question gingerly. Why? After serving various congregations for twenty-two years all over the world, I have come to realize that I'm a big part of the problem. It is not that I'm anticlerical. I'm not. I hold the pastoral office in the highest possible esteem. I also recognize, of course, that pastors aren't the sole problem when it comes to evangelizing. Too few of the baptized across the country embrace the evangelistic task as a fundamental Lutheran value or as a part of their baptismal call, even though they have heard this message repeatedly preached from the pulpit. Forces surrounding our congregations today make evangelizing increasingly complex and difficult. Nevertheless, clericalism has run rampant through our Lutheran congregations in the United States, repeatedly snuffing out any possible flicker of evangelical renewal. Clericalism is one of our ecclesiastical diseases, and the mainline brand of clericalism doesn't embrace evangelizing. This clericalism has lured us all into its web, sucking out much of the evangelical character of the Lutheran movement.

The concepts of "mission" and "confession" have, furthermore, often been mistakenly placed into the crossfire of ideological conflict, making any reconciliation between them almost impossible. The history of Lutheranism in the United States is strewn with examples of this fight.[1] Clergy, as well as many of the baptized, carry this conceptual divorce deep within their personal experience and ministries. These dynamics create havoc for those trying to lift up the evangelistic call within our church today. One can easily get bogged down within the quicksand of these debates. Consequently, I have come to the painful realization that my Lutheran pastoral training never equipped me to bring my confessional heritage into a healthy engagement with mission in the world. This was the lacuna that Pastor Gunter Rahner and others immediately recognized at the German pastoral conference over twenty years ago. It is the same theological gap that renders evangelizing vulnerable today within Lutheranism in our context.

This confession-mission misconnection belongs to the actual DNA of the Lutheran theological system. It is not that we don't have the necessary intellectual resources at our disposal to address this lacuna. It is rather that the necessary theological work just hasn't been done for our own post-Christendom context. James Scherer, the Lutheran missiologist who wrote the 1982 study on evangelism for the Lutheran World Federation,[2] states it clearly: "Luther's own thought possesses a uniquely missionary structure. Here the enormous untested potential of the Reformation for mission practice can be seen."[3] The theology is there, but it is underdeveloped and untested.

The great need of the Lutheran church today is for a renewal of theological vision about evangelizing.[4] This need for a renewed vision about evangelizing is, at its core, not about clergy or the baptized *doing anything*. It is a vision about God's activity in the world through Jesus Christ and our own identification with that activity. The flame of our theological imagination must be ignited around evangelizing. This is a particularly hard message for a church that is suffering from numerical decline. We are a church needing to be evangelized so that we can once again catch a vision of God's amazing activities in the world. God's mission in the world has a church. Evangelizing is at the core of the church's self-understanding. That is the biblical, confessional, and missional picture of being an evangelical church that we strive to rediscover. Or as Pastor Rahner declared after his own conversion on that night over twenty-five years ago, "I'm not leaving this conference until you show me how to evangelize as a Lutheran."

REREADING LUTHERAN HERMENEUTICS: WORD, SACRAMENT, AND CHRISTIAN COMMUNITY

Behind all the books about congregational and spiritual renewal lies one simple quest: to encounter Jesus Christ. We aren't really fascinated, in the final analysis, by the most effective ministry techniques. Trendy mission books often leave us hungry for more theological substance. What we genuinely desire to know is what Jesus Christ himself wants for us, his church, and his world. We want to hear Jesus' word when we go and listen to a preacher. It's that simple. What is Jesus trying to say to us? What is Jesus' will for us today? The same is true when our friends gather around the kitchen table to share insights from Scripture. We desire more than friendship and fellowship. We want to grasp Jesus' word in a real way. This quest has always been the case in our church. We have the clear conviction that Jesus' word and presence are not only for us as Christians, but also for our neighbor, and even for our world of diverse cultures and religions. We imagine that if Jesus were with us as he was with his disciples, things would be different in our struggling congregations. There would be genuine renewal, signs and wonders, transformed lives, and dynamic worship. The oppressed would be freed, the blind would receive their sight, the prisoners would be released, and the year of Jubilee would actually break into our communities. We say to ourselves, "Yes, if Jesus himself were *really* present and active with us, *then* the good news really would be heard!"

Encountering Jesus' word and presence does, in fact, make the real difference in a congregation's life and ministry. But Jesus' word and presence have often been overlaid with too much human baggage. It is our aim to lift up Christ alone (*solus Christus*). However, when all is said and done, it is not the fault of the critics when they find Lutheran preaching so hard to understand or so hopelessly out of touch with the everyday spiritual yearnings of our people. *Christ alone* is often far from the main message. It is true that our Lutheran church is faring better than many other mainline churches.[5] Nevertheless, religious trends in the United States since the 1960s force many Lutheran leaders to wonder, "Why do we possess so little evangelical power?" "What's wrong?"

If our mission in the United States is to be completely comprehended, an honest full-disclosure policy must be risked. If the truth be told, our weaknesses are often self-inflicted, and they are more about the gospel itself than about method or technique. So many people come to Lutheran churches with a genuine desire to hear *good news*, yet they often return home with the uncomfortable feeling that the institutional church is making it too difficult. They are convinced that it is not the word of Jesus himself that puts them off, but rather the superstructure of human, institutional, and doctrinal elements in our ministries.

Why are ministries so ineffectual today in such a large portion of our congregations nationwide?[6] Many Lutherans simply do not have the confidence that their gospel is *good news* to the unchurched, the poor, or those on the margins of our neighborhoods. Consequently, most Lutherans are born into the church, not evangelized into it. How many of our faithful members are finally giving up on our congregations in order to frequent other churches down the street, or worse, no church at all? Many feel pushed in this direction. They want to hear the word of Jesus. They desire to know Jesus in a Lutheran setting. How many finally leave out of desperation that Jesus' word and presence can be heard and experienced more clearly elsewhere.

The problem isn't about technique or style. One cannot overemphasize this issue. It is about the real presence of Jesus in the gospel we proclaim. Shouldn't we ask ourselves, therefore, whether we are acting as obstacles to Jesus and his word? Have we lost confidence in the gospel's benefits for our neighbor? How do we move forward as leaders of a denomination that is struggling to find its way? There is much at stake for our congregations, for our denomination, and for the Christian church's mission in the United States. God's mission is on the move. God's mission has a church. The gift is a call! What a privilege! What a responsibility! What a joyous opportunity we've been given! What should be our next step in developing a vision for mission?

Our proposal is simple: let us rediscover the *evangelical* dimension of our heritage by fully embracing evangelizing as central to our identity. The key to becoming a vital church is to commit to evangelizing as the center of an evangelical vision for mission. This commitment needs to be holistic in scope and rooted in the message of the cross of Jesus Christ. Can Lutherans, in other words, emphasize *justification* and *evangelizing* at the same time? This question sounds strange. It represents a situation filled with irony. But this polarity reflects present realities concerning confession and mission. The key for Lutheran renewal is to learn to reread our theological tradition through the lens of God's evangelizing mission. God has called us to be an evangelical, missional church.

But where do we start? In terms of congregational ministry, this rereading of our Lutheran tradition means first taking hold of our favorite ecclesiastical phrase—*the ministry of Word and Sacrament*. We must do so in a way that frees the church to do ministry, truly, as evangelical mission. The church's whole ministry depends on jealously guarding its evangelical core. This core is our most precious gift. It is our call. The doctrinal emphasis on Word and Sacrament was initially intended to guard that gift and call for mission. This teaching no longer automatically serves this purpose. The results are obvious. It is no use taking refuge in abstract discussion.

When it fights the old battles of Christendom, the Lutheran church knows why it exists. But it does not know how to confront the present or future challenges of mission in a post-Christendom environment.[7] The truth is that no church in our context today can engage in holistic mission without fully accepting the evangelical call; no church is vital or faithful if it cannot give away the faith; and no Reformation church can stand on the doctrine of justification by grace through faith without committing itself fully to evangelical proclamation both inside and outside the church. This is our evangelical identity. Let us reclaim our evangelical heritage by getting back to the basics, back to the Scriptures, and back to the call of Jesus Christ himself. The gift of Jesus Christ in Word, Sacrament, and Christian community is the call to evangelizing.

WORD, SACRAMENT, AND CHRISTIAN COMMUNITY AS THE CALL TO EVANGELIZING

This simple call to evangelical faithfulness begs the catechetical query: If evangelizing is the door that must be opened for Lutherans to enter into a future of holistic mission, *what does this mean*? The answer should be easy for an evangelical church to find. Jesus is not marching around in our context as he walked around the Sea of Galilee two thousand years ago calling disciples to "follow me" while preaching "Repent, for the kingdom of God is at hand." Some want to ask, "If Jesus were actually a leader, a pastor, or a bishop in our church today, wouldn't that make evangelistic ministry much easier?" Our situation, however, calls for a different question to be asked, "What does evangelical witnessing mean today without Jesus being physically present in our midst as he was in Galilee?"

A brief survey of theologians, church leaders, and the evangelistic literature indicates quite clearly that the word *evangelism* is used with a wide variety of meanings. In English, over three hundred definitions of the concept "evangelize" have been proposed in print.[8] Lutherans use many of them. Confusion ensues. A host of variants ranging from "all missionary activity" to "revivals," from "small-group activity" to "political organizing among the poor" are proposed. Evangelism is used to describe every spiritual activity of a local church from soup kitchens to bake sales. The thick fog of such diversity demands a beacon of clarity because we are describing the center of God's mission. Lutherans simply can't make everything they do *evangelism*.

Evangelizing seems crystal clear in the Bible stories when Jesus called, for example, Levi the publican, or James, or John, or Andrew. Jesus calls. Jesus heals. Jesus teaches. Jesus forgives. Jesus preaches the kingdom. When he touched the paralytic or raised Lazarus from the dead, we immediately grasp the power of Jesus' good news for the world. Encountering Jesus' word and presence made the difference. The act of Jesus coming to people, touching them, and calling them to lives of discipleship seems clearer in the biblical stories than in our twenty-first-century lives.

Many Christians instinctively respond to such gospel stories by lamenting, "Since Jesus is no longer living with us bodily, how can we actually 'hear' his voice or 'feel' his healing touch?" Mary could reach out and touch Jesus. Even Thomas, while doubting, got the privilege of putting his fingers into Jesus' wounds. The Syrophoenician woman could debate with the man from Galilee about dogs and crumbs off the table. What are we to do two thousand years later? Have we been left with nothing concrete or tangible? Many Christians murmur that for the disciples, Jesus' call was direct and unmistakable, whereas for them it is much more problematic and ambiguous. They lament, "The biblical picture represents nice stories, but these are not realities for today."

For Lutherans, although attempts to define Jesus only in reference to history are understandable, there is something fundamentally wrong about such an approach, even faithless. Every time we distance ourselves from the living Lord, we are actually retreating from our own evangelical heritage. Why? The heart of evangelical theology and preaching is that Christ is alive and present among us—concretely and unmistakably. Jesus' word and presence are real, direct, graspable, and available for us—today! If faith means anything, it means grasping hold of a sermon or a forgiving word from a friend and declaring, "Amen, I believe these are Jesus' words for me." Clarity on this point is vital for evangelizing. We do not act *as if* Jesus Christ were present in the Christian community. The gospel message is that Jesus, actually, is alive and is really present with us in Christian community as he promised. That's the good news. It's the great gift of salvation.

Jesus does come today as he came to the disciples in Galilee. This message summarizes the witness of the whole New Testament. Jesus gives people life by freely coming to them. This understanding is at the heart of Luther's theology. Luther's view of the *means of grace* grew out of his understanding of the incarnation itself as God's order of salvation.[9] Salvation, in fact, depends on Jesus coming in concrete ways to individuals, to communities, and to the whole world. Now, the secret of Jesus' real presence is this: the way he freely comes to people today is through the proclamation of his word, the celebration of the sacraments, and the life and witness of the Christian community.[10] It is through the spoken, visible, and lived words that God's special grace in Christ is given to a hungry church and a needy world. Salvation depends on the grace of Jesus coming by special means to people and, then, being received by faith. This is consequently how Lutherans must approach both the office of ministry in general and evangelizing in particular. The two are, in fact, joined together as one entity. The office of ministry is the office of evangelizing, because at its core we find Word, Sacrament, and Christian community. Evangelizing begins with the incarnation of Jesus the Christ coming to us through concrete words, physical signs, and real people.

This incarnational understanding of how Jesus comes to us has both a positive and negative dimension. Positively, Christ comes to us concretely through his spoken and visible word. If people are looking for Jesus' coming to them, they need to look no further than the gospel words being shared among Christians in their fellowship, and in their practice of communion and baptism. This is how saving grace happens to people. God's love doesn't remain a secret theory to be studied or a lofty idea to be achieved. God's saving love comes down to us through living words, a bath, a meal, and in the mutual care and consolation among Christians.

There is a negative side, however, to Jesus coming in such concrete ways to people. Jesus, the divine Son of God, also comes *hidden* within these human activities.[11] The challenge, for Luther, was that this incarnational *coming* of God in Christ through gospel words, two simple sacraments, and the Christian community of believers ultimately often kept the good news hidden for many people. For if Jesus comes to us simultaneously as a *human* word, a *human* bath, a *human* meal, and a *human* fellowship, all of these *human* dimensions can become huge stumbling blocks to recognizing Jesus' presence within them. It is, without doubt, the human dimension of Word, Sacrament, and Christian community that often creates the biggest headaches for evangelizing. At times, it renders *hearing* almost impossible. What is the solution? Faith. It takes faith to hear human words like "God loves you" or "follow me," or "given and shed *for you*" from very sinful people—even people you dislike, and still hear Jesus' very call on your life. It is the concreteness of how Jesus comes to us that often poses the greatest hurdle to evangelizing. Incarnation is the blessing and the bane of evangelizing. Christ comes to us concretely in the human events of word, sacrament, and the Christian community. God is coming once again "in the flesh," in fact, in "the likeness of sinful flesh" for our benefit.[12] This is the best of news for us, our congregations, and the world, and it is also the greatest malady for evangelizing today.

In the end, all evangelical ministry boils down to the reality of Jesus coming to people. Jesus' presence makes the difference in people's lives. Consequently,

Lutherans have made Word, Sacrament, and Christian community the sole evangelical centers of all their ministries because this is how we believe that Jesus Christ himself comes in a salvific way to people. In Word, Sacrament, and Christian community, in effect, Jesus still walks along the lakeshore of our world and evangelizes us just as he did two thousand years ago.

Dietrich Bonhoeffer maps out the Lutheran understanding of Jesus' coming in ways that provide parameters for delineating a missional ecclesiology for the church:

> If we want to hear his call to discipleship, we need to hear it where Christ himself is present. It is within the church that Jesus Christ calls through his word and sacrament. . . .To hear Jesus' call to discipleship, one needs no personal revelation. Listen to the preaching and receive the sacrament! Listen to the gospel of the crucified and risen Lord! Here he is, the whole Christ, the very same who encountered the disciples. Indeed, here he is already present as the glorified, the victorious, the living Christ. No one but Christ himself can call us to discipleship. . . .That was true in the same way for the first disciples as it is for us.[13]

This may prove to be Lutheranism's unique contribution to missiology in our context: a definition of evangelizing that ties the word of the cross not to ministry methods, church growth, Christian disciplines, liturgical forms, social status, contextual dynamics, or musical style, but simply to the concrete coming of Jesus in Word, Sacrament, and Christian community. This may prove to be true, that is, if the means of grace among Lutherans can be freed from their Babylonian captivity.

THE CAPTIVITY OF THE MINISTRY OF WORD AND SACRAMENT

If there is any theological phrase in Lutheranism that has suffered martyrdom time and time again at the hands of a careless clergy, it is "word and sacrament ministry."[14] We debated while preparing this book whether to use this cornerstone of Lutheran orthodoxy at all in reference to evangelizing. So often it represents a lukewarm status-quo mentality that lulls clergy into thinking that their present pattern of proclamation, even when obviously unproductive, is, nevertheless, faithful. Lutheran clericalism thrives upon a misuse of this deceptive doctrine. Word and Sacrament ministry has become the safe slogan by which generations of Lutheran pastors in the United States have justified a brand of congregational ministry that has rarely engendered any theological imagination for evangelizing. Lutheran history is strewn with famous examples where *orthodoxy* and *evangelistic practice* were pitted against one another as mortal enemies. This was not done by fellow evangelists striving for increased clarity in their commitment to outreach, but rather by pseudo-Lutherans avoiding at all costs the call to evangelize.

How can Lutherans regain an understanding of Word and Sacrament ministry that doesn't fall prey to a lifeless orthodoxy, but rather feeds a life-giving orthodoxy leading to genuine evangelizing? The risk of using this standard theological designation is real. By guarding this phrase, the newness of the evangelical call might go unheard. However, the risk of not using this theological resource is also real. Overlooking the ministry of Word and Sacrament would mean defining evangelizing while simultaneously abandoning that very aspect of our theological heritage that lifts up a unique and powerful Lutheran contribution to proclamation. Word and Sacrament can and must serve as a wellspring of evangelistic imagination. They are indeed marks (*notae ecclesiae*) of an evangelizing church. Consequently, we embrace *Word and Sacrament* as a dangerous concept, yes, but also as the life-giving core of all evangelical activity. Let us be absolutely clear on this point. An evangelical rereading of Word and Sacrament ministry should be one of Lutheranism's core contributions to an ecumenical mission theology of evangelizing. Thus, we use the phrase "Word, Sacrament, and Christian community" as an alternative reading regarding how Jesus comes to people salvifically.

This uniquely Lutheran contribution to evangelizing has not been embraced by the wider ecumenical community because, unfortunately, it lies in chains within many of our own churches. Many Lutheran congregations stand before the Sisyphean task of attempting an evangelical ministry to a needy world without the means of God's grace being fully liberated from the effects of this debilitating captivity. They have been given the right means for evangelical mission, true, but these means are locked down, chained up, and imprisoned.

Churches of the Reformation hold tightly to the belief that the church is in need of constant reform. The task of reform today must focus on unlocking those chains that continue to imprison the very means of grace given to liberate humanity and all creation. An evangelizing church's first task is to free the church itself from its captivity so that it can fully embrace its wider evangelistic call. The church needs to be evangelized in order to evangelize the world. This call for renewal isn't new within Lutheranism. It is one of the constants of our theological tradition from Luther to the Pietists, from Kierkegaard to Bonhoeffer, from Tumsa[15] to those Lutherans in South Africa who fought against apartheid. And the bells from this reformation tower continue to ring out around the world. *Ecclesia semper reformanda* (the church is constantly in need of reform).

The first step to the renewal of evangelical ministry, consequently, is to recognize that Word, Sacrament, and Christian community have been subjected to a miserable captivity in the Lutheran church throughout this country. Living in Babylon has thus robbed Lutheran congregations of much of their liberty and power for ministry. Luther wrote at a time of church captivity: "I would have one single gift: Jesus, with two means of grace—word and sacrament."[16] This simple message still rings true today within our own captivity. Our problems with evangelizing are deeper than method; they are *means problems*. Our message about Jesus is lifeless because the means of grace have been held within a cultural prison. This captivity is pernicious, it is systemic, it is a cancer that eats away at the ministries of so many Lutheran congregations and agencies around the country. What does this captivity look like?

THE SEVENFOLD CAPTIVITY OF WORD AND SACRAMENT

Captivity One: The Sermonic Cage

Congregations routinely reduce, and then equate, the biblical notion of "the word of God" to a ten- to fifteen-minute homily given on Sunday morning. The sermon, therefore, must carry the *whole* proclamation freight for the *whole* congregation during the *whole* week. This is an impossible feat! It's analogous to caging up a wild animal in a zoo. The cage kills the spirit of the animal. Once Jesus' living word is put into these chains, the baptized never view their task as having anything to do with *the word of God* or evangelizing. Pastors view their whole evangelistic task as preparing the best twelve-minute sermon that they can. Evangelizing becomes caged within a professional activity restricted to a liturgically specified time that is limited to one morning a week.

Captivity Two: Hollow Ritual

The dynamism of the gospel can be easily reduced to mere performance. Here a hollow repetition of comforting rituals is confused with a genuine engagement with the living Lord through baptismal and eucharistic liturgies. The prophets warn of this tendency throughout the Old Testament. The true evangelizing dimension of the sacraments is quickly reduced within our consumer-oriented Babylon to the churchly distribution of religious goods and services. A person goes to the communion rail to receive personal forgiveness, and that's all. Such rituals contain no power for transforming the individual, the community, or the world.

Captivity Three: A Tribal Prison

Tribal prisons severely limit the vision of God's kingdom, defining its borders no further than the boundary lines of one's culture and ethnicity. How often has ethnicity served as a prison for Lutherans in restricting their theological vision for mission? How often has evangelizing basically meant the worldwide expansion of a culturally conditioned form of Christianity? How often have congregations found their evangelizing identity related to national expressions of German, Norwegian, Danish, or Swedish culture? Evangelizing has been polluted time and time again by its complex relationship with various forms of colonialism or power. This is as true globally as it is locally. The missionary dimension of the gospel, its catholicity, is denied in deference to various sociological principles that often boil down to *them conforming to us* or *like evangelizing like*. When evangelism functions from within this tribal prison, it's often not Jesus that is preached but one's own culture.

Captivity Four: The Playground of Class

Since the seventeenth century, Lutherans have placed artificial limits on where they can or cannot witness to the gospel. These limits are often determined as much by class as they are by ethnicity and geography. There is a cultural ethos in our context that refuses to discuss class openly. Clear lines have been quietly but effectively drawn between groups. Many congregations simply accept these divisions between poor and rich, blue- and white-collar ministries, and different neighborhoods without debate or a fight. Today these limits begin by delineating suburban, urban, and rural churches as much by class as by geography. If one does mission across class, it often degrades into mission *for* instead of mission *with*. Mission is thus reduced to a geographically and contextually defined playground inside of which members feel comfortable and safe.

Captivity Five: The Addiction of Clericalism

How often has the Lutheran church lamented the fact that Luther's doctrine of the priesthood of all believers is widely suppressed in our congregations—with few exceptions? Why do our pastors and congregations so easily accept the trappings of clericalism? While study after study exposes the beauty of the biblical principle of the ministry of the baptized, Lutherans can't seem to break their addiction to hierarchical structures of ministry. The price we pay for this addiction is devastating to what God is trying to accomplish in our congregations, in our neighborhoods, and around the world. Evangelizing simply cannot thrive in congregations when restricted to the clergy class.

Captivity Six: Gospel Shrinkage

The Bible lifts up so many beautiful dimensions of what God gives us in Christ Jesus. Lutherans have focused on one of these, the justification of the ungodly. And this is for good reasons. Nevertheless, the Bible stories give a fuller picture of what happens to us when the gospel is preached and Jesus' presence is experienced. The fullness and diversity of these stories must be reflected in our proclamation through Word and Sacrament and our life as a Christian community. The gospel cannot be reduced to just one message, even one that is biblical and beautiful. Neither can the good news be expanded to include every aspect of human hope and liberation. The church's evangelistic efforts are constantly confused by either gospel shrinkage or gospel expansion. This either chains the living word to our own favorite dimension of the gospel or expands it beyond the word of the cross of Jesus.

Captivity Seven: Our Love of Glory, Power, and Success

This is a particular disease in our church life. Every congregation wants to lift up the name of Jesus and preach the gospel of Christ. However, when they speak of Christ, many do so primarily in terms of power, glory, miracles, and success. Certainly, Lutherans embrace the concept of "glory." Our eucharistic liturgy speaks openly of our yearning for a foretaste of this glory in the reign of God. But

Lutherans understand the biblical gospel to be one where glory comes through suffering, resurrection comes through the cross, and new life comes through baptism into Christ. Luther's insight into the theology of the cross assists us as we proclaim the gospel message to a culture that is addicted to power, success, and glamour. Preaching Jesus as the crucified one isn't easy within a culture that is only interested in winners. Any kind of evangelizing that bypasses the cross will elicit either short-term transformation or lifelessness. Short-term success can never substitute for true conversion and renewal.

As Lutherans move from prolonged discussions about evangelizing techniques to a more thorough theology for evangelizing, calls for liberating the means of grace will grow louder. We Lutherans should not react defensively to these voices. These calls are calls to evangelical freedom. For this liberation to happen, Lutherans themselves will need to be evangelized as they accept the call to evangelize. A church-in-mission is always a missionized church. Good news works this way. Here is where the freedom, the power, and the motivation for evangelizing are to be found. Daily baptism, for Luther, revolved around the need for being daily evangelized and renewed. The means of grace are available for the church to do this kind of gospel work. God has given us an abundance of gifts for our evangelical call. Those churches that are freed to use these gifts will also be free to follow the call.

STANDING AT THE FORK IN THE ROAD: SEVEN THESES FOR FREEING EVANGELIZING

What is the answer to our churchly captivity in Babylon? The answer is as simple as it is complex. It touches on the questions of *who* and *where*, rather than *how*. We must return to the Lord who has promised that he will come to us. He comes to is in Word, Sacrament, and Christian community. In other words, the answer is not primarily about theology. The answer is certainly not a task just for evangelical activists. It involves the death and resurrection of a whole church body with much of its theological and cultural baggage. Pride is a difficult hurdle. Few churches suffer from theological pride as much as Lutherans. Fortunately, few Lutherans today would claim that our theology has produced a vibrant evangelizing church in our context. This is a powerful admission (*admissio*) from a confessing church (*confessio*). As God renews our church, our prayer is that our theology and practice of evangelizing will also be renewed so that we can experience the Lord's coming and live. Our prayer is that Jesus would come to us. "Come, Lord Jesus."

Freedom to follow the call to be an evangelizing church is a call to participate in the mission of God in all its dimensions. Jesus' presence makes this possible. There is, consequently, a growing conversation about the theology of evangelizing that moves beyond just methods and strategies. This conversation wants to grapple seriously with the whole missiological understanding of a church that has an evangelizing core. This is not an easy task, especially within our competitive church environment.

Evangelizing falls between a rock and a hard place. The rock is the extraordinary silence on the part of systematic theology on the subject of evangelizing. The hard place is the inability of practical theology to reach any sustained measure of theological consensus on evangelizing praxis. In relation to other religions, our inability to reach a growing non-churched culture and, above all, our inability to pass on the faith to our children, our weakness in evangelizing has been exposed. We stand at a mission crossroads in our context. The contours of this crossroads become increasingly evident as the church wrestles with this gift and the call to be an evangelizing church.

Seven theses serve to describe both the contours of this critical crossroads and how the foundation of Word, Sacrament, and Christian community is a liberating force for renewal and revitalization, not only for Lutherans but for the whole church across the world. The driving concern behind all these theses is to set free the word of God to do its saving work.

Thesis One: Evangelizing Means Simply That Jesus Comes to People

Evangelizing needs to be defined clearly and simply so that it is accessible to all Christians for the purpose of articulating the center of the church's mission. Luther set the tone for this kind of direct but simple language. He defined evangelical proclamation as "what promotes Jesus" (*Was Christum treibt*). The theology surrounding evangelizing is complex, nuanced, and worthy of deep scholarship. Evangelizing itself, in contrast, must model simplicity because it is about *good news* for people. Thus, our definition reads as follows: *Evangelizing is Jesus coming to people.* We might add to this definition that Jesus comes to people through their ears, that is, through *hearing* the gospel. Thus, another definition might read as follows: Evangelizing is an acoustical affair in which Christ comes to people within their particular context through the concrete means of grace.

Now, caution is required at this point. No one definition of evangelizing will ever be sufficient. The Bible points to definitional diversity, rather than any one brand of *witness*. Nevertheless, the verbal dimension of evangelizing must remain clear and uncompromised, whatever else sharing the gospel includes or demands. The aim of evangelizing is Christ's coming. It is this coming that produces responses of faith and obedience in believers and nonbelievers alike by communicating that this good news from God that necessitates Jesus Christ is *for you*. This acoustical event takes place within but must be distinguished from the wider framework of Christian life that is found in words, rituals, community, and deeds. Without Christ's real presence, evangelizing isn't possible. Thus, God remains in control when God comes to people through Christ.

Thesis Two: Evangelizing in the World Happens in Three Ways— In the Spoken Word, in Two Sacramental Acts, and in Christian Community

When speaking today of "the means of grace," we should speak in terms of Christ coming in Word, Sacrament, and Christian community. Two things are true: Word and Sacrament create an evangelizing community *and* the Christian community itself serves as a means of Christ's presence in the world.[17] Therefore, evangelizing functions within an ecclesiological framework. The power of evangelizing is released when Christians gather around the Word and Sacrament, and share in mutual conversation and consolation as a body.[18] This opens up the *office of the keys* by providing Christians with the knowledge of how to give and receive the word of forgiveness. Word, Sacrament, and Christian community establish the means of how Jesus Christ comes to people and how this presence can be salvific and redemptive for the world.

Thesis Three: Evangelizing Both "Gathers and Scatters" and "Sends and Receives"

A missional ecclesiology founded on the means of grace will lead to the renewal of the *sending* and *receiving* (and *gathering* and *scattering*) dimensions of God's word—especially within Lutheran liturgies. Luther's catechetical description of how God's word functions—it calls, gathers, enlightens, and sanctifies (which includes the notion of *receiving* the word from others)—will now need to include *sends*. A church's health should be measured as much by its sending capacity as its receiving capacity. Other churches have often succeeded in neighborhoods where Lutherans have failed. It will be critical for future Lutheran evangelistic efforts to know where God is sending our church, with what message, and why. Sending involves the call to ministry of all the people of God, not just the clergy. The receiving dimension of the word (including the receiving of missionaries into our context) will also need to be relearned, as the church responds to *mission-in-reverse* from those same peoples to whom it has been sent.

Thesis Four: Give the Means to All the Baptized

Evangelizing will succeed when Word, Sacrament, and Christian community are fully freed up to be God's means of grace in the hands of the baptized. A phoenix will rise from the ashes of a declining church as Lutherans rediscover their doctrine of baptism, the baptismal call of all believers to the priesthood, and the relationship between baptism and vocation. Baptismal theology is a richer resource for evangelizing than was once imagined. In particular, the role of vocation is reemerging as one of the most central dimensions of how Lutherans grasp a holistic approach to mission and evangelizing in the world.[19] Consequently, clergy must not only call, but also liberate, equip, and send all the baptized into the world with full authority to use the means of grace to bring Christ to people. Good order should never trump missional necessity. Clergy should supervise and administer the means of grace, not control or dominate them.

Thesis Five: Release the Evangelizing Power of the Eucharist

The evangelistic power of the Eucharist has been largely untapped and is waiting to be discovered more broadly by the whole church. Instead of requiring baptism before communing at the altar (the present ELCA and LCMS policy), more congregations should practice eucharistic evangelism, in which the liturgy is focused on gospel proclamation to all sinners—baptized and non-baptized—announcing that Jesus really comes to them with all his gifts in bread and wine. Our message needs to be, "Come, eat, drink, and believe—the presence of Jesus, God's gift to you." Jesus is the host who is inviting all sinners to table fellowship with him. The Eucharist needs to become more of a banquet feast where invitees come from the highways and byways to receive God's grace in Christ, rather than being an insider feast for family members only (Matthew 22).

Thesis Six: Accept only Evangelizers as Candidates for Pastoral Ministry

Word, Sacrament, and Christian community will function evangelistically when the office of ministry is primarily understood as an evangelizing office (this does not refer, however, solely to the office of evangelist). From the formation of clergy themselves to the equipping of all the baptized for ministry, the pastoral office needs to be the evangelizing office, an office that guides and directs all the evangelizing activities of the whole church. No candidate for the pastoral office should be accepted without these gifts and sense of call. Candidates for the ministry need to be called to gather, enlighten, sanctify, and *send* people into mission. They must not dominate the means of grace, but instead assist and equip the church to rightly proclaim the word, administer the sacraments, and live as a Christian community.

Thesis Seven: Make Adult Baptism and Catechesis the Norm

The means of grace will function evangelically in our post-Christendom culture when adult baptisms and catechesis become the norm from which other forms of baptism and teaching for children draw their lessons. A church-in-mission embraces the call to discipleship for all its people, not just for its children. For this discipleship language to work theologically today, it will need to be brought into dialogue with the dynamic polarity of confession and mission. Confession will help Lutherans make disciples who are grounded in grace. Mission will lead Lutherans into a diversity of themes that describe what God is doing throughout the world, such as contextualization, liberation, humanization, and mission on the margins. In this regard, Lutherans must continue their commitment to ecumenical conversations so that they can grasp the call to discipleship more deeply and broadly.

STANDING AT THE CROSSROADS: EVANGELISM OR EVANGELIZING

Today, Lutherans are standing at the crossroads trying to decide what evangelizing means within this post-Christendom environment. We argue that the biblical and Reformation traditions point to evangelizing as the heart of any missional ecclesiology, even when in captivity. Now that's a Lutheran confession! A church that can't evangelize is like the proverbial dog that can't hunt. If a church is seeking to discover its identity, its purpose, and its very soul, learning to become an evangelizing community is the only door that can open up that future.

A Reformation church standing at this crossroads must ask itself whether the tradition provides the tools that our congregations need in order to evangelize effectively and faithfully. Some authoritative voices have said no, and recent church growth trends point in the same direction.[20] Lutherans need, nevertheless, to stand firm against such voices and recommit themselves to an evangelical identity that is centered on the means of grace and, most important, is one that can liberate us from our captivity in Babylon.

I have learned this from the experience of serving thirteen years as a bivocational pastor of St. Andrews Lutheran Church on Chicago's Southside. Evangelizing, as the core to a missional engagement with the world, is the key to renewal.[21] Statistics tell part of the story. In 1979, church attendance had reached 160 at two services in this mission development congregation, and 100 children were coming to Sunday school. The future looked bright. Ten years later, only eight children were enrolled, five of them from one family.

A devastating lack of missional awareness afflicted St. Andrews during this short period. Members understood their mission as, in the words of a church official, "providing a church home to Lutherans." "Find the Lutherans in the neighborhood and invite them to church" was the evangelistic cry. The church had little sense of ministry to the unchurched, the marginal, the poor, or those who were not of northern European ancestry. The neighborhood changed, but St. Andrews didn't keep pace. Survival became the church's bottom line, its mission. Failure followed.

When I arrived in 1991, the congregation had thirty-five members in worship. I soon heard a laundry list of complaints: there was no choir, the council was exhausted, no one could remember the last successful stewardship program, all our neighbors were Catholic, bigger churches next door had better programs and tons of money to do outreach, and both the church building and the congregation were aging. To survive, St. Andrews needed to discover a vision for mission suitable to its context and size.

In order to become transformed into an evangelizing church, St. Andrews had to let go of clericalism and convert its members into ministers; let go of the myth of size and develop a vision of what a small church can do; move beyond coffee fellowship in its missional emphasis on worship, community, outreach, and food; and leave behind traditional notions of church in order to focus on the congregation's evangelizing on the margins. Church-growth techniques were of little help to St. Andrews as they faced this life-and-death challenge. Church-growth literature would have condemned the congregation years before to the ecclesiastical trash dump. In contrast, putting into place a Lutheran theology of mission centered on evangelizing provided the necessary foundation for renewal.

The hardest hurdle to overcome was clericalism. The congregation was addicted. It placed its hope for renewal on the pastor, not the power of the word of God. "We need a charismatic leader to turn this thing around" was the rallying cry. But it discovered that small churches can turn things around only if the people, clutching the word of God, take complete ownership of the church's administration and ministry. "Since we can no longer afford a pastor, are we willing to do the ministry ourselves?" the congregational president asked. St. Andrews answered yes and decided on a bivocational pastoral model for leadership. I took a part-time call to be the pastor, working between fifteen and twenty hours a week. The people would do most of the work and ministry themselves. It took years, however, to begin to wean the congregation from its clerical addiction, even after mission became the driving focus. Certain ministries remained to the end *clerical* in nature.

The second hardest hurdle to overcome was both defining and actually implementing *mission* with an evangelizing core. St. Andrews developed a mission statement after a long discernment process: "We are sent as a community of disciples and apostles to share God's love." Because we were *sent*, we saw ourselves as a missional community, not a church focused on its own survival. Because we were a *community*, not a collection of individuals, we worked hard to promote fellowship that centered on Word and Sacrament rather than on personalities or events. Communion was celebrated every week. Community meals were organized twice weekly. Bible study was rediscovered. With Word, Sacrament, and Christian community as our missiological base, we explored together what it might mean to live as disciples of Jesus in mission as a small congregation within our context of Chicago. As apostles, we were sent and equipped to participate in God's mission. Our commitment was to bring a ministry of love to our neighborhood. Slowly but surely, we began to learn how to give away our faith as a community. Adult baptisms become normal. Civic organizations praised our outreach to seniors. Members increasingly started to experience their calls into ministry both inside and outside the church.

This specific missional identity didn't emerge from a retreat, a seminar with a consultant, or even a prolonged council meeting. The discernment process took time and it was messy. We made mistakes. But our new evangelical identity started to emerge when we did two things: (1) when we honestly and publicly named our captivities, and (2) when we focused intentionally on the evangelizing power hidden deep within our Lutheran heritage. From this foundation, three specific areas of ministry emerged. Each had the dynamic of evangelizing at its core. The first major emphasis was mission to seniors. The second mission focus was to build an inclusive community of faith where whites, African Americans, Asians, Hispanics, and Native Americans could experience life together as a community, which became their chief witness to the wider community. Finally, our focus was turned toward evangelizing the masses of unchurched and de-churched persons in our neighborhood.

Barring a miracle, St. Andrews will likely never become a leading congregation numerically or financially. Having 160 in worship may be as far as it can grow numerically. St. Andrews will always be a neighborhood church increasingly surrounded by larger congregations. That is the trend. St. Andrews was, nonetheless,

dynamic, growing, alive, and faithful to God's mission. The congregation rediscovered its call. What a gracious gift that call was. Size is never the chief govern-
ing factor that determines a healthy congregation. The real question is whether a
congregation has discovered, named, and committed itself to its evangelical core.

Congregations tend to define themselves in terms of mission because the
church is, by definition, missional.[22] Although Lutherans have not always used the
language of "mission," "missiology," and "missional ecclesiology," mission is exactly
what is meant when we affirm that at the center of all God's mission in the world
is Christ coming to people through the means of grace. At St. Andrews, we studied
other churches that were doing mission effectively. We had to pose the question to
ourselves: "Should we immediately adapt, adjust, or change our own theological
direction to be more successful?" This is a critically important question. What we
rediscovered was that our Lutheran heritage was a solid foundation upon which
to build an evangelizing congregation and escape our own captivity in Babylon.
This project had to be tested. But what a thrill it was for a whole congregation to
witness God's faithfulness when the focus on Jesus' coming through the means of
grace actually led to renewal.

Since the Reformation, Lutherans have challenged the church with an evangelical proposal for theology and ministry. Because of our numerous captivities,
we now face an evangelical challenge of our own. Can a new imagination for mission that is centered on evangelizing actually free and empower a whole church to
embrace its mission to the world? I am convinced that the churches that will be
most effective in reshaping their life as missional communities will discover their
evangelical identities from their Lutheran roots in Word, Sacrament, and Christian community. These are the means by which Christ comes to people. These are
the means that will release people who find themselves to be captives in Babylon.
The communities that can best serve the world will be those who embrace Christ's
coming as the core to their evangelical identities, like St. Andrews Lutheran Church
in Chicago.

As a church, we need to start making the same request that Pastor Gunter Rahner made: "I'm not leaving until you show me how to evangelize—as a Lutheran."

CHAPTER 4

FOR THE SAKE OF THE WORLD

L iberation from the Babylonian captivity leads the church directly into the world to participate in God's mission. One cannot focus on evangelizing without taking seriously the fact that the world is the primary location of God's mission. Scripture presents this story clearly.

God is passionate about the world. God the Creator made all that is and "it was very good" (Gen. 1:31). However, this created world became corrupted when the presence of sin was introduced into the world through the Evil One (Gen. 3:1-7). But God through Christ intervened to defeat the power of sin in the world through triumphing over the Evil One (Gen, 3:15; Col. 2:15). Now God the Redeemer is working through the Spirit to bring back into right relationship all that was lost in the fall by bringing redemption to bear on every dimension of life (Isa. 61:1-2; Luke 4:16-21). Finally, God, through the crucified, risen, and ascended Christ, will one day return as the triumphant King to bring all of redeemed life into a new heaven and new earth where the presence of sin will be removed (Rev. 21-22).

This biblical framework deeply informs our understanding of evangelizing in relation to the world. Whenever we think about God, we need to add the words, "the mission of the Triune God within all of creation." Whenever we talk about the gospel, we need to add the words "for the sake of the world." Whenever we discuss the church, we need to add the words "sent into the world to participate fully in God's mission." Our view of God is not complete without having the world in view, with God in relationship to it as both Creator and Redeemer. The gospel is not fully the gospel if it does not have the whole of creation as its horizon. The church is not fully the church if it does not seek to bring redemption to bear on every dimension of life.

In the discipline of missiology, this perspective is referred to as the *missio Dei*, which is usually translated as "the mission of the Triune God in all of creation." This mission represents a panoramic overview of God's creation purposes in relation to the kingdom of God as inaugurated by Jesus, which introduces God's redemptive intent within God's larger mission to the world. This ties together the creation with the cross, where the church is called and sent to participate fully in this mission. Within this mission, evangelism functions as a more focused activity of the church, where it serves as an essential dimension of the *missio Dei*.

God has a passion that all persons should hear about and be invited to participate in this new life that comes through Jesus Christ. The focus of God's intent is always toward all persons, referred to in the Bible as "whosoever," and meaning *everyone* (John 3:16). God has a passion that this good news should be taken to the entire world that all may hear it. The focus of God's passion is always toward "the ends of the earth," what might be referred to as *everywhere* (Acts 1:8). God has a passion that all of life should flourish—that the mission of God should function within all of creation, and this means *everything* (Matt. 28:19).

God's passion is for the gospel to go *everywhere* so that *everyone* might be invited to receive redemption that relates to *everything*. In God's plan, the church is given the incredible privilege of sharing this good news about new life in Christ with all who have not heard. The gift is a call. The call is a gift. This is the evangelizing task of the church. The mission of God in the world, the *missio Dei*, requires evangelizing in order for persons to have an opportunity to come to know fully the living Christ and experience new life through the Spirit (Rom. 10:14-17). Evangelizing always has this more comprehensive mission of God in view as it announces the good news that God is seeking to bring back to right relationship all that which was lost in the fall.

Evangelizing reveals to the world, through words that can be comprehended, the power of God and God's redemptive purpose in Christ. This is Paul's point when he summarizes his understanding of the gospel in Romans 1:16: "For I am not ashamed of the gospel. It is the *power* of God for salvation to everyone who has faith, to the Jew first and also to the Greek" (my italics). The gospel, conveyed by words that are announced as good news, both contains and reveals God's power. All the power that God brought to bear in the incarnation, life, death, resurrection, and ascension of Jesus Christ is now embedded in the story about Jesus. Evangelizing releases the power of this story into the world. Through the work of the Spirit, this story becomes redemptive in character as it is heard and received through faith by the recipient (1:17).

A BIBLICAL FRAMEWORK FOR UNDERSTANDING THE CHURCH'S PARTICIPATION IN EVANGELIZING AND MISSION

The Old Testament Covenants as God's Stated Intention regarding the World

God's passion for the world is made clear in the Old Testament. After humanity's fall into sin, the story of redemption unfolds around God's continuing concern for the entire world. This is made clear through the various covenants that God made with the human community, starting with Noah (the Noahic Covenant in Genesis 9) and extended through Abraham (the Abrahamic Covenant in Genesis 12, 15, 17), Moses (the Mosaic Covenant in Exodus 19), David (the Davidic Covenant in 2 Samuel 7), and the prophet Jeremiah (the New Covenant in Jeremiah 31). In each of these covenants, God made it clear that the larger horizon of God's intention was always the world. It is especially important to understand that God lodged the particularity of redemption for the whole world in the selection and election of Israel. However, Israel's election was never about privileged status, but rather about being selected for witness and service to the world. Israel was to be a "light unto the Gentiles" (Isa. 42:6; 60:1-3) and a "city set on a hill" (Isa. 2:2-4). Their communal life was to continually bear witness to the redemptive purposes of God so that this redemption would be available to all. The whole world was always in view, that all the nations might come to know the living and true God.

God's covenants in the Old Testament are God's clear statement of intent that in spite of the fall and our own sinfulness, God is not finished with the world. Redemption is not just about some special people being chosen, as an end in itself. God's election of Israel as a particular people was for the purpose of bringing the good news about God to all the nations. Election in the Old Testament was for service, not privilege. The gift is a call. Unfortunately, Israel often turned the focus of its election inward and built barriers to keep the nations out rather then constructing bridges to bring them in (Amos 9:7; Isa. 19:24).

The coming of Christ into the world is in direct continuity with God's intention in these Old Testament covenantal commitments. When Jesus announces at the Last Supper that the New Covenant is coming into full reality through his death and resurrection, he proclaims that the forgiveness of sins is now available to all—*everyone everywhere* (Matt. 26:28). Whenever we announce the forgiveness of sins, we need always to keep the whole of the world in view. Being "in Christ" (2 Cor. 5:16) is never about privileged status, but rather about being selected for witness and service to the world because "in Christ God was reconciling the world to himself . . . and entrusting the message of reconciliation to us" (2 Cor. 5:19). The gift is a call.

Critical to understanding God's redemptive purposes is understanding that the universality of the good news is always embedded in particularity. There is no abstract gospel. Gospel is always clothed in culture and comes to expression through particular people within particular contexts. God's working in this way is clearly evident in God's selection of Abraham and the election of Israel through him. God's working in this way was true even when this particularity regarding Israel appeared to the larger world as scandal. When in captivity, those taken to Babylon under Nebuchadnezzar were instructed to live in their servitude by seeking the welfare of the city where God had sent them into exile, because "in its welfare you will find your welfare" (Jer. 29:1-9).

The implication that became clearer over time in Israel's history was that participation in God's redemption in the world, while anticipating the fully revealed kingdom of God, was more about suffering service than privileged status (see especially the role of the Suffering Servant in Isaiah 53–54). This is a lesson that comes clearly into focus when Jesus tried to help his followers understand that the role of the Suffering Servant of Isaiah 53 must precede the full revealing of the reigning king of Daniel 7. In Jesus' words, "the Son of Man came not to be served but to serve, and to give his life as a ransom for many" (Mark 10:45). This is the same lesson the church throughout the ages is called on to model, and has often struggled with. The gospel frees the church to live in vulnerability in relation to the world, where this vulnerability will often lead us to the margins. All too frequently, the church has sought to amass power at the center in order to build and maintain domain, a domain that is often more about serving the interests of the church than being for the sake of the world.

The Kingdom of God in the Gospels[1]

In the Gospels, one encounters the expectation that a movement is about to be born as a result of the announced presence of the kingdom of God in the person and work of Jesus Christ. This kingdom is present in our midst: "the kingdom of God is among you" (Luke 17:21). It is to be received (Mark 10:15); persons are invited to seek it (Matt. 6:33) and to enter into it (Matt. 23:13) while also looking toward that day when they will inherit it (Matt. 25:34). The coming of the kingdom is about God's power confronting and defeating the power of the enemy, the Evil One (Matt. 4:1-11).

Living into the presence of the kingdom, the redemptive reign of God in Christ, means that illnesses may be healed (Matt. 11:2, 4-5), evil spirits may now be cast out (Mark 1:39), and natural circumstances may be changed (Mark 6:47-52), even as the poor hear the gospel of the kingdom as good news (Luke 4:18-19). Parables are used to explain the kingdom as a mystery that only some have ears to hear and eyes to see (Matt. 13:10-17). The Father gives the kingdom as a gift to the followers of Jesus, and accepting this gift radically changes the way one looks at material possessions (Luke 12:32-33). While the presence and influence of God's kingdom will grow dramatically in the world (Matt. 13:31-32), there are also many who think they are part of God's kingdom who will miss it (Matt. 21:33-44).

Jesus announced that the time of the presence of the kingdom being made manifest in the world was now at hand, and that redemption would now be brought to bear on all of life—*everything*; and that it was his intent to invite *everyone everywhere* to repent and believe this good news (Mark 1:14-15). In order to spread this message, he gathered around himself followers who were to learn to "fish for people" (Mark 1:17). The expectation was that these followers would serve as the foundation of the church that Jesus would himself build. "I will build my church" (Matt. 16:18). Anticipating his death, Jesus prayed not only for his followers, but also for all who would come to believe in him through their testimony (John 17:20). Following his death and resurrection, as noted above, Jesus made it clear that his followers were to take the message of salvation, rooted in God's kingdom (the redemptive reign of God in Christ), to all people—*everyone*; and to the ends of the earth—*everywhere*; and to bear witness to its truths in relation to all of life—*everything* (Matt. 28:19-20; Luke 24:47).

Jesus also conveyed to these followers that they would be led in this work and empowered to carry it out through the presence of the Spirit among them (Luke 24:49; John 14:25-26; 20:22). Jesus clearly anticipated that a movement, persons who later came to be known as Christians (Acts 11:26), and a new type of organization, what came to be called the church (the ecclesia as a *called out* community), would grow out of the work of these followers as they were led and taught by the Spirit (Matt. 16:18; John 17:20).

The Church in Relation to the Kingdom—Missionary by Nature

The key to understanding the nature, purpose, and ministry of the church is to understand its relationship to the kingdom of God. This kingdom of God as announced by Jesus—the redemptive reign of God in Christ—clearly anticipated that there would be a community of believers built up around the twelve apostles who would carry the message of the good news about the kingdom to the world. Jesus does not provide a lot of specific content about how this community of believers would be organized and how it would function, but it is clear that the Spirit's presence within it and the Spirit's working through this community would make this new organization unique in the world.

They would be *empowered* by the Spirit, doing even greater things than Jesus himself had done during his public ministry (John 14:12). They would be *taught* by the Spirit, learning how to discern the leading of God and the working of God's redemptive purposes within particular contexts (John 14:26). They would be *led* by the Spirit into the world and empowered to participate fully in God's mission, which Jesus identifies as beginning with the announcement to the world of the forgiveness of sins (John 20:21-23). The presence of the Spirit and the Spirit's teaching and leading the church gives birth to a church that is missionary by nature. The church's very existence in the world has to be understood in missionary terms. The church cannot help but participate in God's mission in the world. This is part of what it means to be the church. To do less would be contrary to its nature.

The kingdom of God, the redemptive reign of God in Christ, gives birth to the church through the work of the Spirit. The church's nature, purpose, and ministry are formed by the reality, power, and intent of the kingdom of God. Understanding the redemptive purposes of God that are embedded within the kingdom of God provides an understanding of the church being missionary by nature. This has profound implications for an understanding of evangelizing and mission. Evangelizing and mission are not just activities the church takes on as part of its responsibility to serve God in the world. They, like other aspects of the church's life such as worship, discipleship, and fellowship, are embedded as inherent practices in the very nature of the church.

The church does evangelizing and engages in participating in God's mission in the world because it can do no other. It was created for these purposes. These purposes are encoded within the very makeup of the nature of the church. This shifts the focus of evangelizing and mission away from just being activities engaged in out of obedience to being activities that the church participates in because they are part of the very nature of the church. The gift is a call.

In this regard, it is critical to understand the relationship of the biblical imperatives to the biblical indicatives. Matthew 28:19-20 is built around the key imperative "make disciples," but this imperative is premised on the fact that those receiving this expectation are already a changed community empowered by the Spirit. This is reflected in Matthew 5:13-14 where the believing followers are reminded that they are already the "salt" and "light" of the world. This is an indicative statement of fact. The same point is made in Acts 1:8 where the followers of Jesus are told that they "shall be (Jesus') witnesses." This is also an indicative statement of fact. To express it as a double negative: you cannot not be Christ's witness if, in fact, you are empowered, taught, and led by the Spirit. The book of Acts becomes the explication of this new reality. It begins at Pentecost as the intensive indwelling of the Spirit takes place within the community of 120 believers gathered together in Jerusalem and quickly spreads into a growing church that soon spills over into the larger world.

Evangelizing and Mission in the Book of Acts[2]

It is clear from even a cursory reading of the book of Acts that God is passionate about getting the message of the good news about Jesus Christ out to the world. The Acts of the Apostles (probably better titled The Acts of the Spirit) provides an account of what the followers of Jesus experienced after the Spirit came upon them. The author structures this book around the Spirit's activities of ensuring that the gospel would be taken to everyone, all the way to the ends of the earth, and that it would address all of life—*everyone, everywhere, everything.* Jesus had made it clear that this was God's intent (see Matt. 28:19-20; Acts 1:8), but the church struggled to bring this intent of God into their shared practices.

Under the Spirit's leading, and oftentimes in spite of the church's reluctance, the gospel continued to cross boundaries and become contextualized within new cultural settings. The hermeneutic used by the author of Acts to shape the content of the book makes a direct connection between the sharing of the good news about Jesus with three results: (1) the spreading of the gospel message, (2) the growth of the church, and (3) the influence of the gospel and the growing church within various cultural contexts. There are regular references to growth taking place, both in terms of people coming to faith in Christ, *evangelizing*, and the broader redemptive influence of the gospel coming to bear on the social and cultural settings into which it became contextualized, *mission.*

EVANGELIZING. In the book of Acts, we find the church participating in evangelizing through the work of Spirit. Persons bore witness to the good news about Jesus Christ, which resulted in the growth of the church. The following examples illustrate this ministry of evangelizing to *everyone, everywhere*:

Acts 1:8: "you will be my witnesses . . ."
Acts 2:41: "that day about three thousand persons were added."
Acts 2:47: "And day by day the Lord added to their number those who were being saved."

Acts 4:4: "But many of those who heard the word believed, and they numbered about five thousand."

Acts 5:14: "Yet more than ever believers were added to the Lord, great numbers of both men and women."

Acts 6:7: "The word of God continued to spread; the number of disciples increased greatly in Jerusalem . . ."

Acts 9:31: "Meanwhile the church throughout Judea, Galilee and Samaria . . . was built up . . . [and] it increased in numbers."

Acts 11:21: "The hand of the Lord was with them, and a great number became believers . . ."

Acts 12:24: "But the word of God continued to advance and gain adherents."

Acts 13:48-49: "as many as had been destined for eternal life became believers. Thus the word of the Lord spread throughout the region."

Acts 14:1: "a great number of both Jews and Greeks became believers."

Acts 14:21: "After they had proclaimed the good news to the city and had made many disciples . . ."

Acts 16:5: "So the churches were strengthened in the faith and increased in numbers daily."

Acts 17:12: "Many of them therefore believed, including not a few Greek women and men of high standing."

Acts 17:17, 34: ". . . he argued . . . in the marketplace every day with those who happened to be there. . . . Some of them joined him and became believers . . ."

Acts 18:8: "and many of the Corinthians who heard Paul became believers and were baptized."

Acts 19:10: "This continued for two years, so that all the residents of Asia . . . heard the word of the Lord."

Acts 19:20: "So the word of the Lord grew mightily and prevailed."

MISSION. In the book of Acts, we also find the church participating through the work of the Spirit in God's larger mission in the world. This resulted in God's redemption being brought to bear on all of life. The following examples illustrate this larger mission of God to *everything*:

Acts 2: As the gospel was shared in households with slaves and masters their relationships changed as both encountered Christ and then had to reencounter one another.

Acts 2 and 4: Those with excess resources sold these in order to share with those in need.

Acts 6: The leaders heard the communal complaint and addressed injustices in the distribution of food to the Gentile widows.

Acts 6: As Jewish priests became Christians, their whole life orientation in relation to Judaism was redefined.

Acts 9: As Samaritans became Christians, their social status was redefined in relation to Jewish Christians.

Acts 9: Becoming a Christian led to good deeds and acts of charity by Dorcas on behalf of those in need.

Acts 15: The race relations between Jewish Christians and Gentile Christians were redefined by the gospel.

Acts 16: The role of women in relation to church leadership was redefined by the gospel.

Acts 19: The church in Ephesus challenged, through alternative practices, the underlying religious, social, and economic structures, resulting in significant cultural change.

This hermeneutic in the book of Acts regarding evangelizing and mission anticipates the continued expansion of the church throughout the ages. The book ends with the word continuing to be proclaimed by Paul in Rome as a witness to this expectation (Acts 28:30-31).

Within the evangelizing and mission that took place in Acts, there are indications that some intentional strategies were used. Being sent necessitates making strategic choices. For example, the Twelve chose to go to the temple daily to proclaim the good news about Jesus, even when forbidden to do so. In similar manner, Paul and those working with him made it a regular practice of trying to win converts in the synagogues among Jews of the Diaspora as the foundation for planting reproducing churches in key commercial centers of the various provinces of the Roman Empire. As churches were planted, they moved on to the next province, working their way westward.

The church's strategic engagement in evangelizing normally results in expanded mission and the growth of the church. However, the expanded mission and growth of the church under the leading of the Spirit is characterized in Acts as much by conflict, disruption, and surprise as it is by any planned strategy. The Spirit empowers, teaches, and leads the church, even when the church fails to discern, understand, or engage the fuller purposes of God in living out its missionary nature. Examples of this also stand out in the book of Acts.

EVANGELIZING AND MISSION IN RELATION TO GROWTH FROM CONFLICT IN ACTS 6. The complaint of the Hellenists because their widows were being neglected in the daily distribution of food led to a decision to add additional leadership to the church. This resulted in expanded ministry, which in turn facilitated even more growth, where even many in the priesthood became Christians.

EVANGELIZING AND MISSION IN RELATION TO GROWTH FROM PERSECUTION IN ACTS 8. Jesus had made it clear that the apostles were to go from Jerusalem to the ends of the earth. But they stayed in Jerusalem. Finally, a persecution scattered the disciples throughout Judea and Samaria—although, interestingly, the apostles still remained in Jerusalem. The disruption caused by this persecution led to substantial growth from among the Samaritans, persons on whom Jewish Christians looked down as being inferior. These Jewish Christians were now required to change their worldview and to reorder their relationships with the Samaritans, something Jesus had indicated would happen on several occasions in the Gospels (see the story of the Samaritan woman in John 4 and the parable of the good Samaritan in Luke 10:29-37).

Evangelizing and Mission in Relation to Growth from Ministry on the Margins in Acts 11. Also as a result of this persecution, some of the Gentile proselytes to Judaism who later became Christian converts returned home to Antioch. Here they started sharing the faith directly with other Gentiles, without requiring them to become Jews in order to become Christians. This ministry was a surprise to the church in Jerusalem and following the Jerusalem Council eventually became the foundation for the mission to the Gentiles. Both the gospel and the church in the New Testament period were redefined in light of this. What began on the margins came to the center.

Evangelizing and Mission in Relation to Growth from Divine Intervention in Acts 16. In working their strategy of taking the gospel to the next province, Paul's mission team was hindered by the Spirit from entering either Asia to the west or Bithynia to the north. In the midst of their confusion, God redirected the team through a vision to go over to Macedonia. This divine intervention shifted the location of the planting of churches from the east to the west once the Aegean Sea was crossed.

Evangelizing and Mission in Relation to Growth from New Insights into Gospel and Culture in Acts 10 and 15. Peter's understanding of the gospel was dramatically reframed by an encounter, first with God in a vision, and later with Cornelius who was a Roman centurion. While Peter wanted to claim that certain Jewish practices were theologically grounded, God made it clear that they were, in fact, culturally bounded. What God called clean was to be understood as clean. Peter's strategy, in light of his understanding of the gospel as being shaped by the ceremonial practices of Judaism, would never have taken him to the Samaritans or to Cornelius. God intervened to disrupt and reframe Peter's understanding of the relationship of gospel and culture, although Peter still continued to struggle to fully accept Gentiles as fellow believers in Christ.

In all of these cases, the church encountered significant change that was neither planned nor anticipated. No strategy was in place that directly led to the growth of the church from these influences. The church was led by the Spirit to move in new directions, which resulted each time in new growth taking place. Two patterns are evident. There is planned activity that leads to growth—a *strategy*, as illustrated in the work of the apostles and Paul's mission team. But there is also the *Spirit's leading* of the church through conflict, disruption, and surprise into new and unanticipated directions that result in growth. When considering evangelizing and mission, it is essential to have a strategy, but it is also essential to be alert to the unexpected leading of the Spirit. In summary, it might be said of the Spirit's leading the church in the book of Acts that a church that is not changing is a church that is probably not being led by the Spirit.

Evangelizing and Mission in Paul's Letters

Although a full treatment of Paul's views on evangelizing and mission exceeds the scope of this chapter, it is helpful to note the framework that Paul develops in thinking about these matters. We find that Paul had a profound belief in the power of the gospel as the basis for changing the lives of people who had faith in God's reconciling work in Christ (Rom. 1:16-17). His personal ministry was shaped by a passion to take this message to *everyone everywhere* so that an offering of the Gentiles might be given to God through Christ in the power of the Spirit (Rom. 15:16). He was always willing to go to those places where others had not gone or would not go (such as Spain, vv. 28-29), in order that this good news might come to the hearing of all. For Paul, it was essential that this message be shared verbally so that persons had opportunity to respond by faith to the grace that God was so desirous of giving to them (Rom. 10:14-17).

Paul understood this good news, when it was accepted by faith, to result in a personal transformation (Rom. 8:9-11) that radically reoriented one's life, where all things have become new (2 Cor. 5:17). Not only does this message come to us as good news, but those who are in Christ become the ambassadors of this good news to the rest of the world so that *everyone everywhere* might learn of this (vv. 18-20). Paul understood that the words that are spoken in evangelizing need to be accompanied by demonstrations of the power inherent in the gospel through the work of the Spirit (1 Thess. 1:5). He also understood that people who respond to this message and begin to live in accord with it become, therefore, an evangelizing community to others (vv. 7-8).

Paul, however, also understood the larger eschatological reality represented in the sharing of the good news. In Christ, God defeated and disarmed the principalities and powers (Col. 2:15), so that now through the life and witness of the church these very principalities and powers are themselves unmasked (Eph. 3:10). Engaging in evangelizing always looks toward the redemptive possibilities regarding *everything*, even as it passionately seeks to bring the message of good news to *everyone everywhere*.

In the biblical framework outlined above, we find a church that is living between the times. It lives between the now and the not yet. The redemptive reign of God in Christ is already present, meaning that the power of God is fully manifest in the world through the gospel under the leading of the Spirit. But the redemptive reign of God is not yet fully complete as the church looks toward the final consummation when God will remove the presence of sin and create the new heavens and new earth.

Lutheran Confessional Foundations for Understanding the Church's Participation in Evangelizing and Mission

The biblical story presents a picture of the church as being missionary by nature, such that it carries out evangelizing and engages in mission because these are embedded within its very life. The key premise of the biblical story is that you have to start with the world in order to understand the story of salvation. A missional hermeneutic is required to correctly read Scripture. It says that God is passionate about God's created world, and desires to bring everything into reconciled relationship with the living God.

An interesting question to consider is whether the Lutheran confessional tradition is consistent with this understanding of the missionary nature of the church when read through a missional hermeneutic. It is important to ask, "Are there theological foundations in the Lutheran confessional tradition that correspond to this understanding of the church and its participation in evangelizing and mission?"[3] In the following section, selected themes from the Lutheran confessional tradition are read from the perspective of this missional understanding of Scripture and the church. Reading these themes from this perspective invites a fuller imagination about how, in fact, the gospel is for the sake of the world.

Law/Gospel Hermeneutic

God's mission within all of creation has in view that all of life should flourish. Understanding the first and second uses of the law clarifies this point. We find in the first use of the law a capacity to restrain sin, but we also find here the development of structures and practices that allow life to flourish in every dimension. The focus here is on living life in the world from the outside in, where God's law serves both to protect and permit. It is always critical to remember, however, that in God's revelation the law is always accompanied by gospel. The second use of the law makes clear to us our own sinfulness, but also tells us that through Christ the power of sin to have dominion over us has been defeated. New life, a life lived through the power of the Spirit, is now available. The focus here is on living life in the world from the inside out, where God's gospel serves to empower us to experience the abundance of life (John 10:10).

Augsburg Confession—Article VII: The Church

The Augsburg Confession develops an understanding of the church around Word and Sacrament. What is critical to understand is that Word and Sacrament are inherently missional. They invite the church into an understanding of and participation in God's mission within the world. One cannot hear the word or participate in the sacraments without having the world in view.

The Sacrament of Baptism enfolds persons into the new eschatological community that is living between the times. Through the Spirit, the water with the word brings new life to these persons and gives new meaning to their lives. Their vocational identity is made clear: they are children of the living God called to participate fully in God's mission in all the world. The law and gospel, which are made clear by the word, provide perspective on God's creation purposes and God's intent that the message of the good news of the forgiveness of sin should go out to *everyone everywhere*, and that redemption should be brought to bear on every dimension of life, *everything*. Through the Spirit, God's people are empowered to participate in God's mission within the world.

The Sacrament of the Lord's Supper invites persons to receive the body and blood of the risen Christ, the very presence of Jesus. As they do, they acknowledge and celebrate the eschatological future that has already begun. The future heavenly feast that will one day take place in the presence of the living God is already in view in our partaking of the eucharistic meal. And the good news that redemption in all of life is now available is also prophetically being announced (Matt. 8:11-12; 22:1-10; 26:26-29; Rev. 19:9). The intention is that all people are invited to believe in the risen Christ so that they may receive forgiveness of their sins. All who partake of the meal have full access to this redemptive reality. The Eucharist is inherently evangelistic. In a related way, the Eucharist echoes the groaning of all of creation as it anticipates its release from the bondage of sin that, though still present, will one day be removed (Rom. 8:18-25).

Word and Sacrament, in calling, gathering, enlightening, and sanctifying the believing community, are also sending this community into the world. The church's participation in Word and Sacrament is directly connected to the church's participation in God's mission in the world. Evangelizing and mission are as much a part of the church's corporate life—in what it means to be the church—as are worship, discipleship, and fellowship. Properly speaking, none of these can be separated from the very nature of the church.

Liturgy as Enactment

It is helpful here to consider the concept of "liturgy as enactment." Liturgy is a communal practice of the Christian church where Word and Sacrament become most visible and are most readily available. While we need to understand that Word and Sacrament are more than just liturgy, we also need to understand that they are enacted in a unique way in and through liturgy. The horizon within liturgy is always the world. Liturgy as enactment represents the power of the cross and resurrection being released, first among the gathered community, but then into the world as the church is sent to participate fully in God's mission. As such, liturgy becomes the location that both symbolizes and mobilizes the release of God's redemptive power into the world.

Enactment as anticipating the reality of the eschatological future: As the church gathers around Word and Sacrament, it does so with the eschatological future in view. The church knows that its life is not limited to this present world. While it lives in this present world, it is not subject to the powers of sin and death as its final fate. There is good news. There is a different future that awaits the community of faith gathered by the Spirit in the name of Jesus. In this regard, the practices of the gathered community represent a dress rehearsal of the eschatological future that will one day belong to persons of faith in Jesus Christ. The theme of this part of the dress rehearsal is celebration. God's people are entering joyfully into the future that is already present, a future that will one day be fully theirs.

Enactment as preparing for participation in God's mission in the world: As the church gathers around Word and Sacrament, it does so with the world in view. The word is about good news for the sake of the world. The sacraments are about empowering the church to participate fully in God's mission for the sake of the world, even as they are an open invitation to the world to encounter the presence of the living and true God. The practices of the gathered community represent, in this regard, a dress rehearsal of the anticipated engagement that the gathered church will have as it is dismissed and sent into the world.

The theme of this part of the dress rehearsal is suffering service, in which the church learns to live in vulnerability in relation to the world, often on the margins. God's people joyfully consider ways in which they can shape their lives and give voice to sharing the good news of the gospel with others in the world around them. They do so knowing full well that the principalities and powers of the Evil One are present. This is what the Bible refers to as our joy in suffering (Rom. 5:1-5). The good news cannot be shared without evoking an encounter. It is an encounter between the redemptive power of the gospel and the oppressive powers of the Evil One, which hold persons in bondage to sin and corrupt the structures and practices within the cultural context. It is an encounter that often results in suffering for the sake of the gospel.

Smalcald Articles—(Part III, Article 4): On the Gospel

One of Luther's important contributions in conceiving of the church in relation to the gospel was to recognize the social reality inherent in its life. Redeemed persons are to be in relation with one another just as they are now in relation to God. He refers to this in the Smalcald Articles, where we read:

> We now want to return to the gospel, which gives more than just one kind of counsel and help against sin, because God is overwhelmingly rich in his grace: first, through the spoken word, in which the forgiveness of sins is preached to the whole world . . . ; second, through Baptism; third, through the Holy Sacrament of the Altar; fourth, through the power of the keys and also the mutual conversation and consolation of the brothers and sisters. Matthew 18:20: "Where two or three are gathered," etc.[4]

It is interesting to note that the same two marks of the church identified in the Augsburg Confession, Article VII—Word and Sacrament—are listed here as gifts of the gospel along with one other *mark*: the power of the keys in relation to mutual conversation and consolation. According to Luther, the gospel creates a church that is characterized by three marks: the word, the sacraments, and the power of the keys in relation to mutual conversation and consolation—Christian community. It would appear that God's forgiveness of our sins invites us to actively, even proactively, forgive one another. This is an understanding of the assembly of the church as being a *social community* where persons are in relation. The church is a community created by the Spirit that gathers in assembly around Word and Sacrament. As such, it is a community that is both holy and human. The Spirit's presence within this community through Word and Sacrament is complemented by the Spirit's presence within this community in and through the relationality of those present. This is given expression through the fruit of the Spirit: our changed corporate nature (Gal. 5:22-23). It is also present in the ministries of the persons in this community. These are given expression through the gifts of the Spirit: our individual contributions in being members one of another (Rom. 12:3-8).

Exercising the power of the keys in relation to mutual conversation and consolation is the process where God's people as a social community develop the fruit of the Spirit while also cultivating the gifts of the Spirit. This underlies the process of sanctification, where God's people seek to become conformed into the very image of Christ. It gives direction to the reality of every member's contribution to the body, as well as their vocation in the world. God's mission is deeply affected by both dimensions. As God's people are conformed into the image of Christ, they become a *sign, foretaste*, and *instrument* for announcing the presence of the redemptive reign of God in Christ to the world.

Their communal life, built up through a mutual conversation and consolation that is shaped by the Spirit, is a *sign* that heaven has already begun, and the presence of the future is made evident to the watching world. This communal life is a *foretaste* of this new eschatological reality that is already present, that persons in the world can see, taste, touch, and partake of. In doing so, they encounter the living and true God through the community of believers. This communal life is also an *instrument*, as the church is sent into the world to participate fully in God's mission. This participation takes place both individually and corporately. Through all the baptized, the church acts out the redemptive purposes of God in the world within and through the vocations of each individual. The church as a community also acts out the redemptive purposes of God in the world as a suffering servant who willingly bears the burdens of the world (see Phil. 2:1-11).

Luther's Small Catechism—The Third Article

As the church lives between the times, it is a community that models the new reality of redemption within a fallen and broken world. As it gathers, it gathers in the name of the risen Christ. As it gathers, it gathers around Word and Sacrament. The word is God's presence in the midst of the community as it is read and spoken. The sacraments are physical elements that are God's presence in the midst of the community to be partaken of by those who are present. Luther made this clear in his explanation of the Third Article on the work of the Spirit, where he defines the Spirit's work as calling, gathering, enlightening, and sanctifying those who are gathered.[5]

Luther's statement of the work of the Spirit was profoundly missional in the context in which he was working, which was a version of Constantinian Christendom that was being set up under the jurisdiction of the German princes. To be born into the emerging territorial church meant that one would be baptized into the church. The church community and the social community were the same. In light of this, Luther did not make explicit the sending of the church into the world because this was inherent within his assertion of the Spirit calling, gathering, enlightening, and sanctifying the church. Clearly implicit, even if unexpressed within Luther's explanation of the work of Spirit, is the point that the church was, in fact, inherently already *sent* into the world since it was already fully inhabiting the social context. The Spirit that calls, gathers, enlightens, and sanctifies the church also *sends* it into the world. It is fair to say that if Luther were writing his third article commentary in our contemporary context, one in which the world and church are not coterminous as the same social community, that he most likely would have added *sent* to the list of the Spirit's activities.[6] This addition, needed in our context, is illustrated in the recently adopted mission statement of the ELCA.

The Gospel as Good News in Every Context

Evangelizing is the verbal sharing of the good news about Jesus Christ with others. It is to be engaged in both individually and corporately by the community of faith as it seeks to participate fully in God's mission in the world. But to be good news, the gospel must make sense to those who are hearing it. It must reflect the promise embedded in the incarnation—that the Word becomes flesh. In becoming flesh, Jesus Christ as the living Word became understandable, knowable, and accessible. The importance of the incarnation as a foundation for understanding the contextual character of both the gospel and the church is expressed well by the Lutheran World Federation in its "Nairobi Statement on Worship and Culture":[7]

> Jesus whom we worship was born into a specific culture of the world. In the mystery of his incarnation are the module and the mandate for the contextualization of Christian worship. God can be and is encountered in the local cultures of our world. . . . Contextualization is a necessary task for the Church's mission in the world, so that the Gospel can be ever more deeply rooted in diverse local cultures.

Jesus as the incarnate good news took on the particularity of his context. But even in his particularity, he retained his universal relevance.[8] This is part of the mystery of the good news of Jesus Christ. In its particularity, we find the promise and the reality of its universality. Just as Jesus, the living Word, took on the particularity of a specific context, so also the gospel of the good news about Jesus Christ is inherently translatable into every particular cultural context with a view toward being universally applicable.[9] This means that it can become good news to *everyone, everywhere*, about *everything*, in language and within cultural expressions that are understandable, knowable, and accessible. Through this translatability, this same gospel of good news invites persons to come to know the living and true God and to become enfolded into the worldwide church.

Just as the gospel is inherently translatable to every cultural context, so also the church is inherently translatable in the same way. The church that is professed as being catholic, as stated in the Apostles' and Nicene creeds, is able to find expression *everywhere*. This same church, then, has the inherent ability to live *every place*, to become contextual within any and every setting. The church that is missionary by nature inherently seeks its contextuality—it seeks to become responsive within and adaptive to every context in which it finds itself.[10]

These premises regarding the inherent translatability of the gospel and the church have profound implications for evangelizing and mission. The church is responsible to translate the good news of the gospel, along with its own organizational reality, into every cultural context that it encounters. To do so requires that the church plan strategically for this work even as it seeks to discern the leading of the Spirit. This often comes through conflict, disruption, and surprise. Through strategy, as well as through discernment, the church must engage the principalities and powers of every context with the redemptive power of God. This sets up three very important dynamics regarding evangelizing and mission. Each finds its fuller expression in relation to the others.

The Church Reads and Relates to Each Context

Since both the gospel and the church seek to become contextual within every cultural setting, the church actively and intentionally seeks to read and relate to each particular context. This activity of *reading and relating to the context* is essential if the message of the gospel and the forms of the church are to be understandable, knowable, and accessible. The current context of the United States is complex in character, but it is helpful to provide some reading of this context in order to discuss ways in which the gospel and church might become more responsively contextualized to those who do not yet know and worship the living and true God. Two dimensions are addressed here as illustrations of what is required for reading our context in order to engage in the work of evangelism and mission. While this reading is focused primarily on the macro level, these examples are relevant as well at the micro level for most locations.

A globalized and multicultural context: One of the profound changes in the past few decades within our context is the emergence of a globalized and multicultural reality. While we have always been connected to the larger world and have always had new immigrants, two significant shifts occurred during the last half of the twentieth century. One shift involves the changes in information technology and communication systems. These new technologies have dramatically shrunk the globe—both our conception of it and our access to it—in terms of people having direct and immediate access to the larger world. This shift is captured in the metaphor of *global village* where we are now encouraged to *think globally while we live locally*. How do churches that were shaped by institutional patterns of stability and continuity now present the gospel within a rapidly changing context that is being reshaped by immediate access to global information?

The other shift relates to the changing patterns of immigration. The laws enacted in the 1960s through the 1980s dramatically shifted immigration patterns through increasing flows of persons coming from Latin America, Africa, and Asia.[11] These flows largely represent communities of color and are reframing our national consciousness from one of a largely white domain that spoke of communities of color as *ethnic* minorities, to a shared multicentered, multicultural understanding of our identity. How does the church, shaped largely by an ethos of dominant white culture from decades past, now present the gospel as good news to persons living in a multicultural and multicentered context?

A postmodern context: The argument about whether we are living primarily in a modern world or whether we now find ourselves in a postmodern context continues to elicit energy. What some have labeled as *the postmodern turn* during the past forty years informs us that we now find ourselves living in the midst of both.[12] Something significant has shifted in our worldview that might be labeled *post*modern, even as much of the *modern* world continues to function. From the perspective of the gospel and the church, there are some aspects of the postmodern that might best be labeled as problems to be addressed—a tendency toward relativism and nihilism, the evaporation of substance within the commodification of symbols, the privileging of desire over reason, etc. So also, problems need to be addressed regarding the continued influence of modernity—the loss of the particular within abstraction and universalizing, objectifying the subject, overreliance on technical reason to solve our problems, and so on.

From the perspective of the gospel and the church, there are other aspects of the postmodern that might best be viewed as bridges to be utilized, such as the focus on community, the emphasis on spirituality, the value of the particular, and the role of irony. So also, there are aspects of the modern that continue to serve as bridges: the importance of truth, a commitment to shared human rights, and the value of the individual.

Both the modern and the postmodern present problems yet offer bridges as the church seeks to bring a contextual gospel to bear within our context. Careful discernment of both cultural forces needs to be part of the communal life of congregations as they seek to bring a gospel to *everyone everywhere* that addresses *everything*.

Each Context Reads and Changes the Church

Interestingly, just as the church is responsible to read and relate to its context in order to better translate the gospel and specific church forms, so also the context reads and changes the church in relation to its efforts to present the gospel. It is evident that views of the gospel and the church in the larger society are filled with stereotypical images. But usually some element of truth is embedded in such stereotypes. It is helpful to name some of the ways in which the gospel and various forms of the church are portrayed within our larger social order. Four examples are provided below of what is present among the wide array of congregational forms. Such images need to be addressed, for sometimes the church can become so overly contextualized that the integrity of the gospel becomes compromised. Sometimes the world is allowed to change the church too much.

The *village-folk church* is often evoked as a quaint expression of a time gone by. The pastoral view comes to mind of the small New England community that has a church building with its high steeple standing at the center of the village. Here is a congregation that, although once serving at the center of society, no longer appears to be relevant to the modern, secular world. Historically, these congregations functioned primarily as ethnic enclaves that served their own kind. While they are useful for purposes of eliciting feelings of nostalgia, the relevance of such congregations for addressing the contemporary world is readily dismissed.

But how many Lutheran congregations still function as expressions shaped largely around the pattern of an ethnic-based, village-folk church? How irrelevant do they appear to the world around them?

The *institutional-program church* is often portrayed as a type of social-service delivery system that addresses human needs in functioning as yet one more community-based, volunteer organization. While this is helpful in expressing some aspects of the church's participation in God's work in the world, the conception of the transforming power of the gospel is often lost amid the various programs that seek to address human needs. Such congregations are often conceived of as being primarily venders of religious goods and services. How many Lutheran congregations present themselves to the world as functioning primarily as service-oriented, institutional-program churches? What type of gospel, and what good news, is being portrayed to the outsider?

The *suburban-family church* is often pictured as a congregation that seeks to protect family values by providing a safe place for educating and raising children. While expressing one set of biblical values around the family, these congregations often become homogenous communities that tend to buffer themselves against cultural diversity and thereby tend to deny another set of biblical values regarding inclusiveness and racial reconciliation. Suburban congregations are typically viewed as institutions that have commodified the good life by packaging it for safe consumption for those who can afford to live in the suburbs. How many Lutheran congregations function as suburban-family churches in a safe and affluent location? To what extent has the gospel become captive in such congregations to cultural patterns such as seeking homogeneity, valuing economic success as the criteria of one's worth, and desiring upward mobility as a primary pursuit?

The *personal-rights and political-coalition church* is one more type of church that is often portrayed by the larger society as a congregation that is organized around a particular issue, usually a controversial one. Its core identity is formed around this issue, where members join in support of it and organize politically both within the church and the broader community to advocate for it. In their doing so, the content of the gospel is usually collapsed into advocacy for that particular issue, and the function of the church is usually organized around political coalitions that support it. How many Lutheran congregations reflect the characteristics of a personal-rights and political-coalition church? What type of gospel does the world hear from their corporate life and witness?

THE GOSPEL AND RECIPROCITY

One of the interesting things about the leading and teaching of the Spirit in the church is that over time the gospel brings about a reciprocity. Reciprocity occurs when the cultural group that brought the gospel to another context is itself changed over time by those who received the gospel. An example of this in the book of Acts is Peter's encounter with Cornelius (Acts 10). This story is as much about the continuing conversion of Peter as it is about the conversion of Cornelius. Another example is the spillover effect of the persecution in Acts 8 that resulted, seemingly circumstantially, in the development of the Gentile church in Antioch (Acts 11). The former Gentiles who became Jewish proselytes came to Christ as Gentile-Jewish Christians. Upon arriving back home in Antioch, these Christians started proclaiming a new understanding of the gospel. Given time, the gospel that was proclaimed as "salvation by grace through faith plus nothing," came to be accepted as the gospel of the entire church (Acts 15). What began on the margins came to the center. Reciprocity took place within the Jewish-Christian community as it came to reckon with the Gentile-Christian community.

This pattern of reciprocity has important implications for the church in our context. One can see this pattern at work, for example, through the slave culture that was introduced into the colonies in the eighteenth century, which was brought to its full operation in the nineteenth century. During this time, the gospel was often preached to the slaves on the plantations by slave owners, usually with a view toward bringing order and control among the slaves. Some converted slaves were even permitted to sit in special sections in white congregations. But a deeper transformation was taking place within slave culture. What became known as the *invisible church* was formed, where Christianity became the deeper religion of identity, formation, and even revolt within the slave community. The invisible church functioned as an alternative society for the slave community, in which social, political, and economic issues were deeply woven into spiritual perspectives as being the rightful concerns of the church.[13]

Following the Civil War, much of the invisible church became institutionalized into black denominations. Though segregated and marginalized for decades by a policy of separate but equal, given time the power of the gospel embedded in these churches was released into the broader society through the civil rights movement. A transformative reciprocity took place within the whole of society in the United States through this movement. It was a movement that called both the church to accountability for its complicity in racism, and society to accountability for its denial of constitutional rights to all its citizens. Through this movement, the United States was changed forever.

A similar pattern now appears to be at work through many of the newer immigrant communities that are emerging in our context. For several centuries, white churches in the United States sent missionaries around the world. Their proclamation of the gospel and efforts to plant the church in these foreign countries eventually led to the formation of scores of national churches and multitudes of congregations around the world. Interestingly, many of these are now represented within the immigrant communities in our context. The conception of the church as a white-domain institution is now in process of being reconceptualized as a church that has both a multicultural identity and a multicultural constituency.

Many of these newer immigrant churches are also bringing their own missionary activity into the United States, where they view this new location as being in need of hearing the gospel. This reciprocity is calling white churches to reframe their conception of church and to reimagine their understanding of the gospel. The church is in need of developing new forms of mutuality and discovering new patterns for shared practices. Many white churches that have grown used to exercising domain are now in process of learning new practices of experiencing the power of the gospel from the position of being made vulnerable to the *other*.

Given these realities, we need to ask, "What does an evangelizing congregation look like?" This is a crucial question to consider because of the important role local congregations play in the participation of the church in God's mission in the world.

CHAPTER 5

CALLED OUT OF OUR COMFORT ZONE

> *"I said I wasn't gonna tell nobody, but I just couldn't keep it to myself—what the Lord has done for me."*
>
> —*Traditional African American gospel song*

Evangelizing is more about *who we are* than *what we do*. Every congregation is a Christian community of God's people who gather as an assembly of baptized members. But a congregation as a gathered community is much more than just an organized group of people with common intentions. Congregations are the creation of the Triune God and find their identity and purpose in their relationship with God. The word used in the New Testament that is translated as church is *ekklesia*. *Ekklesia* means to be "called out of," and implies being called out for a definite purpose. Congregations are Christian communities created and *called out* by God for the purpose of participating in God's mission in the world. They do not exist for their own sake; congregations exist for the sake of the world. Congregations being *called out* means they are, of necessity, also being sent into the world to participate in God's mission through evangelizing.

Announcing the good news is what a congregation does, but it does this because of what it *is*. If a congregation believes that evangelism is just another program to be added to the nine other things it is responsible for doing, it misunderstands the church's *being-ness* and its participation in the *missio Dei*.

To speak of the *mission* of the church is to speak of its task in general. This broader term embraces *evangelism*, namely the more specific aspect of the preaching or proclamation of the gospel of Jesus Christ. More exactly, "the terms are near-synonyms, the one concentrating on the act of sending, the other on the purpose and content of the sending."[1]

The content of the sending is about God's love being abundantly poured out in Christ for a hurting world (John 3:16).[2] It is the story of a missional God who desires to redeem all of creation. In Christ, God desires to reconcile the world to Godself. The church is called to participate in this mission of reconciliation. *A congregation's purpose is to tell the story of God's gift revealed in Jesus Christ.* Telling others about Jesus is not another program to be employed periodically when the membership decreases. Evangelizing is what we do because of whose we *are*! Evangelizing is the result of our being sent for the sake of the world. We are evangelized when we gather as a Christian community, and we are sent from this gathering to evangelize the world. We can do no other. Congregations, by nature, are living witnesses to the risen Christ.

While all congregations share an essential unity in Christ—their being-ness, congregations are also individually different. No two congregations are the same, whether in a church body or along the same street. Congregations are diverse geographically, socioeconomically, racial-ethnically, and politically. A demographic report on congregational life in the Evangelical Lutheran Church in America at the beginning of the twenty-first century indicates that:[3]

- An average size congregation is 470 baptized members
- The majority of congregations are small with fewer than 350 members
- Fifty percent of congregations are located in rural or small town areas
- Nearly one quarter of congregations worship with less than 50 in attendance each Sunday
- Twenty percent of congregations report no called pastor
- Only congregations in distant suburbs of large cities are showing significant growth
- Four percent of congregations have more than 1,500 members
- In general, ELCA does not do well in predominantly nonwhite settings

These statistics provide a snapshot profile of the sixth-largest Protestant church body in the United States. Further review of the demographic data reveals that overall membership is decreasing while the number of small congregations is increasing, and this comes at the end of a decade-long evangelism strategy between 1991 and 2001. One might ask what went wrong. Why is there a continuing decrease in membership, especially after so much effort was expended in the evangelism initiative?

Individual congregations are asking similar questions. Congregations that have introduced outreach programs are not necessarily experiencing either sustained growth in worship attendance or increased participation in the life of the congregation. These congregations, frustrated, are asking, "What are we doing wrong?" The more relevant questions to ask are, "What are we *being*, and what do we believe is our *purpose*?"

During the ELCA evangelism initiative of the past decade, members were surveyed about their evangelism witness and invitation to others. The responses were mixed. It was noted that "the vast majority of members in the vast majority of con-gregations are yet to be convinced that evangelism is a significant and important part of their lives or the mission of the church."[4] At the end of the decade, the report concluded that the core of the issue was the *lack of a heartfelt attitude for evangelism.* Frankly, the report revealed that the *culture* in the vast majority of congregations did not support intentional evangelical witness or inviting others to faith.[5] It is now clear that, on the whole, ELCA congregations are not evangelizing.

There is no exact formula or perfect plan for congregations to use in being called and sent by God for the sake of the world. However, an evangelizing culture can be, and must be, nurtured. This requires that a congregation and its members *listen, discern, speak,* and *act* from a deep awareness of the privilege God has given them to announce the good news of the gospel of Jesus Christ to the world. The gift is a call. This awareness is best developed through an intentional prayer life, one that seeks to say *yes* to God and to God's mission in the world. An evangelizing culture is evident when members of the congregation are simply unable to keep the good news to themselves. In this kind of an ecclesiological posture, God's pur-pose for the congregation is revealed. God's promise of reconciling the world in Jesus Christ becomes clear, and God's calling the church to participate in this min-istry of reconciliation becomes evident. These insights are revealed in Word and Sacrament as well as in the mutual consolation and conversation of the gathered Christian community. The congregation itself is a *living* witness to the promise of God, and it becomes a place of promise for the world to which it is sent. The evangelizing congregation embraces the gift and call of the Spirit as the Spirit is sent *in, with, and among* God's creation.

As places of promise, congregations are simultaneously *being and becom-ing,* as the Spirit creates them and sends them into the world. If congregations in the Evangelical Lutheran Church in America are going to grow spiritually and numerically, we will need to develop a culture of evangelizing. If we are convinced that evangelizing is something we *do* rather than who we *are,* we will continue to struggle with both our spiritual and numerical growth. If we are willing to leave our comfort zone and trust the Spirit to guide us to live out our *being,* we have the opportunity to step into a future of faithful witness for the sake of the world.

CONGREGATIONS AS MISSIONAL COMMUNITIES

The Triune God creates the church and sustains it through the gifts of Word and Sacrament by the power of the Spirit.[6] Our *being-ness* and *sent-ness* are inextri-cably linked. The gift is a call. The gift—*being*—is a call—*sent.* Both of these are ontological and existential realities of our relationship with a missional Triune God. They express our created identity. The Christian community is an expression of God's intention for bringing reconciliation to everyone, everywhere.

God's gathered Christian communities—congregations—are called to par-ticipate in God's mission in the world. Created, called, and sent by God, these communities are places of promise. As places of promise, God calls congregations to participate in the mission of reconciliation in Christ. They do so by first gathering around the means of grace to hear the witness of the gospel message, even as they prepare to bear witness to that message.

> Christians gather for worship . . . for morning or evening prayer, for services of the Word or devotions, to mark local and national festivals, and for important life occasions such as weddings and funerals. Christians also gather in their own homes for prayer, Bible reading, and devotions.[7]

When the congregation gathers, it preaches the gospel, administers the sacraments, and engages in mutual conversation and consolation. What a congregation experiences when it is gathered is the *formation and transformation of its culture*. This leads to its empowerment for ministry in the world. The gathered and sent Christian community is, by nature, an evangelical witness.

We observe these patterns in the early gatherings of God's people in Acts.

- The followers of Jesus gathered on the day of Pentecost waiting to be *baptized with the Holy Spirit* (Acts 2:1-4).
- The first converts gathered for *teaching, fellowship, breaking of bread and prayer* (Acts 2:41-47).
- The apostles gathered for *prayer* in the temple and *taught and healed* in the name of Jesus (Acts 3:1-10).
- Followers of Jesus gathered and *prayed for boldness to speak* the word of God with boldness (Acts 3:31).
- These early believers gathered and *distributed the shared possessions* to any who had need (Acts 4:33-35).

Prayer, fellowship, teaching, healing, breaking of bread, and baptism marked these early gatherings of the Christian community. In essence, the people *listened, discerned, spoke,* and *acted* as they lived into their new life in Christ.[8] Those who gathered *listened* for the voice of the Spirit. They often received explicit direction while praying. The believers also listened to the voices of the surrounding community. Sometimes these voices were in opposition, but even then the Christian community found opportunities to share the love and healing power of Christ. These early Christian communities learned to *discern* among the political and social demands of their context and their new life in Christ. Discerning God's will for their corporate life was a foundational part of their communal experience. These Christian communities were also *speaking* communities. They spoke out in Christ's name and were willing to suffer if necessary. The book of Acts is so named precisely because of the *acts* performed by the Spirit *in, with, and among* the people of God. The sign of God's reign was present with them as the Spirit worked through them.

Those who first gathered were also initially sent into the world by being scattered through a severe persecution. As a result of this persecution, they "went from place to place, proclaiming the word" (Acts 8:4). In time, this forced *sending* became known as the mission to the Gentile nations. Peter shared the good news about this mission in Caesarea and reported to the church in Jerusalem that "the Holy Spirit fell upon them just as it had upon us at the beginning. . . . And they praised God saying, 'Then God has given even to the Gentiles the repentance that leads to life'" (Acts 11:15-18). The initial *sending* of the church occurred as a result of persecution. But as a result, it soon became evident to all that Christianity was not supposed to be an insiders' religion. God's mission was, in fact, for the whole world, and God was calling the church to intentionally participate in this mission. This meant that the church would not, and could not, be made up of only one racial, ethnic, or national group. The mission of God being for the whole world meant, of necessity, that it was God's purpose for the church to be multicultural and multiethnic.

THE WORK OF THE SPIRIT IN THE CONGREGATION

When we review the life of the early church as recorded in Acts, it is evident that the believers were not alone in their efforts to witness. The Spirit worked through them as they shared their faith. Luther's understanding of the work of God's Spirit is that the Spirit calls, gathers, enlightens, and sanctifies the church. As presented in the previous chapter, we are choosing to add *sends* to the Spirit's work, in light of the context in which we minister. This understanding of the Spirit's work is a reference to the relationship we share with God in the *missio Dei*.[9] Jesus sent the Spirit to empower the church and fulfill the promises of God.

The Spirit works through the people of God with grace given to each. The Spirit is promised as a helper to assist the Christian community in its witness (John 16). God's power is given for evangelical witness (Acts 1:8). As congregations live into Christ's costly call of evangelizing, the Spirit sends them into the world and empowers them for mission.

The Triune God is a missional God who brings good news to the world through Jesus Christ. God's action inaugurates a ministry of reconciliation for the sake of all creation. The church is God's missional community, called to participate in this ministry (2 Cor. 5:17-21). The congregation, therefore, is God's primary agency for announcing the good news of the gospel.

Congregations, as missional communities, are sacramental. Their life together in the world is the word made flesh. This shared life together can be understood as communal discipleship, where mutuality, reciprocity, and the ministry of reconciliation are both experienced and demonstrated. As noted in the references from Acts, these practices include prayer, teaching, giving, proclaiming, worship, and serving. These practices are to be engaged in both corporately and individually. And these practices need to be *biblically grounded*—deeply rooted in scripture; *historically informed*—shaped by the historic Christian faith; and *culturally relevant*—responsive to the realities in every particular context.

The congregation acts because God has acted! Jesus said, "As the Father sent me, so I send you" (John 20:21). God sent Jesus because of God's love for the cosmos. God listened to the cries of creation and responded with grace and mercy. The epitome of that response was the sending of the Son (John 1:14). God's mission in the world continues in and through the congregation, which includes listening to the cries of people, communities, and all of creation. An evangelizing congregation finds ways to listen, discern, speak, and act in its context.

CREATING AN EVANGELIZING CULTURE

Evangelizing is not a program or set of gimmick-laden activities. It is a corporate *attitude of the heart* of a congregation. It is embedded and expressed in the congregation's culture.[10] Evangelizing demonstrates a congregation's passion for Christ and its compassion for the world God created. It is congregational living into Christ's costly call.

Why should a congregation be interested in an evangelizing culture? If evangelizing is not understood as something a congregation *is*, the congregation will fail to fully embrace the gift as call and will misunderstand its mission. Congregations are missional because the one who created them is missional. Created by the Spirit and fed through Word and Sacrament, the congregation is uniquely positioned to receive and offer God's gift of forgiveness both to the gathered community and to the world. As a congregation lives into this call, it engages in core activities that frame and direct its actions. There are four such activities that are foundational to a congregation's life of *being*. Congregations need to *listen, discern, speak*, and *act*. In relation to these core activities, research by the Evangelical Lutheran Church in America's 2001–2003 Evangelism Strategy Task Force indicates that growing, missional congregations tend to demonstrate in common the following best practices.[11]

- Clear vision of God's mission
- Make disciples
- Deeply involved in Bible study and prayer
- Inspiring worship
- Lay leaders use spiritual gifts in daily life
- Invite, welcome, and integrate newcomers
- Engage community and serve its needs and work for community transformation
- Leadership that boldly witnesses to Christ
- Deal openly with change and conflict

In order for a congregation to clarify its vision of God's mission, it must *listen* to God's word, *discern* its context, *speak* the vision, and *act* in ways that allow the vision to take shape in its corporate life. Likewise, members must listen to one another's voices and those of potential members, discern needs and opportunities, speak the gospel as truth to everyone, and act in love. Being deeply involved in Bible study and prayer assists a congregation in learning to listen, discern, speak, and act. It is important to note that these functions are not linear or sequential. A congregation is a living organism that dynamically relates to a changing context. Let us consider these four core activities as they apply to creating an evangelizing culture: Listen, Discern, Speak, Act.

Listen

Many voices compete for our attention in today's culture. Learning to listen requires intentionality and focus. It is often a challenge simply to hear one's own voice, let alone the voices of others. The noise and pressures of life crowd out our thoughts and dull our hearing. In Luke 10, Jesus says that Martha is worried and distracted by many things but that there is need for only one thing. Mary, her sister, chose to focus on Jesus' teaching. Jesus said that Mary chose something that would not be taken away from her. This text is not about a choice between service and study. It is about how we become distracted and how our worrying often causes us to forget who we are and why we exist. With so many demands on our time, we must choose what will receive our attention. It is the same with congregations. They must choose to whom they will listen. It is easy for congregations to become distracted by the many activities and ministry opportunities.

It is important for congregations to remember *whose* they are and take time to listen to what the Spirit is saying to them about God's mission. God is seeking to reconcile the world to Godself in Christ. This mission is not debatable. The invitation to be reconciled has been given. The word of welcome is being declared to the world from a cross and an empty tomb. In Luke 14 and Matthew 22, the parable of the banquet says that those invited to a great dinner refused to come. On hearing this, the king sent servants into the streets to invite everyone they found to the feast. God is passionately persistent about the new life offered in Christ. Jesus said, "Whoever welcomes one such child in my name welcomes me" (Mark 9:37). Congregations listen to God's word of welcome for the world in Scripture, preaching, and the sacraments. They also listen and hear the many voices in their context and the world. Creating an evangelizing culture means intentionally listening for the voice of the Spirit, especially in prayer.

Why prayer? Prayer is our communion with God. The place of prayer is essential in creating an evangelizing culture in a congregation. Corporate praying is a discipleship practice that grounds a congregation in fellowship with one another and with God. We are given examples in Acts of how the Spirit works with the church through prayer. Direction, comfort, and insight are available to congregations. God has sent the church an Advocate, the Spirit, who leads the church in mission and helps the church communicate the message.

Several years ago I visited Nairobi, Kenya, during a Lutheran World Federation Mission Conference. While there I worshiped at Uhuru Highway Lutheran

Church. Pastor Schmalzie told us a story of how the congregation had been transformed. When he first arrived, the congregation was worshiping with a few dozen people and had a pressing debt of over $10,000. The building needed repairs, and there was a complete sense of hopelessness. There was no energy for moving forward. After forty days of fasting and prayer, the congregation felt led to hold a service of exorcism. Pastor Schmalzie was not sure about the service but supported the lay leaders in their idea. The service was characterized by a rededication of the space and the people to God, much like an affirmation of baptism, when we renounce the devil and confess belief in the Triune God.

The service was a turning point. Shortly following that event, the debt was paid, attendance went from 25 to 225, and the offerings went from $15 a week to $600. Also, the people began to see mission opportunities that they had not seen before. The first was in the office building directly across the street from the church building. The members recognized an opportunity to offer Bible study and prayer for the workers. After that, the congregation began to reach out to the wider community and serve neighbors outside the city. The day I worshiped there, the congregation was filled with love, hope, and joy in the Lord. People of all ages were everywhere. The congregation had been transformed from death to life!

Discern

Evangelizing congregations listen to the voice of the Spirit in and through community. But even with our best efforts at listening, it is not always easy to interpret what is heard. Congregations must practice discernment along with listening in order to be equipped for mission. To discern means to perceive, recognize, or differentiate. Discernment includes awareness, sensitivity, and seeing as well as hearing. It implies understanding and wisdom. Jesus taught that seeing with only the natural eye is a limited point of view. The story of the man born blind in John 9 illustrates this truth.

Congregations are called to see beyond apparent problems to the possibilities for engaging in mission. Congregations are called to envision a future with God. Discernment implies vision beyond natural sight. Without a vision congregations are left with only the harsh realities of any given day. The congregation in Nairobi, Kenya, had seen the building across the street for years but had not discerned the mission opportunity. In order for that congregation to move forward and change, it needed to *see* things differently. It needed to change its perspective. After discerning the opportunity, the congregation reached out to serve its neighbors.

As a congregation seeks to cultivate an evangelizing culture, it engages in processes to discern its context, assets, community alliances, and areas for growth and change. It focuses its attention on what God is doing and has already done in its locale. In *Studying Congregations,* Robert J. Schreiter writes, "What makes congregations the special places they are is that they are focused on God, in whom they live, move, and have their being. Their members congregate to remember how God has acted in the history of the world and in their own lives. They congregate to discern what is happening to them and to the world today, and to listen for where God is leading them."[12] This listening and discerning process is crucial for an evangelizing congregation.

Congregations in the United States are increasingly encountering a multicultural context. Yet many of these congregations have not discerned that the presence of these people who are different from themselves may, in fact, be a gift to them. This is certainly true in the Evangelical Lutheran Church in America. I was involved with an ELCA congregation that was leasing space from another ELCA congregation. The congregation that owned the building was dying. There were perhaps five to ten worshipers on any given Sunday. The community had changed years ago, and the current members no longer lived nearby. The congregation that was renting space for its ministry was African American. When I arrived, the two congregations were involved in conversations that were to result in a transfer of the facility from the older, white congregation to the African American congregation.

When I left, they were still negotiating! It seemed as though the white congregation was not ready to come out of its comfort zone to receive the gifts of new people. It was not willing to release control of the facilities so that another congregation could emerge. While both congregations attempted to listen to each other, discernment of the mission opportunity was missing. If congregations are unable to discern beyond their own needs, they will not create an evangelizing culture or live fully into their *being*. The discernment spoken of here is *seeing that leads to transformation*. It is a perception that is nourished by passion and an insight that opens up new possibilities.

The Evangelical Lutheran Church in America's membership is 97 percent white. A lack of membership from communities of color remains, despite the denomination's goal since 1987 to become at least 10 percent multicultural in its membership. The opportunity before the church is great; the challenge to change our culture is even greater. Whether or not we are able to rise to these opportunities will determine our future viability as a denomination.

SPEAK

To evangelize is to announce that God's good news is "for you."
—*Richard Bliese*

The congregation *speaks* God's word of forgiveness. What a gift! The congregation first hears the word spoken through Scripture, preaching, and the sacraments. It then speaks this word among its members and in the world. Evangelism is a verbal activity embraced by a sacramental lifestyle.[13] This spoken word is to be lived! The congregation lives this word as it forgives and manifests reconciliation for individuals, families, and the community. Thus, the congregation corporately and individually participates in the ministry of reconciliation as Christ's body in the world.

It is not only important for a congregation to have a vision, but also to speak that vision. As the congregation lives its vision, it talks about it and verbalizes it in as many ways as possible. Words have power. What we say matters. What we speak shapes our lives. The early church prayed to be able to speak the word of God with boldness. Creating an evangelizing culture in our congregations means speaking the name of Jesus boldly. It means telling the story of God's love over and over again. It means speaking the truth in love.

The words spoken in the gathered Christian community prepare us for activity in the world. Proclaiming the gospel in the world is our gift and our call. Evangelizing congregations prepare their members to speak the grace-filled "for you" in the world and to act boldly in Christ's name. Congregations are places for learning God's story, for teaching people how to connect it with their own story, and for developing an ability to talk about it. Evangelizing that does not include catechesis is incomplete!

Once, when my daughter was four years old, I shared a Bible story with her. She smiled as she looked at the pictures and listened to me tell the story. Slowly her face saddened and she began to cry. When I asked her why, she replied, "Mommy, I see pictures of you and Daddy in the book, but where am I?" She had seen pictures she thought resembled her father and me but no picture that looked like her. I hurried to find the picture of a child to put her at ease about being part of God's story. People need to be able to see themselves in God's story.

We study the Bible to get to know more about God in hopes of getting to know more about ourselves as God's people. Evangelizing congregations help people to learn God's story and understand how they are a part of it. Learning God's story, our story in it, and how to communicate both to others is basic preparation for Christian discipleship and for giving verbal witness to Christ.

ACT

If our listening and speaking do not lead to *action*, then our faith is dead. To be alive in Christ is to act in Christ's name. Christ lives in us for the sake of the world. Jesus gave a command to those who follow him to "go into the world" and "baptize and teach." We call this text the Great Commission because it is about what congregations *do*.[14] Congregations are especially equipped to carry out this call.[15]

Congregations who understand themselves as missional communities are intentional about the gift and witness of baptism. Baptism is a public witness to the new life God offers in Christ and is the means of grace God uses to incorporate individuals into the body of Christ. It is a sign that we are buried and raised with Christ. It inaugurates a life of discipleship that is rooted in the Great Commandment (John 13:34). The call to love one another as Christ loves us is the gift we give to the world. The gift of love is a powerful sign of God's reign in the here and now.

Baptism is the beginning of a new relationship in Christ and initiates a daily dying and rising. Followers of Jesus needs to be taught about this gift they have been given. Baptizing and teaching are inextricably tied in evangelical witness. These twin practices characterize congregational evangelizing. The parish education of the congregation is part of its baptismal ministry. Indeed, all the baptized require lifelong learning, along with daily reappropriation of the wonderful gifts given in baptism.[16]

The good news of the reign of God is announced as the Scriptures are read, preached, sung, taught, prayed, and celebrated in the sacraments. As a sacramental and confessional church, Lutherans are well equipped to baptize and teach. Our strong sacramental practice of baptism engages Christ's command as the inauguration of a life of discipleship. Luther's emphasis on daily returning to our baptism points to the believer's lifelong learning experience and ongoing catechetical journey.

Evangelizing congregations are places of inspiration to action for the lifelong learner. They support and encourage their members to serve in the world. People want to understand their purpose and mission in life. When individuals are affirmed in their vocational callings and equipped to serve within them, they experience more joy and vitality in life. Congregations can provide opportunity for small-group gatherings, training, and points of service in the local community and beyond.

A central task for the congregation is to equip the members to live their faith in the world. Pastors were not given any greater gift at baptism than anyone else to share the good news. While Scripture states that there is a charism for evangelists, the whole body of believers shares the call to announce the gospel. Apostles, prophets, evangelists, pastors, and teachers are given to equip the baptized for the work of the ministry (Eph. 4:4-13). It is vitally important for congregations to provide these equipping opportunities and to support the ministry of the baptized in the world. Members are to be taught to *listen, discern, speak,* and *act* so that the gift of God is shared with others, inviting them to a new life of faith in God through Jesus Christ.

The concept of the *priesthood of all believers* is a natural means to embrace the call to every member to share the good news. Russell Briese writes that "it is a gift and task in the same breath."[17] Luther understood this call as primary to the believer's faith life. James Scherer notes this when he states, "According to the Reformer, every Christian was called by baptism to be Christ to his or her neighbor. Wherever the word was proclaimed and true believers gathered by baptism, these had the right and duty to work for the spread of the kingdom."[18] The whole church is called by God to participate in the *missio Dei.* The call to follow Jesus was not given to an institution but to human beings. This calling is also the gift and call to every baptized person. All the baptized become the church's missionaries in the world. The individual who is saved by grace through faith and gifted with the promise of God is an essential witness of that experience. This means that equipping members to share their faith is a central task for a congregation. Luther believed that the baptized needed to know what they had received and what they were called to share with their neighbor.

Educating the baptized was a primary function of the church in Luther's mind.[19] Briese argues that Luther's "concept of the Priesthood of All Believers meant that each of these baptized people have evangelism as a normal activity of their (Christian) life."[20] Resources like the Small Catechism were to be put into the hands of every Christian to prepare them for a life of faith and witness in the world.

The challenge today is to create an understanding that permeates congregations so that the call to share the good news is not optional. This call must be considered as the natural implication of baptism. Sharing the story of God's actions in Christ and inviting others to faith is then an *act* that flows from the being of every believer. Given this baptismal-missional understanding, congregations prepare individuals for witness and service in their daily lives. The people of God are sent to continue *being* Christ's body—good news for the world.

Ministry of Reconciliation

The evangelizing congregation has an understanding of the importance of relationships and the need for the ministry of reconciliation. How congregations address change, conflict, and healing are keys to their vitality. The ministry of reconciliation is centered in the announcement of "forgiveness—for you." Restored relationships, healing, and freedom characterize the ministry of reconciliation in the life of Jesus Christ and in a congregation. The restored relationship between humanity and God opens the door for restoration between humans and creation.[21] In Ephesians 2, there is a further word about God's action to reconcile the world.

> But now in Christ Jesus you who once were far off have been brought near by the blood of Christ. For he is our peace; in his flesh he has made both groups into one and broken down the dividing wall, that is, the hostility between us. He has abolished the law with its commandments and ordinances, that he might create in himself one new humanity in place of the two, thus making peace, and might reconcile both groups to God in one body through the cross, thus putting to death that hostility through it. (Eph. 2:13-17)

This ministry of reconciliation is at the heart of the ministry of the church. It is needed both for the life of the church and for the sake of the world.[22] A foundational text for the biblical witness of this ministry is in Paul's letter to the Corinthians. Paul says that God was in the Christ reconciling the world—*gift*, and entrusting to us the ministry of reconciliation—*call*.

> So if anyone is in Christ, there is a new creation: everything old has passed away; see, everything has become new! All this is from God, who reconciled us to [Godself] through Christ, and has given us the ministry of reconciliation; that is, in Christ God was reconciling the world to [Godself], not counting their

trespasses against them, and entrusting the message of reconciliation to us. So we are ambassadors for Christ, since God is making [Godself] appeal through us; we entreat you on behalf of Christ, be reconciled to God. For our sake he was made to be sin who knew no sin, so that in [Christ] we might become the righteous of God. (2 Cor. 5:17-21)

FORGIVENESS

New Testament usage of *katallasso,* reconciliation, in 2 Corinthians 5 means "to change from enmity to friendship or to make peace and live in harmony."[23] This kind of reconciliation implies forgiveness. Without forgiveness there is no true reconciliation. The congregation serves as the corporate body that receives and offers forgiveness in evangelical witness to the life, death, and resurrection of Jesus Christ. The confession and absolution enacted in the assembly represents and points to the reign of God on earth. It is a realized eschatological witness to the world.

When individuals receive the gift of forgiveness, they are empowered to use this gift within their everyday world and, thereby, continue the ministry of reconciliation. This is an empowerment born of love. It is a new power that confronts the principalities and powers and breaks the hold of sin in the world. This power is grounded in the powerlessness, agony, and humiliation of the cross.[24] Reconciliation requires embracing a power born of love to transform broken lives and relationships.

In classical Protestant theology, the emphasis found in Romans 5:6-11 is on a reconciliation that is the result of Christ's atoning death. God reconciled and justified humanity through the death of Christ. Another emphasis, embraced by Roman Catholic tradition, is on the love of God that is poured out on humanity through Christ, as described in 2 Corinthians 5:17-20.[25] Here the point is made that *anyone in Christ is a new creation.* There is a new relationship with God and a new understanding of God's creation. We need to hold both of these theologies together in the light of mission. Romans 5 explains God's act of love—a love that led to the atoning death of Christ and our justification—to be for the purpose of bringing the message of reconciliation to the world as described in 2 Corinthians 5.

The church is the living body of Christ. What the church receives from God, it *becomes* and gives away. These gifts transform and empower us to be gospel-bearers in the world. God's grace and gift of forgiveness received in Word and Sacrament are not only for the church, but also for the healing of the world.

HEALING

The ministry of Jesus was characterized by healings. The *gift of healing* is a gift of the Spirit to the church (1 Cor. 12:9). Healing has always been a part of God's story with God's people. The congregation has an opportunity to receive and give this gift. In addition to prayers for healing and the laying on of hands, the congregation can be a place of healing for those in the assembled Christian community as well as those in the broader community who are hurting and alone. The grace of acceptance can be the healing experience that persons need in order to face another day. The evangelizing congregation creates opportunities for all the baptized to share this gift freely in the congregation and with the broader community.

There is a story in the Old Testament of a man who needed healing (2 Kings 5). He was a person of wealth and power. His name was Naaman. Through a young servant girl taken in a raid into Israel, Naaman learned about a prophet who could heal his disease. When Naaman finally contacted Elisha the prophet, he was told by Elisha's messenger to take a bath seven times in the Jordan River. Naaman was insulted that Elisha did not speak to him directly. He also felt there were cleaner rivers in his own community for bathing. Healing was available without price, yet he tried to pay for it. Healing was a gift he need only receive from someone else.

Naaman's search for a cure brought him face-to-face with the boundaries of his comfort zone. If he was to receive this gift, he would have to cross national, ethnic, and social class lines. Naaman was fortunate to have wise servants traveling with him. His servants convinced him to follow Elisha's instructions. Naaman came out of his comfort zone and received healing. He also formed a new relationship and gained respect for a community unfamiliar to him. This story alone is illustrative of the network of community involved in one person's healing. It also reminds us of the interdependent web of creation; for example, the river was a key factor in Naaman's healing. The ministry of reconciliation is for the healing of the world.

FREEDOM

Christ has set us free, both to *be* and to *become*. The freedom that Naaman needed to open himself up to the gifts of another community is given to us in Christ. We can be there for our neighbor in redemptive ways because of God's mercy and grace in our lives. The evangelizing congregation needs to express this freedom and encourage its members to live in it. The gift and call of God sets congregations free to live, forgive, and serve in the world. Some of the most exciting stories of congregational vitality are about service. Congregations that serve in the world, from building houses to feeding the hungry, experience renewed energy. As a congregation listens, discerns, and speaks, it also acts. The freedom to act in service to the neighbor is a mark of an evangelizing congregation.

This freedom is the consequence of a costly call. The gift of God that forms the gathered Christian community also calls that assembly to live its life for the sake of the world. The gift came through the suffering, death, and resurrection of Jesus; and the inherent call to follow Jesus into the world that God loves is the cost of discipleship.

Then [Jesus] began to teach them that the Son of Man must undergo great suffering, and be rejected by the elders, the chief priests, and the scribes, and be killed and after three days rise again. . . . He called the crowd with his disciples, and said to them, "If any want to become my followers, let them deny themselves and take up their cross and follow me. . . . For those who are ashamed of me and my words in this adulterous and sinful generation, of them the Son of Man will also be ashamed when he comes in the glory of his Father with the holy angels."
(Mark 8:31-38)

The call to discipleship for Lutherans cannot be separated from the cross, its suffering, and the glory of God revealed in Jesus Christ. Lutheran evangelical witness is found in the tension between law and gospel, saint and sinner, cross and glory. Lutherans understand the gift of God as forming and transforming them for cruciform witness and service in the world.[26]

Congregations listen, discern, speak, and act out of an understanding of what God has done for them in forming and transforming them into a sacramental community. This means that they become vulnerable, as God was vulnerable in Christ. Congregations are called to *martyria*—to witness in and through suffering for the sake of the world.

The purpose of God sending Christ and, subsequently, the church is that all might receive life and be reconciled to God. Congregations that understand their missional nature will identify with being sent as central to their purpose. So, we return to the question, "Why does a congregation evangelize?" Because it is part of its very nature and is central to its purpose!

Context

The world in which congregations are called to evangelize is diverse and complex. The previous chapter outlined the mission context that we face in the United States. Let us look briefly at how a congregation lives out an evangelical witness within a particular location in this context. The people, civic and business structures, sociopolitical environment, and cultural traditions of a given area shape and define a local community. Congregations participate in the *missio Dei* in a particular location. It takes intentionality to name the realities and powers present in any particular location. This discerning process begins and ends with prayer. Praying with and about the community is fundamental to a congregation's evangelical witness.

As a congregation lives out its witness, it engages the particularities of its place and the people of its locale. We also know that a congregation that is open to innovation and change is better equipped for positive engagement with its context than one that is inwardly focused and resistant to change.[27] In order to announce good news to the world, congregations are called to turn outward to the community where they are planted and to *listen, discern, speak*, and *act*.

Congregations are obviously shaped by their communities. There is already an interdependent relationship, whether or not the congregation acknowledges it. As congregations discern their mission context, they must ask reflective questions about where God is already at work in the community and among the people present there. They must also critically inquire whether they are ready to receive the gifts of those who are different from themselves.

God's mission is for the sake of the world. Therefore, context is a key factor for congregations. Every congregation must discern and analyze its context for mission within the wider contextual realities of the world. Local mission contexts in the United States are changing. Communities across the country are becoming more racially and ethnically diverse. The number of languages other than English spoken on a given day in our public schools continues to increase. While the United States reports 257 million Christians out of a population of 305 million, it is still the fourth-largest mission area where persons claim no religious affiliation.[28]

This data also indicates that there are a large number of people who are yet to become part of any faith community. While there are numerous people in our population who claim no faith affiliation, the number of people becoming part of traditional Protestant congregations is declining. We now know that the majority of congregations associated with mainline denominations, especially in urban areas, are declining. However, Bethel Lutheran Church, an urban ELCA congregation in Chicago, Illinois, serves as an exception.

Bethel Lutheran Church's mission context is one of a declining population. Over the past two decades, the community has lost thirty percent of its population.[29] This area of the city of Chicago is a microcosm of urban America.[30] In addition to a declining population, Chicago's West Side community is profiled with the following issues.

> Struggling Black households representing 49.7 (percent) of all households . . .
> Concerns which are likely to exceed the national average include: Neighborhood Gangs, Racial/Ethnic Prejudice, Affordable Housing, Neighborhood Crime and Safety.[31]

Bethel's community context requires that the congregation live into its *being-ness*. Only this approach can provide an understanding of God's gift of grace and how it can be appropriated in daily life in this context. Given its locale, Bethel was not expected to experience membership growth. According to projections based on trend lines, Bethel should have closed its doors a decade ago. However, over the past decade, membership has increased.

The pastoral and lay leadership made a commitment to first of all be welcoming and hospitable. This communal understanding is characterized in the saying, "Bethel Lutheran Church, the friendliest church in the world!" While it may sound simple or trite to some, this saying has become part of the consciousness of the members and they act it out. It is part of creating and supporting an evangelizing culture. Bethel routinely listens to its community through surveys, gatherings, and civic meetings. Bethel's Bible study and prayer life consists of several small groups as well as corporate study and prayer. Another saying in the congregation is "We begin our ministries on our knees."

Bethel is a place of promise for its community. It has created an evangelizing culture by listening, discerning, speaking, and acting. There are many opportunities for ministries of reconciliation, healing, and hope. There are daily demands for survival that involve the usual stresses for families and individuals. But there is also a strategy for seeking and creating a positive future, a future that envisions the presence and power of God at work in their congregation and in their community.

Although Bethel's story is about a particular context, all congregations bear witness by their very presence no matter where they are located. The gathering of God's people is a sign of God' reign—that the redemptive presence of God is active in the world. When diverse communities of God's people gather, no matter where they are located, they all share something in common—they are *places of promise*. God's presence is promised in Word, Sacrament, and Christian community. Christ's presence through the Spirit in the gathered community is the gift of God.[32] This gift of good news becomes enfleshed as the assembled corporate body of Christ enacts the liturgy and is sent into the world. The reign of God is revealed in this corporate body at worship and through its life and work in the world. As the people of God are gathered and then sent in all of their diversity, the *evangel* is given voice both corporately and individually.

EVANGELIZING IN SELF-ORGANIZING SYSTEMS: IN, WITH, AND AMONG

How might a congregation organize itself for evangelizing? As congregations announce good news to the world, they also announce it to themselves. As they evangelize, they are evangelized! Congregations are ultimately called to pass on the faith. It is the *how* of this transmission that is of interest to us. God's mission is intended to continue in, with, and through God's people. Evangelizing is not the whole of the congregation's mission, but because it is an expression of our *being-ness*, it is the heart of a congregation's mission.

In the decade review of evangelism for the years 1991–2001 conducted by the Evangelical Lutheran Church in America, the report concluded that congregations that had a sense of mission and purpose and were open to innovation and change were the most effective in evangelism over the long term.

—*See ELCA,* Toward a Vision for Evangelism Report, *2001, p. 13*

The ELCA's study on evangelism made an interesting discovery. They found that even if a congregation used proven programs and was intentional about training its members, but did not have a sense of mission and purpose and an openness to change, it was unable to sustain growth over time. Usually within a few years, growth ended and plateau or decline set in.

Insights from the social sciences help us understand that congregations function as nonlinear, self-organizing systems. Self-organizing systems are intentional, have a purpose, and are open to change. They must be in order to survive. In nature, cells within organisms move *in, with, and among* their environment. They have specific intentions or purposes but are permeable and transformable. We need to think of congregations in terms of being interrelated teams or cells of activity rather than as rigid organizational structures. If we think about a system of ministry teams or cells that interact to create, form, and change in response to opportunities, we open ourselves to more possibilities.

Congregations need clarity of purpose to stay healthy and vital. In a congregation's inner life, there are deep symbols and rituals to remind it of its basic purpose. These signs may be taken for granted and can become stale. Yet they are ever present and ready to provide insights, nurture, and empowerment. The gifts of word, bread and wine, water, fellowship, music, and song all work to evangelize those gathered in Christian community. Worship, study, and a life of fellowship are opportunities for evangelizing inside of the gathered community.

These forming and transforming processes are part of our everyday Christian life. In this system, evangelizing takes place in the ministry cells as well as within the congregation as a whole. For example, worship is not planned in isolation from the rest of the congregation. Intersecting cells that have an understanding about why and how a congregation worships share a sense of the congregation's mission and are better able to contribute to its worship practices. This may seem a bit messy for some. However, messy does not mean without order. As we are learning from quantum physicists, there is order in what may at first appear to be chaos.

In her book *Leadership and the New Science*, Margaret Wheatley makes the argument that "to stay viable, open systems maintain a state of non-equilibrium, keeping themselves *off balance* so that the system can change and grow. They participate in an open exchange with their world . . . every organism in nature, including us, behaves in this way."[33] The openness to change in the world around it, to which Wheatley refers, provides the system or congregation with the opportunity to shift and adjust.

Wheatley suggests that openness to the environment over time creates a stronger system. She says that partnering with the environment increases capacities and resourcefulness.[34] Translated to congregational life, this means that when congregations operate as self-organizing systems, they interact with their community and the world around them. They form alliances and partnerships that strengthen both the community and congregation. Congregations that open themselves to the resources around them can become stronger centers for mission.

Evangelizing that is *in, with, and among* allows the world to penetrate the congregation. By that we do not mean that congregations should compromise the gospel for the sake of the world. We mean that congregations open themselves to what God is already doing in the world. How would worship change if we were to look for God outside the church walls and include what we found—or what found us? How might our service change if we discerned and appreciated being served by the people in our community?

Self-organizing systems demonstrate the value of change that comes from death but issues in new life. As Christians, we have a fundamental belief in this principle. Our theological convictions about death and resurrection position us to embrace change and transformation. Yet letting go of old ways and allowing change is a struggle for most congregations.

The paradoxical nature of self-organizing systems is intriguing to consider, especially as a way of thinking about organizing evangelizing congregations. The systems give up their present form in order to recreate themselves in new forms. This process is reminiscent of Christ taking the form of a human in order to bring new life for creation (Philippians 2). Below are summarized some of the characteristics of self-organizing systems:[35]

1. Open to their environment
2. Being and becoming
3. Resilient rather than rigid
4. Self-reference—choose a future path congruent with their identity
5. Stability over time
6. Freedom and order

The paradox of being and becoming exemplifies our understanding of who we are as people of God. We live in the *already* and *not yet* of God's kingdom. We are God's agents in the world, yet we are saints and sinners. Congregations are evangelical witnesses by their very being, and yet they are in process of living out their evangelizing culture.

Another relevant paradox for congregations is that of freedom and order. Christ has set us free to live our lives in this world, yet there is a responsibility to God's mission that frames our freedom. In self-organizing systems, there is freedom to make decisions that is guided by a clear sense of organizational identity. This allows the whole system to get stronger. The organization is less controlling but more orderly.[36] In congregations where members have freedom to use their gifts and make ministry decisions based on the congregation's mission and purpose, the congregation is stronger and is more likely to flourish and grow.

GROWTH

So far, little has been said about growth. Evangelizing is about growth. Are congregations who are intentional about inviting and welcoming, baptizing, teaching, and equipping the baptized only interested in being bigger? The question for congregations today is less about numbers and more about purpose. Of course, given the fact that numbers represent persons for whom Christ died, yes, we are interested in numbers. After all, it is the people represented by the numbers that interest God. However, for a congregation to become fixated on arguments about *church growth* only takes energy that would be better applied to understanding and living its mission and purpose.

We can certainly speak of growing *deep*—that is to say, growing deeper in faith. However, when this becomes simply a convenient way to avoid addressing growth in numbers, it is not helpful. It is also less than helpful to try and play faith-fulness and growth against one another as if they are mutually exclusive. A more insightful conversation would be about whether a congregation can be faithful and *not* evangelize. When a congregation understands its purpose and engages its mission because it is living out of its *being*, there is growth. Members grow in their faith, and the corporate body grows in its evangelical witness.

CONCLUSION

This chapter began with a definition of the church as being "called out." It is important to understand the historical roots of what *ekklesia* means in terms of *being called out*. In Greek city life, an *ekklesia* was called when there was a need for the rightful citizens of a city-state to come together in public assembly to give determination to matters of public interest. In relating this understanding to the use of this term for the church by the New Testament biblical writers, we find that the church is *being called out into the world to speak public truth*. This understand-ing means that in pursuing the development of an evangelizing culture, congrega-tions are *being called out of their comfort zones*. They are being called out to be the people of God for the sake of the world. They are being called to live in, with, and among the world for which Christ died.

Responding to this call places the congregation on the edge of society rather than in its center. The hurting world awaits the gift that was given *for us all*. Jesus' ministry was characterized by his relationship with the poor, sick, and outcast. His mission was to announce good news to society's forgotten (Luke 4). How a congregation invites and welcomes those most different from it is a sign of its missional understanding and faithfulness to the call to follow Jesus. Jesus takes hospitality to the outsider personally (Matthew 25).

God's cosmic hospitality in Christ sets the tone for God's people to evangelize. As congregations say *yes* to God's mission, they are transformed. God was faithful to those first congregations in Acts, and God remains faithful to us today. We must remember that the mission belongs to God and that we are called to participate in that mission. The gift is a call.

In Acts 8, Philip went into Samaria. Philip left his comfort zone and shared the gospel with people from whom he had previously been separated. Signs and wonders were done where the apostles and followers gathered. Their story grew as they reportedly "turned the world upside down" (Acts 17:6). Imagine what would happen if our congregations trusted God and *came out* of their comfort zones into the world!

Congregations are not alone in bringing good news. Congregations are called *to evangelize* within the broader participation of the church's apostolic engagement of the world. St. Paul uses the metaphor of the body to describe the interdependent nature of the baptized. In 1 Corinthians 12, Paul writes, "For just as the body is one and has many members, and all the members of the body, though many, are one body, so it is with Christ."

While Paul was writing about individual members as part of a congregation, the analogy holds for congregations as part of a wider church. Congregations are part of the larger *ekklesia*. This larger body has a historical witness that unites it with the church eternal. A congregation's story continues what God has already been doing in the church and in the world. The third article of the Apostles' Creed reminds us of the unity a congregation has with the one holy catholic church and the eternal nature of God's apostolic mission. This helps congregations understand why they are called to live outside their comfort zone.

CHAPTER 6

NAVIGATING DIFFICULT QUESTIONS

A colleague at my seminary says that there is one commandment that almost every Lutheran never breaks. Given the Lutheran reputation for being soft on law and big on grace, this may come as a surprise. It's the commandment recorded in Mark 1, where Jesus has just cured a man of leprosy. Jesus then says to the fellow, "See that you say nothing to anyone." A good many Lutherans, indeed some Lutheran congregations, says my colleague, have *never* broken that commandment![1]

The remark may sound like a caricature of Lutherans and Lutheran congregations. But it is no secret that in our church context, predominantly Protestant in orientation, Lutherans have functioned as a subculture, unable or perhaps unwilling to relate within the broader culture. Garrison Keillor on National Public Radio has relentlessly lampooned the subcultural mentality of Lutherans. As immigrants from the various territorial churches in Europe, Lutherans transplanted their values, traditions, congregational structures, and theological understandings to the new land they inhabited. As a result, Lutherans in the United States represent significant ethnic, linguistic, and cultural diversity. This diversity has subtly contributed to significant theological debates and conflicts among Lutherans. Yet, collectively, Lutherans have sought to forge a unified identity that is centered on a confessional heritage. And they have used this to distinguish themselves from the larger Protestant culture of North America.

The situation, however, is changing after nearly three hundred years of Lutheran history in this country. Despite the Lutheran desire to maintain a distinct theological heritage, our society now views them, for the most part, as just another mainline Protestant denomination. The boundaries that distinguished Lutherans as a subculture within the religious landscape are rapidly fading. They are becoming part of a cultural Protestantism of the United States that is now experiencing a continual erosion in allegiance. The National Opinion Research Center (NORC) at the University of Chicago reports that the number of people who claim to belong to Protestant churches in the United States has declined significantly from 1993 to 2002, from 65 to 52 percent.[2] During the same time, the number of people who said they had no religion went up from 9 to 14 percent. The survey suggested that by 2004 the percentage of Protestants would likely fall below 50 percent.[3]

The declining membership of mainline Protestant denominations is also true of Lutherans in the United States. Between 2001 and 2003, Lutheran membership declined by 86,000.[4] The rate of attrition in Lutheran membership is causing alarm among some Lutherans and is leading to a search for evangelistic strategies or renewed congregational efforts to reverse this trend. This decline, no doubt, is part of the general trend toward a *churchless* ethos of the American society. Postmodern values, rapidly growing religious plurality,[5] and economic disparity within our society radically question parochial worldviews or theologies. In the face of such challenges, it is tempting for Lutherans to focus attention on coping mechanisms such as self-identity, confessional purity, or the right liturgical practices. Such strategies are safer than daring to risk our identity and our congregational life for the sake of the gospel!

This chapter approaches the task of evangelizing from the perspective of the religious, social, cultural, and economic realities presently facing the church. It raises some difficult and critical questions that evangelizing must take into account if it is to be relevant in today's world. Because these questions are difficult, the reader must be cautioned that there are no quick and ready answers. Nonetheless, an attempt is made here to grapple with and offer relevant perspectives. The aim is to critically and constructively explore the adequacy of certain Lutheran theological resources for the church's task of evangelizing the world.

BOLTING THE DOORS OF THE CHURCH

Not too long ago, my wife, who is a pastor, was invited to do supply preaching at an urban Lutheran congregation (ELCA) that was on the verge of shutting its doors. The congregation had few members, but an endowment had kept them going even without a full-time pastor. The congregation was a victim of white-flight to the suburbs. On this particular Sunday, I accompanied my wife to worship. A dozen people were present. They were mostly older persons with long-standing connections to the church. Many had been baptized, confirmed, or married there and were unwilling to let go of *their* church!

Within minutes after worship began, an usher got up and walked to the front door, surveyed the churchyard, and then bolted the door. The same usher would get up every fifteen minutes or so, walk to the front door, unbolt it, survey the churchyard, and then bolt the door again. Sitting in the back pew, I could not help but observe this ritual action. After worship, I asked him about what was going on in the churchyard. I had thought the usher was looking for any latecomers stranded outside the main door. His response was something I had never imagined. He said, "I was only making sure that our cars parked in the churchyard are still there or not broken into. You know, this neighborhood has changed. We don't trust them folks out there!"

The "them" referred to African American and Latino folks who had taken over the neighborhood. The fear of the *other*, whether racial, cultural, or religious, is perhaps the foremost stumbling block for Lutheran outreach in our culturally diverse and religiously pluralistic society. Reared within a subculture, many Lutherans are not only fearful of others who are different from themselves, but also lack the necessary social or cultural skills to relate to them. In Lutheran history in the United States, the subculture performed the evangelizing task with little effort. If you were born into the subculture, your church affiliation was already defined. Going to church on a Sunday was assumed. But today the reality is different. Our broader culture is no longer homogeneous, either racially, culturally, or religiously. In this context, *believing* is increasingly jettisoned from communal belonging, and *faith* is seen as a matter of personal preference.

It may appear startling to some Christians in our society to realize we live in a world of religious plurality. Christians are increasingly becoming a subculture among other religious subcultures. One may dare to say we are believers of one religion among many other religions in our society! A realization of this reality could be unnerving to some Christians. For others, the very *experience* of religious and cultural diversity raises profound questions about their own self-identity in a postmodern culture.

What Are We About?

In his novel *The Book of Lights*, the Jewish author Chaim Potok narrates the story of a Jewish rabbi and his companion traveling in Kyoto, Japan. As the travelers were passing by a Shinto shrine, they saw a man standing in front of the shrine holding a book and swaying back and forth. Watching this scene, the rabbi asked his companion, "Do you know whether our God is hearing the prayers of this man?" The companion replied, "I do not know, I have never thought about this." "Neither have I," replied the rabbi. "If he is not, why not? If he is, what are we about?"[6]

This story illustrates the dilemma of Christian evangelizing in a world of religious plurality. Profound questions are raised: Why must we engage in evangelizing? Is it because God is absent in the lives of others and therefore they lack the experience of God's love and forgiveness? If God is absent, what do we make of our belief that God is the creator of all and that all humans have their being in God? If God is present, what is the relationship of our message to the religious life of our neighbors? Are Christians the only ones who have access to God's forgiving love and grace, and are others destined to hell and damnation unless they accept the Christian message? Do we adopt a viewpoint that civility demands, that we don't foist our faith and views upon others? If so, why bother to evangelize? Is our current enthusiasm for evangelizing prompted by desperate desires to boost our dwindling church membership? Or is our evangelizing grounded in a genuine commitment to a costly call of what it means to be a Christian?

These are not rhetorical questions. In our pluralistic environment, we must wrestle with them because they are real questions that affect the life of congregations. Congregational preaching and teaching have a tendency to steer clear of such troubling questions. We must raise them, however disturbing they may sound, in order to reexamine the foundations of our theological understanding of the evangelizing task.

Evangelizing in a World of Religious Plurality

Christian evangelizing presupposes a fundamental commitment to Jesus Christ as Lord and Savior of the world. This claim is embodied in our baptism and our incorporation into the body of Christ. The church announces this claim in and through its various ministries. But in our context of growing religious plurality, such a claim comes under serious questioning. It has become a contested claim. Exclusive religious claims in our society are understood as being arrogant, fundamentalist, or fanatical. Many in our world flatly reject claims about the superiority of one faith over others. Others would argue that the diverse religious options must be respected and, therefore, any attempt at overt evangelizing is an infringement of the rights of another faith. Some even think that exclusive allegiance to one faith is a restriction on the religious freedom of the individual![7] The term "proselytism," which means inducing people to convert, has acquired a pejorative connotation for many people, including Christians. How one distinguishes between legitimate witness and proselytism is now a matter of debate.[8]

It's against My Constitutional Right!

Hamtramck, a small town outside Detroit, was in the news recently concerning a controversy over public prayers. The main mosque in the town began broadcasting—over loudspeakers—the call to prayer, which in Islam occurs five times a day, 365 days a year. The invocation in Arabic lasted up to two minutes and could be heard throughout most of the town. Suddenly, tension arose in this ethnically and religiously mixed town, where more than forty percent of the inhabitants were born outside of the United States.

"They've crossed the line," said some. "It's no different than the tolling of the church bells," said others. A resolution to allow the call to prayer was passed by the city council, and the residents of Hamtramck are now grappling with issues of religious freedom. A longtime resident stated the issue thus: "I used to say I wasn't prejudiced against anyone, but then I realized I had a problem with them [Muslims] putting Allah above everyone else." Said another, "My main objection is simple, I don't want to be told that Allah is the true and only God. . . . It is against my constitutional right to have to listen to another religion evangelize in my ear."[9]

The story illustrates the dilemma of evangelizing in a pluralistic society. Some are tempted to simply capitulate to the pressures of society and abandon the evangelizing task of the gospel, lest we offend others. It seems many in our churches are doing precisely this. But what religious plurality demands is not a withdrawal from engagement with others. Rather, it forces us to offer a reasoned articulation of the necessity of our faith that goes beyond the mere citing of certain scriptural mandates. In fact, the very context of religious plurality provides such a rationale for evangelizing.

Discussions about religious diversity are often understood in *static* terms, as if faiths lived in their own individual silos or ghettos. On the contrary, religious plurality is far more *dynamic* in most contexts where we encounter continual interaction between people of different faiths. This interaction is enhanced today through religious advertising on radio and TV, in newspapers, and especially through the Internet. Interreligious jostling is an inevitable aspect of pluralist societies. People are constantly being exposed to the religious worldviews of different faiths. In this context of *dynamic plurality*, each faith is now forced to articulate its distinctiveness and rationale within the same public space it shares with others. The fundamental question is inevitably raised: "By *what authority* do religious people make their claim for exclusive truth and allegiance?"

In other words, plurality, explicitly or implicitly, demands public accountability and articulation on the part of every faith and religious person.[10] "Why are you a Christian?" "Why are you a Muslim?" And so on. A true recognition of religious plurality makes every faith inherently evangelistic or missionary, demanding of every religion that it articulate its distinctive claims. It is the very nature of contemporary religious plurality that prompts religious faiths to compete with one another for people's allegiances, while outwardly professing a tolerant view of other faiths. The challenge for a religion today is how not to appear intolerant while making universal faith claims.

For the Christian faith, the contemporary reality of religious plurality is not a new phenomenon. The Christian church through the ages has lived in diverse religious contexts. Yet there is a new problem today, especially in Western societies. We need to ask, "How can Christians authentically profess their faith in the midst of other faiths while acknowledging the values of other faiths and beliefs?" This is the challenge of religious plurality for the evangelizing task of the church.

BY WHAT AUTHORITY?

Christians have traditionally responded to questions of authority by citing biblical texts as their mandate for the evangelizing task. The "apostolic imperative,"[11] as stated in the four Gospels and the Acts of the Apostles, is typically used for this purpose. "Go . . . make disciples . . . baptize . . . and teach" (Matt. 19:28-30); "Go into all the world and preach the gospel to the whole creation" (Mark 16:22). In Luke's gospel, "repentance and forgiveness of sins should be preached in his [Christ's] name to all nations, beginning from Jerusalem" (Luke 24:47); in John, "As the Father has sent me, even so I send you" (John 20:21); and in Acts, "You shall be my witnesses in Jerusalem . . . and to the ends of the earth" (1:8).

These texts, it is claimed, provide the foundations for evangelizing the world. And when these texts are read in conjunction with other, exclusivist, texts, the question of authority gains a sharper focus. The sending of the disciples into the world is usually grounded in an absolute claim about Jesus and the work of salvation he accomplished. Two texts in particular are often cited to make this exclusive claim: John 14:6, "I am the way, and the truth and the life; no one comes to Father but by me," and Acts 4:12, "And there is salvation in no one else, for there is no other name under heaven given among mortals by which we must be saved." These two texts are central to the Christian tradition, but how we read these texts in the context of religious plurality is an issue today.

These two crucial texts are often cited by Christians not only to indicate their own commitment to Christ, but also to draw negative conclusions about the faith of another. The tendency has been to read these as texts of comparative religion, where they are used to announce the Christian faith while denouncing the faith of other religions. Lifted out of context, these texts can become slogans of Christian triumphalism.

The intent of John 14:6, however, is not to deny access to God the Father apart from Christ. In the Gospel of John, the Word who is incarnate in Jesus is the same Word that from the beginning was life and as such was also the true light coming into the world to enlighten everyone. This text occurs in the dialogue between Jesus and Thomas. Jesus has disclosed to his disciples that he is going to his Father's house to prepare a place for them (v. 2) and the disciples know the way to the place he is going (v. 5). Thomas, wanting to get a further insight into where Jesus is going, asks the question, "How can we know the way?" Jesus' response indicates the path that he is taking. The way to the Father is the "way of the cross." This is the "truth" and "life" of his mission. The statement of Jesus is in fact a call to his disciples to follow the way of the cross that Jesus has shown to them. This interpretation is reinforced by Jesus' encounter with Thomas in John 11:16, where Thomas seems to be the only disciple who has understood Jesus' mission. It is further strengthened by Thomas's encounter with Jesus in his post-resurrection appearance in John 20:24-29, where he now wants to make sure the resurrected Christ is in fact the crucified one. A careful reading of John 14:6 suggests that this text is a profound testimony to the mission of Jesus by the "way of the cross," and, read in its context, is not intended as a universal statement denouncing any other way to God the Father.[12]

A similar process of interpretation might be applied with regard to the other much-quoted text, Acts 4:12, with its affirmation that there is no other name given by which we may be saved. The statement is the climax of a series of narratives in Acts 3 and 4 and is related to a healing miracle. Peter said to a man lame from birth, "In the name of Jesus Christ of Nazareth, stand up and walk" (Acts 3:6). In 4:9 he is still discussing with the Jewish authorities "this good deed done to someone who was sick" and "how this man has been healed." In response to the question, "By what power or by what name did you do this?" Peter makes a bold confession, "There is no salvation [i.e., healing] in anyone else . . . there is no other name . . . by which we must be saved [healed]." Both the Greek noun (*sōtēria*) and the passive infinitive (*sōthenai*) mean to heal, make whole, or save. Thus it makes sense to translate the text as referring to a healing rather than the broader meaning of salvation, and to understand it as a specific appeal to Jewish leaders to accept the Messiah.

These biblical texts read in their context offer a profound testimony and *positive witness* to the reality of Jesus Christ. To use them as texts of comparative religion in order to denounce other faith traditions is to misuse them. Together with other *sending* texts, these *exclusive* texts need to be used judiciously in a pluralistic world. The biblical witness to faith in relation to other religious traditions must not rely exclusively on a couple of texts. The entire biblical witness (with some exceptions) is more positive and far more open to other people than we recognize.[13] Christian evangelizing therefore ought not become a *negative witness* against others or a denunciation of the faith and beliefs of others, but a positive engagement with others.

There is another dimension to the question of authority. We now also live in a *multi-scriptural* environment. Citing certain exclusive texts from one's own tradition is often counterbalanced by equally exclusive texts from the Scriptures of another. *Whose* texts, *whose* Scriptures, *whose* interpretations are most authoritative in a multi-scriptural society? But not all religious traditions rely solely on texts or written Scriptures as their source of authority. They also rely on sources such as: "experience," "tradition," "creeds," "religious leaders," "gurus," "rituals," and "doctrines and dogmas." Therefore hurling biblical texts at others is often counterproductive. The New Testament tells the story of Christian faith centered on Jesus Christ. Its authority lies in the persuasive power it has to invite people to become part of that story. Christian evangelizing is about telling the whole story and not about citing certain texts.

THE LUTHERAN EXCLUSIVISM: THE *SOLAS*[14]

For Lutherans, the theology and doctrines of the Reformation have provided another foundation of authority. Lutherans are often hesitant to adopt a literal reading of biblical texts and have developed an articulated theology of Scripture. The written Scripture is seen as the *formal* principle and Christ is the content or the *material* principle. The old patristic dictum of the church, *extra ecclesiam nulla salus* (outside the church there is no salvation) in Lutheran self-understanding meant *extra Christum nulla salus* (outside Christ there is no salvation). The Lutheran tendency toward exclusivism, therefore, is derived from a doctrinal interpretation of biblical texts. The absoluteness of the Christian claim is thus articulated in terms of the "Lutheran *solas*": *solus Deus, solus Christus, sola gratia, sola scriptura, solo verbo, sola fide*, and so on. The doctrinal language of "God alone," "Christ alone," "grace alone," "Scripture alone," "word alone," and "faith alone" are all intertwined, and they reinforce claims of Lutheran exclusivism. If anything, the *solas* mark the boundaries of faith and make an issue of the "scandal of particularity."[15]

The Lutheran *sola*s by their very nature make exclusive Christian claims. But they do so in the form of a circular argument. In a multi-faith society, a generic affirmation of faith in "God alone" may not meet a great resistance (except of course by atheists!). However, the Lutheran hermeneutic is not content with a theocentric view of reality that easily accommodates other religious beliefs in terms of grace and truth. The Lutheran view of "God alone" is imposed with a decisive limitation in the claim, "Christ alone." But this "Christ alone" claim does not represent a "cosmic Christ" or a "universal logos." Rather, it points to the historical Jesus Christ. The Lutheran way of interpreting Christ is invariably tied to *faith* in Christ, which in turn comes by the hearing of the word (*ex auditu*). The *word alone* is not any word, any good word, not even the words of Scripture, but a word of promise that points to *grace alone*. The *grace alone* refers back to what God has done in and through *Christ alone*.

The series of qualifications the Lutheran hermeneutic imposes on understanding the faith leads to an impression that Lutherans are intent on keeping the gospel as exclusive as possible so that Christian engagement with religious plurality is possible only according to our terms. The *sola*s appear to draw a rigid boundary between believers and outsiders. Put differently, it seems that the Lutheran understanding of evangelizing precludes a positive dialogue with persons of other faiths unless others subscribe to the doctrinal claims of Lutherans. Lutheran evangelizing appears to be no different from the exclusivism practiced by some other Christians.

THE LUTHERAN INCLUSIVISM:
THE DIALECTIC OF LAW AND GOSPEL

Thoughtful Lutherans may question an exclusivist reading of the Lutheran *sola*s. Rightly so. The Lutheran *sola*s are, of course, only one side of the Lutheran dialectic of engagement in the world. The intent of the *sola*s, despite their exclusive claims, is not to erect a mighty fortress around Lutherans. Lutheran theologians have sought to temper the exclusive claims of the *sola*s by pointing to the dialectic of "law and gospel," along with the corresponding distinctions between the "left hand of God" and the "right hand of God," and the "realm of creation" and the "realm of redemption." Many have argued that the dialectic of law and gospel, and the other corresponding distinctions, are not intended to draw a rigid boundary between Christians and others in the world.

God is the creator of the world, and therefore all people have some knowledge of God and God's law, and if God's law is the foundation of all human laws, Christians and others are subject to them. Thus, in the realm of creation, all humans live in mutual interaction with one another without distinction. Since God relates with all people through the modality of the law, which is grounded in human reason and natural law, Christians must engage in dialogue with others and appreciate their social and moral contributions. Lutherans, therefore, can affirm and cooperate with all spiritual, moral, and societal values that uphold justice, peace, and the integrity of God's creation.

The Lutheran dialectic of law and gospel, however, stops short of affirming any *salvific values* in the realm of creation. Though all people, regardless of their faith convictions, are subject to God's law and its restraining and sustaining function in the world, only Christians have the knowledge of the redemptive work of God in Christ Jesus. All people have an element of natural theology in their faith stories, but not all people have a sure and certain knowledge of Christ. Those who do not explicitly profess the name of Christ lack the experience of a gracious God and are therefore engaged in works of self-salvation. The Lutheran "yes" to the world of religious plurality in God's creation, it turns out, is a decisive "no" to the religious values and claims of others! Because others lack a proper knowledge of Christ through faith, their faith and beliefs lack any *salvific* validity. Whatever knowledge others possess, especially people of other faiths, is "ambiguous," "insufficient," and "incomplete." Because others lack a proper knowledge of Christ and salvation, they lack the gospel.

The Lutheran dialectic of "yes" and "no" to the world of religious plurality may provide a basis for Lutheran engagement in evangelizing the world. It allows us to encounter others positively as God's children, to live and work together in ordering our world. It encourages Lutherans to share the good news of Jesus Christ with those who have not heard the gospel and to invite them to be participants in God's kingdom inaugurated by Jesus Christ. But the Lutheran dialectic of law and gospel can also instill a negative bias against others because they lack the gospel and may lead our efforts in reaching them into a *crusading evangelism* (more fully described below). Despite the positive values that we may find in others, they are ultimately deficient in their understanding of God and salvation. Therefore Lutheran evangelizing becomes a word of judgment against others. But then, what is the point of a dialogical engagement with others if ultimately all their religious values are deficient or insufficient? Christian dialogue with others in this case becomes a disguised form of monologue!

Toward a Lutheran Theology of Engagement: The "*Simul*"

The traditional Lutheran *solas* have made Christian engagement with others problematic because of their claim to exclusivism and exclusion. And the Lutheran dialectic of law and gospel is not without difficulties in our attempt to articulate a relevant theology of evangelizing that is not condescending toward the beliefs of others. In Lutheran theology, the law and the gospel are categories that help understand God's dealings with the world. They are primarily analytical tools and not categories of judgment. They represent two modes of God's relation to the world. They are to be distinguished but not separated. The dialectic therefore insists on holding together *simultaneously* two divergent modes of God's activity in the world.

The dialectic of the *simul*, which we understand as "simultaneously," is a fundamental presupposition of almost all Lutheran doctrinal affirmations. Lutheran theology understands that God's revelation is *simultaneously* hidden and revealed; God's activity occurs *simultaneously* through the work of the left hand and right hand; Christ is *simultaneously* human and divine; the saving activity of God is *simultaneously* through law and gospel; the Christian is *simultaneously* a saint and sinner; the sacrament of the bread and wine is *simultaneously* the body and blood; the kingdom of God is *simultaneously* present here and now and not yet. This emphasis on the *simuls* in Lutheran theology opens up possibilities for a positive engagement with all people in our world. A proper understanding of the *simuls*, in fact, pushes us away from an exclusive stance in matters of faith and invites us into an inclusive engagement with people.[16]

The Lutheran *solas* hold us back by their exclusive claims, while the *simuls* thrust us into an open stance toward the world. They are thus juxtaposed in a dialectical relationship. The *solas*—"Christ alone," "faith alone," "grace alone"—provide the necessary anchor for our participation in the world and our encounters with people of other faiths, or no faith. Without such an anchor, our conversations with people become ambiguous and lack any particular religious commitment. But if the *solas* alone were to prevail, our conversations would become restricted. The *solas*, in order to be effective anchors of faith, need the *simuls*.

The Lutheran *simuls*, on the other hand, by affirming God's inclusive love for the world, free us to affirm the reality of God's grace and truth in the world, wherever they may be found. The *simuls* recognize that God is at work in both the law mode and gospel mode. This occurs whenever the Christian community hears the word and receives the sacraments. But this same God is also at work among other peoples in and through the dialectic of law and gospel. It is part of the biblical testimony that God is active in creation in love, and insofar as Christ is the medium of creation, God's love finds expression also among people of other faiths. The Lutheran *simuls*, therefore, encourage us to confidently explore the mysterious ways in which God is present among other people, and we may even meet Christ among them.

If the *simuls* alone were the criteria, without the *solas*, Christians would have no reference point for their engagement with others. We would have no way of distinguishing the authentic from the spurious or the divine from the demonic. The *simuls* are grounded in the *solas*. The *solas* and the *simuls* therefore need each other and must be held together. A tension exists within these two categories of understanding, pushing us in two different directions simultaneously. But, in holding on to this tension, we are provided with a foundation for a Lutheran theology of evangelizing.

DIALOGUE AND CHRISTIAN EVANGELIZING

If the *solas* provide the necessary authority and commitment to faith, the Lutheran *simuls* provide the courage for engagement with people. The dialectic of the *solas* and *simuls* captures a profound tension inherent in the biblical witness regarding God's dealing with humankind. On the one hand, in being created in God's image, God's *universal love* and grace are bestowed upon all people irrespective of people's beliefs (Acts 14:17). God has written God's law into human hearts and therefore judges and saves persons according to God's mysterious will (Rom. 1:14-16). Therefore, it is unhelpful to use the language of "unreached" to refer to people who are not Christian by faith. It sort of begs the question, "Unreached by whom?" It does not mean that God has not reached them. It is a fundamental Christian conviction that God's love is *universal* and embraces all people, whether they acknowledge it or not. On the other hand, God has shown God's commitment to humanity through the *particular love* demonstrated in the cross and resurrection of Jesus Christ. God desires to save all people and bring them to the knowledge of truth through the one mediator between God and humankind, Jesus Christ (1 Tim. 2:4-5). These two affirmations remain in tension, and Christians cannot fathom nor resolve this inherent tension in biblical witness.[17]

Christian evangelizing and mission are an affirmation of this tension, and the church's evangelizing efforts must be grounded in this tension. Not to respect this tension may result in the development of a crusading mentality. The Christian understanding of God's love—both universal and particular—has not always been transparent in Christian praxis. A Hindu friend once remarked, "When Christians speak of love, it makes everyone nervous!" Christian history is full of examples of such negative witness.

As those who have experienced the particular love of God in Christ Jesus, Christians are called to bear a *positive witness* to what God has done in their lives. A positive witness is respectful of the faith and convictions of others, even if they appear alien or contradictory to our faith. Recognizing the inherent tension between God's universal love for all and God's particular love in and through Jesus Christ helps us to understand that Christian evangelizing is not merely a task to be performed or an act of obedience to a biblical command. Rather, it is a joyful public affirmation of God's marvelous deeds in the life of a Christian. In a religiously diverse society, such witness occurs most notably through public conversation and dialogue with people of other faiths, or no faith, at various levels and for different purposes. Christian evangelizing therefore is not antithetical to interreligious dialogue. Authentic dialogue presupposes that the partners are committed to their respective faiths and willing to share in open and honest discourse.[18]

A meaningful dialogue is a two-way conversation and presupposes a mutual sharing and listening and not a covert form of monologue. In this process, Christians not only bear witness to their faith in Jesus Christ, but also listen to the faith experiences of others. What Christians hear about the faith and the convictions of others may appear strange and confusing, because other faiths have their own logic and distinct frameworks of meaning. Engagement in dialogue requires patience and understanding. It is in the process of dialogue that Christians discover the mysterious ways in which God is touching the lives of others. It is in *learning the language of the other* that Christians are better able to communicate their faith, as well as make it commendable to others.

Christian evangelizing is not a religious debate. It is not a marketing technique or a manipulation of the other. Its intent is not to negate the other or view the other with condescension. As a positive witness, Christian evangelizing does not seek to disfigure *other names* or *saviors* in order to proclaim the name of Jesus Christ. Christians in dialogue must willingly acknowledge "whatever is honorable, whatever is just, whatever is pure, whatever is pleasing, whatever is commendable, if there is any excellence and if there is any thing worthy of praise" (Phil. 4:8) that is found among others.

Such an acknowledgment of the values found among others may trouble some Christians. They may feel that it negates the age-old conviction that Christians alone possess the true knowledge of God and that they alone have been saved. The position articulated in the preceding paragraphs may be charged with promoting compromise and as rejecting the traditional Christian assumptions about other religious faiths. It might even be asked, "Why bother with evangelizing if others have valid religious convictions?" The answer is simple: "Christian evangelizing is not a competition for religious market share in a pluralistic society, nor is it an attempt to recruit people to fill our empty pews." Christians engage in evangelizing because they love their neighbors as themselves and therefore are not hesitant to share their deepest religious convictions with their neighbors.

Christians need not be perturbed that others claim to have "found meaning in life" and to have experienced "salvation" through their faith and religious tradition. If this breeds insecurity in the minds of Christians, then our evangelizing effort is not based on the certitude of faith but rather on our fears and insecurity brought about by a pluralistic society. Acknowledging the positive values found in the faith of our neighbors neither puts an end to Christian evangelizing nor negates Christian claims. It opens new relationships with others. Christian evangelizing as a ministry continues, and Christian friendship and dialogue are further strengthened. Conversion to the Christian faith may or may not happen in dialogue with people of other faiths. However, that is not the burden of the Christian, but is solely the work of the Holy Spirit. All we offer in dialogue is the gift of the gospel of Jesus Christ that we are privileged to share with others.[19]

Christian evangelizing among people of other faiths therefore requires courage for dialogue in humility. Following the way of Jesus, it seeks to reconcile people, establish new relationships, and build communities of faith in a religiously pluralistic society. Authentic Christian witness presupposes a relationship with people and a willingness to engage with others. But such an engagement also presupposes that one is grounded in one's own faith and is convinced of its truth.

Evangelizing as the Practice of
a Theology of the Cross

The approach suggested in the preceding section makes it clear that Christian evangelizing is neither about a crusading spirit nor an attempt to undermine the convictions of others by asserting the superiority of the Christian faith. Christian evangelizing follows the way of the cross by adopting a *crucified mind* in our engagement with people. In the language of Lutheran theology, it is the practice of the theology of the cross. The basic text of the theology of the cross is in Paul's first letter to the Corinthians (1 Cor. 1:18-25). The passage reveals that Paul is trying to reach out to both the Jews and the Gentiles. For the Jews, the cross was a stumbling block and an offense, and to the Gentiles, it was nothing but foolishness. "But to those who are the called," says Paul, "Christ the power of God and wisdom of God" (v. 24). However, in the history of Christianity, "the power of God and the wisdom God" have all too frequently been usurped by humans and transformed into an ideology of human power and domination. The symbol of the cross has become at times a distorted symbol of subjugation and oppression of the other.

Coffee and Croissants

In 2003, Pope John Paul II beatified a seventeenth-century Capuchin priest who is perhaps most famous for preventing a Muslim invasion of Europe. When the Ottoman Turks besieged Vienna in 1683, the priest, Marco D'Aviano, led the Christian armies to victory. Legend has it that when the Turks fled, they forgot their black coffee—leaving it to the triumphant Viennese, who named their new favorite beverage cappuccino after the Franciscan order to which D'Aviano had dedicated his life.[20]

The same context of the defeat of the Ottoman Turks is also the occasion of the birth of a delicate pastry, the croissant. It was invented to celebrate the Viennese victory. The crescent shape of croissants was intentional. The central symbol of Islam was eaten as a symbolic act portraying how Christendom had turned back the evil hand of the Muslim.[21]

These two bits of trivia are a painful reminder of the history of conflicts between Christians and Muslims, which continue to this day. The cross, as a symbol of suffering and death, has been a source of suffering and death to millions of people in world history. It was a symbol of the Crusaders of the eleventh century. In the course of history, the words *cross* and *crusades* became intertwined and came to symbolize Christian intolerance, aggression, and colonial expansion. It became an expression of *violent evangelization* in many parts of the world, especially in Latin America. The symbol of the cross played a significant role in the event of the Holocaust. Some Christians would prefer to blot from memory such Christian atrocities. A few days after the 9/11 terrorist attack, President Bush made a reference to a "crusade" against terrorism, which created an uproar among Muslims and unease among others.[22] The fact that the cross has served the purposes of extremist ideologies in the world may warrant a judicious use of this symbol in evangelizing.

The sense in which the phrase a "theology of the cross" is invoked here has nothing to do with such triumphalist, oppressive, and crusading notions of Christian evangelizing. As used here, the phrase is drawn from Luther's Heidelberg Disputation (1518),[23] where he contrasted the "theology of the cross" with the "theology of glory." Drawing on the insights of St. Paul, Luther indicated that a true knowledge of God is revealed in the sufferings of the cross rather than through God's works in creation and history. A theology of glory, in Luther's view, is oriented to human pride and self-glorification, whereas a theology of the cross points to the appearance of God in lowliness and weakness and amid the sufferings of the crucified Christ.[24]

In his own feudal context, Luther did not explore the full potential of a theology of the cross as a liberating force in Christian social involvement.[25] He did not adequately draw out the political and socioethical implications of his own theology. But today others have done so, noting the liberating message that affirms God's solidarity with the suffering, abused, exploited, oppressed, or voiceless people of the world. In our context of profound human suffering, such a reinterpreted understanding of the theology of the cross is critical for engaging in Christian evangelizing.

THE CROSS OF THE RISEN CHRIST

The message of a theology of the cross is fundamentally God's identification and solidarity with the sufferings in the world. But that identification finds its meaning only in relation to the event of Christ's resurrection. Without the event of the resurrection, the cross of Christ may appear as a glorification of pain and suffering. If the message of Good Friday is primarily about the painful death of a man, it has no ultimate significance or special meaning. Countless people die every day as violently as Jesus did. What distinguishes this particular death at Calvary is its inextricable link with the resurrection of Jesus and the message of Easter Sunday.

Any articulation of a theology of the cross, apart from a theology of resurrection, leads to a distortion of the Christian message. It is the event of the resurrection that redeems the sufferings of the cross and points to the efficacy of the cross as the cross of the risen Christ. The event of the resurrection is an eschatological event that unveils the profound meaning of the cross. It points to the life-transforming message of the cross to all humanity. The church's evangelizing message is not only a testimony to the event of cross and resurrection but is also a concrete realization of the power of that message in the lives of all people. The cross of the risen Christ stands as the symbol of God's abiding commitment to participate in the sufferings of humanity.

The cross of the risen Christ stands as a clear antithesis to all forms of violent, triumphalistic, and crusading evangelizing or any practice of ecclesiastical imperialism. A theology of the cross of the risen Christ takes as its point of departure the reality of the brokenness of the human spirit and human community.[25] Christian evangelizing, in the posture of the cross of the risen Christ, proclaims a message of divine solidarity with those who are broken, oppressed, or marginalized, and points to God's transformative intent of offering fullness of life to suffering humanity. This posture is not a *posture of pretension*, but rather a *posture of participation* in the life of the suffering people of the world. It is an incarnate evangelizing that seeks the healing of the world and strives toward wholeness of life in community.

Luther succinctly observed in his Heidelberg Disputation, "A theology of glory calls evil good and good evil. A theology of the cross calls the thing what it actually is."[27] If we transpose Luther's insight into our context, it means that Christian evangelizing cannot be oblivious to the involuntary suffering of people because of injustice. Christian evangelizing, by explicitly naming the demonic and dehumanizing realities of our world, seeks to confront them and call them to accountability in the presence of God. The cross thus becomes a word of judgment against all, including Christians, who participate in the structures of injustice. Proclaiming the justice of God in a sinful world is the prophetic dimension of our evangelizing commitment. Christian evangelizing therefore cannot be oblivious to the social and political dimensions of the cross.

Saturday People

The Lutheran doctrine of "justification by faith" is fundamentally God's affirmation of life in a world of human bondage to forces of death and defeat.[28] Too often, justification has been interpreted by Lutherans in a way that is divorced from the painful realities of this world and focused instead on individual guilt. As a result, the preaching of the theology of the cross and the resurrection has been reduced to simply being an acoustical affair. The verbalization of the message of the gospel has been understood as the essence of evangelization. There is biblical support for such an auditory view of evangelization, as found in Paul's famous remark, "How are they to believe in one of whom they have never heard? And how are they to hear without someone proclaiming him? . . . Faith comes from what is heard" (Rom. 10:14-17).

Nonetheless, for a countless number of people in our world the reality of the cross being present in a perpetual Good Friday is an everyday reality. These are the "crucified people"[29] who die every day experiencing the reality of Good Friday but without a following Easter. They experience pain, violence, and suffering but seldom the hope of the resurrection. Many people are caught between the darkness and despair of Good Friday and the hope and promise of Easter. They are the *Saturday people*, who are so near and yet so far from experiencing the reality of God's liberation in their lives.[30] They are like Moses, who could see the Promised Land from a distance but could not enter it. For many of the crucified people of the world, even a glimpse of the promised land seems impossible. They die on Saturday! For them, the theology of the cross is neither an eschatological reality nor a mystical experience. They experience hell as a present reality and heaven as a meaningless concept!

Christian evangelizing, taking its cue from the cross of the risen Christ, seeks to enter into the agonies of those suffering people with the message that God understands and participates in their misery and suffering. Through Christ's suffering, God seeks their liberation from bondage and enters into their broken lives. It is not a message of false hope that somehow things will all be set right. The history of humanity, in a sense, is also a history of human suffering, a *passion* history, and the good news that Christians are called to proclaim is precisely that God in Jesus Christ seeks to embrace human suffering in the most intimate way that humanity can ever see and understand. It must be recalled that God's embrace of humanity occurred on the periphery, at a place called Golgotha, the place of the skull! The broken and crucified people of our world usually live at the margins of our society.

The evangelizing message that Christians are called to proclaim is grounded in a *theology of embrace* (see Luke 15:20). The cross of the risen Christ embraces the crucified people of the world, and in that embrace the meaning of resurrection becomes a reality in people's lives. Evangelizing then is more than an acoustical affair but must be grounded in the practice of authentic discipleship. It involves both the *preaching* and *practice* of the cross and resurrection. Evangelizing that does not meet the test of the cross is not a liberating message but pious propaganda! Too often, our evangelizing efforts pay little attention to the social and communal context of people. The gospel cannot be proclaimed in a sociopolitical vacuum. The church's evangelizing message not only calls for the repentance of sinners, it also stands in solidarity with the victims of sin and works for the transformation of life in the midst of suffering.[31]

EVANGELIZING IN A POSTMODERN WORLD

The cross of the risen Christ has been seen as an oppressive symbol by many, while it is a sign of hope for others. But for a large number of secularized people, it is nothing more than a plus sign (+) or a mere fashion accessory! Many in the postmodern generation do not grasp the significance of the cross. The retrieval of the profound meaning of the event of the cross and resurrection is therefore part of the task of the evangelizing mission of the church. The popularity of Mel Gibson's movie *The Passion of the Christ*, despite its distortions and glorification of violence, is in part attributable to the strangeness and incredulity of the story of the crucifixion of Jesus. The movie touched the emotions of a postmodern generation that grew up for the most part outside the church. Many of these persons have been deeply skeptical about the truth claims of the church.

It is a documented fact that our society is comprised of a significant number of *churchless Christians* or *unchurched Christians*. These are people who do not feel the need to associate themselves with any organized religion or become part of a Christian community. These *churchless Christians* seem to be estranged and disillusioned with established churches and have sought alternative forms of community. The existence of such self-professing Christians outside the fellowship of the church has been a challenge to Christian evangelizing efforts. A good deal of Christian evangelizing effort has therefore focused on bringing them in, or what is sometimes referred to as "re-evangelization."

Polls show that ninety percent of the inhabitants of the United States believe in God. But this perspective does not translate into belonging to a religion. In addition to the NORC survey cited earlier, another survey states that the number of people unaffiliated with any particular religion in the United States has doubled between 1990 and 2001, from seven percent to fourteen percent (roughly 30 million!). Presumably this has happened among Christians, since the proportion of the population classified as Christian declined to seventy-seven percent in 2001, down from eighty-six percent in 1990.[32] Stemming the congregational exodus is a priority for most churches. It appears that there is now a growing number of *nones*, those without any explicit religious affiliation. The church's evangelizing effort has an uphill task in the midst of a declining allegiance to the institutional church. There is no contrary evidence to indicate that this faith trend will be soon be reversed.

In addition to the challenges of religious plurality and the reality of suffering masses of people, Christian evangelization must also confront the challenges of our postmodern worldview. It is notoriously difficult to define this worldview, for we are still in transition from a *modern* to a *postmodern* condition. Postmodernism means different things to different people and represents different perspectives in art, painting, architecture, literature, pop culture, and philosophy. For our purposes, suffice it to note that this emerging worldview is skeptical of any absolute claims of truth or any narrative that claims to be universal. Thus the Christian story of God's universal love in Jesus Christ is questioned for its claims or simply placed alongside other stories. Postmodern people no longer search for the one system of *truth*. This skepticism about any "meta-narrative" or a universal story has served to "delegitimize" and "decenter" the church's story and has made it appear less plausible. Instead, postmodern sensitivities are oriented to the formation of a "centerless" society and a celebration of "local" communities where diversity, difference, and plurality flourish.[33]

THE NEXT GENERATION

The television series *Star Trek: The Next Generation* completed its final season in 1994. In many ways, *The Next Generation* was an updated version of the earlier *Star Trek* series. As Jean-Luc Picard's new breed of explorers took over the command of the redesigned spaceship *Enterprise* from Captain Kirk's crew, the creators of the series discovered that their audience was in the midst of a subtle paradigm shift—modernity was giving birth to postmodernity. The new series reflects those changes.[34]

The Next Generation has a crew that is far more diverse than the original *Star Trek* crew, including species from other parts of the universe. This change represents the broader universality: humankind is no longer the only advanced intelligence. Also, the quest for knowledge has changed. Humankind is not capable of completing the mandate without the help of other species. The rational thinker Spock is replaced by Data, an android with perfect intellect but who lacks human emotions. Data sees himself as incomplete and seeks to be human. The presence of Counselor Troi, a woman gifted with the ability to perceive hidden feelings, adds a nonrational, intuitive dimension. The new series distrusts the rational and questions appearance as being reality. The older series, but in a typical modern fashion, generally ignored questions of God and religious belief, while *The Next Generation* shows interest in the supernatural as embodied in the character know as Q.

Whether this analogy accurately fits the emerging postmodern worldview, the new series contains helpful elements for exploring evangelizing in our contemporary age. Many aspects of postmodern worldview run counter to Christian assumptions, such as the rejection of any meta-narrative and the denial of objective truth. Postmodern skepticism over any unifying center of reality radically questions Christian claims about Jesus Christ. It mocks authority, questions moral absolutes, and destabilizes the knowledge that we have accumulated over time. Such a worldview, together with the fact of religious plurality in our society, is indeed contributing to a crisis of confidence among Christians. The temptation has been to abandon making any Christian claim and to go with the flow. Or, we avoid engagement with the postmodern generation by adopting a bunker or cocooning mentality whereby we consider ourselves as resident aliens in a strange new world. These approaches will not help the church. The articulation of the Christian faith, however, need not be wedded to modernist assumptions. As a matter of fact, modernism was no friend of Christianity! A constructive engagement with the postmodern worldview requires us to rethink evangelizing in relation to the contemporary sensitivities of Western culture.

THREE-DIMENSIONAL ENGAGEMENT

The evangelizing church has yet to discover effective methods of communicating with the next generation. However, at least three dimensions of engagement with postmodern culture are worth exploring. They are presented here *not* as strategies but as ideas for further reflection.

First, the postmodern generation sees a disconnect between what the church professes and what it practices. Lutheran theology may explain this hypocrisy in terms of saint/sinner dialectic, that the church is a redeemed as well as a fallen community. For the postmodern generation that distrusts rational explanations, the claims of the gospel are evaluated in terms of the character of the believing community. Members of the next generation are searching for evidence as to how the Christian community embodies the gospel in its communal praxis and its life together. Evangelizing activity needs to be a communal activity more than functioning as individual encounters. What difference the story of Jesus makes in the life of a Christian is not a matter of individual testimony (a modernist assumption), but must be narrated in relation to the community of believers. It is the believing community's relationships that best embody the story of Jesus in concrete terms that the next generation can comprehend.[35]

Second, the postmodern worldview rejects a propositional understanding of truth. The Lutheran tradition has always defined itself doctrinally, and the language of our tradition tends to be insider's language, or a subcultural language. Whether our theological/subcultural language communicates to the next generation is an issue worth pondering. In the emerging culture of biblical illiteracy, the message of the gospel articulated in terms of doctrinal orthodoxy will hardly communicate to the postmodern mind. What our concepts of "sin" and "grace," "estrangement" and "reconciliation," "resurrection" and "atonement" mean in contemporary culture is not really a matter of appropriate translation of these concepts into the language and idioms of contemporary culture. (The term *save* now belongs more to the realm of computers than to theology!) More important, how these terms are embodied in the praxis of the community may best serve the evangelizing witness of the church. George Lindbeck has argued that in a "postcritical age" the believing community's ability to internalize the biblical "sagas and stories, its images and symbols, its syntax and grammar" may be more crucial than theological articulations, however edifying or orthodox, that turn attention away from Scripture.[36]

Third, it must be noted that the postmodern generation may have turned away from institutional religion, but it is not irreligious. The next generation is more fascinated with *spirituality* than *religion*. The old-time preaching of heaven and hell doesn't impress them or scare them. And yet there is a serious interest in exploring the dimension of *mystery*. This, perhaps, explains in part the popularity of the *Left Behind* series, a fictionalized premillenarian account of the end times. Thus a recovery of the dimension of mystery in Christian proclamation may help our engagement with a postmodern culture. After all, at the heart of the Christian message lies the profound mystery of God's incarnation in the midst of the mundane world that defies rational explanation!

Conclusion: Learning to Be "Guests" in the Midst of Others

The thread that ties together the three divergent themes addressed in this chapter is this: *engagement with conviction*. We need to engage with people of other faiths with Christian convictions through interreligious dialogue in our context of religious plurality. We need to practice a theology of the cross as engagement in solidarity with those who are suffering and broken. We need to respond to the emerging spirituality of the postmodern generation in a three-dimensional engagement that involves communal praxis. The point is, there can be no evangelizing without active engagement with people. The practice of the theology of the cross and the dialectic of the *solas* and the *simuls* are distinctly Lutheran resources that encourage our engagement with people with courage and conviction. There are no quick and easy solutions or surefire strategies of engagement that can enhance or ensure the evangelistic outreach of the church. The challenge of forming authentic communities of Christian disciples is, and will remain, an issue till God's kingdom comes! The urgency to mobilize and redirect the church's energy in evangelizing the world must, however, be grounded on a realistic appraisal of our sociocultural realities.

In the present context, some may long for the return of a bygone era when the church was at the center of the town or society. But the reality is that the church today finds itself a marginalized community and a subculture in the midst of others. The contemporary church is fully aware that there is no possibility of resurrecting the old Christendom, whose obituary was written long ago. The church today must compete with a cacophony of voices in society just to be heard! There is little doubt that Western societies will increasingly feel the impact of religious plurality, which by all accounts is here to stay, and the influences of a postmodern culture. Congregations that feel immune from the pressures of religious plurality and postmodernism, or are indifferent to them, are deluding themselves or setting themselves up for a rude awakening!

Despite the efforts of some conservative Christians to thrust Christian values yet once more into the public arena, the church today increasingly finds itself relegated to the margins of society. The Christianization of society is not the goal of evangelization. Even the European churches, which have had a long-standing relationship with the state, have begun to jettison this relationship. What the churches should strive toward is the formation of local communities of authentic disciples embodying the cruciform pattern of Jesus' life, death, and resurrection.

From this perspective it may be fortuitous that the church in our context finds itself today in the margins of society. It is by being situated at the periphery that the witness gains its authenticity and credibility. This *decentering* of the church makes it possible to realize that the church itself is to be a recipient of its evangelizing effort. Its mission includes the formation of local communities of disciples who are nourished by Word and Sacrament for their engagement in the world. The metaphor of periphery is more than a spatial or geographic category, and can also be viewed as a theological category. The ministry of Jesus by and large took place in the periphery and among the marginalized. The event of the cross unfolded at the periphery. Following Jesus therefore is to meet him at the periphery. The periphery is the place of discipleship. If Christ is the *center* of Christian evangelizing, then wherever he is becomes the center.[37]

As a community dispersed to the periphery of society the church witnesses to the story of the cross of the risen Christ. That the church finds itself as a diaspora should energize it for active engagement. The church is now one religious community in the midst of other religious communities. It represents one sacred story in the midst of other sacred or secular stories in our society. It has no privileged status, and its absolute claims are met with distrust in our society. The church must now learn to be a *guest* in the midst of others in a religiously and culturally diverse society. Learning to be a guest in the midst of others is precisely the focus of its evangelizing engagement with people. "Christians learning to be guests" assumes a posture of humility and vulnerability, and it embodies the message of the cross of the risen Christ it seeks boldly to proclaim and to live by.

AFTER THE DEATH OF EVANGELISM— THE RESURRECTION OF AN EVANGELIZING CHURCH

The Lutheran tradition originated as a confessional theological movement. At the heart of this movement was and is *the centrality of the Gospel of Jesus Christ*. Beginning with Luther and the early Reformers, concentration on justification by grace through faith in Jesus Christ alone has been the centering focus. All theology is then ordered in relationship to this nonnegotiable center: the proper distinction between law and gospel; the theological use of the law as preparation for the gospel; Word, Sacrament, and Christian community as the means of grace; baptism as daily death to sin and resurrection to new life according to the promise of the gospel; preaching as the living word of the gospel today; the real presence of Jesus Christ in Holy Communion; theology of the cross; the message that the gospel sets the believer free from sin and free for the neighbor; and an ordering of the world that guarantees a realm for the free proclamation of the gospel (two-kingdoms teaching). Each of these theological assertions functions to preserve the centrality of the gospel of Jesus Christ as the church's greatest treasure. How could such a tradition, grounded deeply in gospel-centered theological convictions, be so ineffectual in evangelism?

In developing our constructive proposals about evangelizing, the authors of this book have also analyzed the shortcomings of Lutheran practice. It is clear that we are critical of the lack of effectiveness of the Lutheran churches in the United States as participants in the fulfillment of the Great Commission. This failure of the Lutheran churches in the practice of evangelizing must drive us to repentance.

This chapter takes a final look at three of the most pervasive obstacles that prevent a more effective engagement by Lutherans in evangelizing: clericalism, the privatization of religion, and ethnic idolatries. The failure of the Lutheran churches in the practice of evangelism should humble us and open us up to learning from others. This chapter also explores some of the lessons about evangelizing that Lutherans in our context need to learn from others: Evangelicals, Pentecostals, the historic black churches, the Roman Catholic tradition, partners from the global church, and even other religions. We have much to learn, and we need to be open to what others have to teach us.

At the same time, we clearly affirm that the gospel-centered theology of the Lutheran heritage is not inherently antithetical to the practice of evangelizing. As we argued in chapter two, the gift of the gospel entails a call to evangelize. We propose that a Lutheran centering in the gospel of Jesus Christ has something essential to contribute to the future of evangelizing in our context and beyond. Although few authors have offered an explicit Lutheran perspective on evangelizing, those who have made a contribution, like Russell John Briese or Robert Kolb, have demonstrated that Lutheran theology is inherently evangelical.[1] The authors of this book likewise begin with the assertion that the gospel of Jesus Christ is intrinsically evangelizing. What needs to occur in order for Lutherans to claim and practice this theological affirmation?

What needs to occur is nothing short of the *death of evangelism*. By this we mean that the prevailing opinion about evangelism as one *program* in the church, among many other programs, must die. Evangelism has been reduced to one function of ecclesial existence and to the work of a committee alongside many other committees. In the worst-case scenario, evangelism has been reduced to an activity used to prop up the survival of the institutional church. Only when we begin to worry about church attendance or finances do we begin to consider the need for evangelism. The deeply rooted conviction that evangelism is an optional *program* of the church must die.

What do we imagine for a church in which evangelism has been put to death? We pray for *the resurrection of an evangelizing church culture* by the power of God. By culture we mean "the total body of belief, behaviors, knowledge, sanctions, values and goals that mark the way of life of a people."[2] No longer will evangelism be one program or ministry function alongside others. Rather, engagement in evangelizing will become so rooted in our identity as a church that speaking the name of Jesus Christ and telling the story of what God has done for us will become as natural as talking about our families. A culture is something in which we are immersed, something we pass on to the next generation. A culture entails a way of being—how we live and how we die. A culture involves a particular way of speaking and acting. A culture is embedded in symbols and rituals that permeate existence. Like the proverbial fish that cannot distinguish itself from the water in which it swims, we need to become so immersed in an evangelizing culture that our communities of faith cannot help but tell the story of Jesus and his love.

Evangelism as a mere program of the church is the deadly enemy of an evangelizing church. Treating evangelism as a program instills in us a false sense of security that it has been taken care of. Such a view is a tremendous obstacle in the development of the fundamental culture shift toward evangelizing that we believe is imperative for the future of our church. We need to become an evangelizing culture, and the culture change that we advocate requires that we leave our comfort zone. May God resurrect a culture of evangelizing that permeates the life of our church on every level!

THE DEATH OF EVANGELISM

The paradigm that reduces evangelism to being a program of the church largely emerged in the nineteenth century. Two aspects of American culture especially influenced this: (1) the privatization of religion, and (2) the American interest in colonization.

According to Sidney Mead, religion in the United States exchanged its public voice for the privilege of being tolerated by the state.[3] Increasingly the voice of the churches became subdued in the public square, as religion itself became a matter of private opinion. In order to overcome this marginalization, the church invented a rationale and programs to counteract its relegation to the private sphere. *Evangelism* was born as an attempt to challenge Christians to bring their faith to public expression. This particular form of evangelism was greatly influenced by the spirit of revivalism and a decisional theology.

The nineteenth century also saw the emergence of evangelism through the mission societies that were formed to spread the gospel to the ends of the earth. Among Lutherans the missionary impulse was born of Lutheran Pietism.[4] Both freestanding mission societies and the denominationally based global mission efforts mobilized the church to greater faithfulness in carrying out its worldwide evangelism work.[5] Peoples in foreign lands needed to be converted to the Christian faith. Tragically, most efforts at global evangelism became too deeply intertwined with the colonialism and cultural imperialism to which they were attached.[6] The nineteenth century bequeathed to us a tradition that understood evangelism as a program to overcome the privatization of religion and as a dimension of colonialism.[7] This is a dubious inheritance.

Evangelism, isolated as a particular program of the church, needs to die. Unfortunately, evangelism continues to be perpetrated by most Lutheran congregations as a program where it is the property of the clergy and the few laity willing to serve on an evangelism committee. Evangelism as a program tends to be the property of those with specialized training. As such, it is often relinquished to the entrepreneur, the TV evangelist, or a consultant. Evangelism as a program is an agenda item at a church council meeting, rather than the very business of the whole church. Evangelism as a program of the church must be put to death. There are three aspects of what must die.

Clericalism

At the heart of the Lutheran confession is the affirmation of Word, Sacrament, and Christian community as the means of grace. Through these means, God in Christ meets us to forgive our sin, deliver us from the powers of evil, and promise us eternal life. The centrality of Word and Sacrament in Lutheran theology places a great emphasis on the event of preaching and the celebration of the sacraments. Pastors are those ministers whom the church calls to give leadership in local congregations in the stewardship of Word, Sacrament, and Christian community. Properly understood, the gifts given to ordained pastors for this ministry are not *higher* or *greater* than the various gifts given to other members of the body of Christ. They are particular gifts needed within the body of Christ, but they are not superior gifts. Rather, the gifts of ordained pastors should be in service of equipping "the saints for the work of ministry, for building up the body of Christ" (Eph. 4:12). The work of the pastor is a ministry of service under the yoke of Christ for the sake of freeing the baptized for their daily ministry in the world through the power of the gospel.

Clericalism is a major distortion of the office of pastor that does great harm to the ministry of the baptized. It undermines efforts at developing an evangelizing culture. In a church governed by clericalism, a hierarchy is established in which the gifts of the pastor are viewed as *higher* than those of the lowly laity. Pastors are placed on a pedestal as the church's highest authorities. The baptized are disempowered, thinking they are not educated, skilled, or prepared enough to engage in evangelizing. Evangelizing becomes a specialized activity that requires the credentials of a professional. Instead of equipping the saints for the work of evangelizing, clericalism silences the baptized, who subordinate and relegate their own ministries to the ministry of a pastor. The pastor is the one who does the ministry for the laity.

Clericalism is a reality in many of our congregations. It developed over centuries and has a wicked grasp on the life of the church, stifling both the ministry of pastors and the ministry of the laity. As a result of clericalism, many pastors feel a sense of isolation from the baptized. Instead of healthy partnership, pastors find themselves saddled with unrealistic expectations and frustrated by the lack of participation by members in the ministries of the church. Thereby, the baptized fail to understand that their gifts are to be used in service to others in every walk of life, including their evangelizing testimony to others. Ministry is reduced to what pastors do; the ministry of the baptized is reduced to partaking in pastoral activities.

If an evangelizing culture is to be resurrected after the death of evangelism, the first major obstacle that will need to be overcome is our penchant for clericalism. No congregation can become an evangelizing culture as long as it clings to the notion that the pastor is *the* educated and superior minister who does evangelism on its behalf. In an evangelizing culture, the work of evangelizing is the calling of every baptized member of the body of Christ. God grants gifts for evangelizing to each one. Giving testimony need not be polished or packaged. It only needs to be an expression of one's experience with God. To overcome clericalism will require nothing else than a culture change.

The Privatization of Faith

As with clericalism, the historical factors leading to the emergence of a privatized faith are long-standing. One of the implicit assumptions about the separation of church and state is that religion belongs to the private sphere, whereas the public sphere belongs to the brokers of power—in business, labor, law, and government. This means that the particulars of one's faith belong to the realm of personal opinion and should not be imposed on others. The historical instances of religious intolerance are so horrific that we have agreed not to allow religious belief to become the basis for oppression and violence. There is something, on the one hand, very right about this idea of religious tolerance. On the other hand, the resulting privatization of faith short-circuits the truth claims of the Christian faith, that there finally is one God—Father, Son, and Holy Spirit—whose mission is to bring all people to faith in the gospel. It confines evangelizing to a circumscribed circle of those who earn trusted access to one's thoughts and values.

In the modern world, faith (or spirituality, to use today's common idiom) has had an important function in providing hope to individuals when they confront major life challenges. Individuals appeal to a higher power when dealing with loss of a job, divorce, illness, death, or other crises. Whereas *spirituality* commonly refers to values that are adopted by particular individuals in their personal quest for meaning, *faith* is typically formed in a communal process together with others. Whether it is known as "spirituality" or as "faith," the one defining characteristic today is that religion is a very private matter. The content of one's faith is something that finally is nobody else's business. Faith commitments are highly cherished and are to be respected as the private property of the individual.

This privatization of faith presents two formidable obstacles to the development of an evangelizing church culture. *First*, it leaves the baptized reticent in speaking of their faith or sharing it with others. While faith is a deeply held conviction and belongs to one's inmost core of beliefs, it is not something to be shared. In fact, I would choose to speak on almost any other subject before I would disclose this precious story to another, for fear that the gift would not be honored. Because faith in God is a closely guarded secret, this magnifies the difficulty of ever putting into words what one truly believes. The privatization of faith means that we build walls to protect our deepest convictions. In doing so, we do not learn to articulate these convictions so that their significance can be communicated to others. We keep our faith under wraps.

Second, given our tendency to regard faith as private, we view the sharing of faith with other people as a violation of their own right to privacy in religious matters. We fear offending others' right to privacy by any attempt to impose our faith upon them. The last thing we want is to be accused of being a religious fanatic. We want to avoid being identified with TV preachers or door-to-door evangelists who force their ideas on others without respecting their right to privacy. We are to be tolerant of the freedom for others to either formulate their own religious faith or to have no faith at all. Religion is a private concern, where I have no right to think that what I believe is any better than what you believe. We live in peaceful coexistence, each guarding our religious beliefs and keeping them from getting in the way of our mutual goodwill.

The phenomenon of privatized religious belief is heightened in the postmodern era. The postmodern is distinguished by the absence of any grand story or "meta-narrative" that gives a common identity to diverse peoples.[8] In the post-modern era, each subculture develops its own story of identity that it sets along-side the identity story of every other group. All of these stories simply coexist, with none of them attaining normative status over the others. Taken to its ultimate con-clusion, the postmodern era becomes a time in which each and every individual claims a personalized story, including a very idiosyncratic faith story. The goal is not to reconcile these different stories, but rather to allow them to live alongside each other, mutually enriching the whole. In such an era, the resistance to evange-lizing reaches its apex. What right do I have to try to convince others that my faith story has significance for them?

If evangelizing culture is to be resurrected after the death of evangelism, a second major obstacle that will need to be overcome is the privatization of faith. While maintaining deep and genuine respect for others, it will be necessary to risk sharing the story of one's own faith in a natural way. It will be necessary to trans-late into words the commitments of one's privatized faith and discover a language that articulates one's feelings in a way that connects with the experience of others. It will be necessary to believe more strongly in the reality of the Triune God's love and grace in Jesus Christ than in the right of others to maintain strict privacy in matters pertaining to faith. To overcome the forces that lead to the privatization of faith will require nothing less than a culture change.

Ethnic Idolatries

The Lutheran churches in the United States originated from the immigration of Lutheran peoples from Northern Europe. The history of Lutheranism in the United States has been largely a process of reconciling the various Northern Euro-pean ethnic groups through the mergers of church bodies. First, we witnessed a complex process moving toward reconciliation of Germans, Danes, Norwegians, or Swedes within their respective language and culture groups. Then we saw the uniting of the various ethnic traditions into ever larger unions. The formation of the Evangelical Lutheran Church in America, as with its predecessor church bodies, has been achieved mainly as the joining together of distinct Northern European ethnic groupings. Unfortunately, in this process, black, Latino, Asian, or other ethnic groups have always been marginal to the primary Northern European Lutheran mainstream.

It is understandable that ethnicity and language have been uniting features of Lutheranism in the United States. But an identity based inordinately on ethnic culture and language serves as a major obstacle to the emergence of an evangeliz-ing culture in the ELCA. Yes, every particular ethnic culture and language is a gift of God that contributes to the richness of the many diverse cultures in which God is at work. To be German or Danish or Swedish or Norwegian is not to be despised. Each ethnic culture has particular gifts to be celebrated among the variety of cul-tural traditions. The problem emerges when particular ethnic and cultural tra-ditions take primacy in defining what it means to be a Christian or a Lutheran. To make German, or Danish, or Swedish, or Norwegian identity primary is to substitute ethnic particularity for baptismal identity in Jesus Christ as the defining characteristic of Christian identity. Whenever this occurs, ethnicity becomes an idol that needs to be rejected. Far too often, our own ethnic idolatries have blocked the development of an evangelizing culture.

Ethnic idolatry prevails in the church wherever any ethnic identity is celebrated to the exclusion of other ethnic backgrounds. This may be detected in the stories that are shared, the jokes that are told, the foods that are eaten, the customs that are practiced, or the songs that are sung. God seeks to become manifest in a world of many cultures through a rich variety of particular ethnic forms and languages. However, ethnic idolatry occurs where a single ethnic culture takes precedence to the exclusion of other ethnic cultures. The particularity of God's activity working in each culture must not be interpreted as God's exclusive activity through any single ethnic culture.

Baptism into the name of Jesus Christ is the basis for an identity that relativizes all other identities, including those of ethnic background. On the day of Pentecost, the Holy Spirit created a community of faith in Jesus Christ that transcended the strictures that define ethnic and language groups (Acts 2:1-21). While each ethnic and language group continued to speak in its own respective language, the Spirit created a communion that transcended all ethnic divisions. Identity in Jesus Christ stands at the center of ecclesial existence. While they are truly good gifts of God, ethnic origins did not separate the faithful into separated and competing camps.

Given the predominance of Northern European origins for Lutherans in the United States, intentional strategies need to be implemented that proactively counter our proclivities toward ethnic idolatry. These include intentional strategies for welcoming new ethnic groups into the church; the introduction of hymns and worship materials from other cultures to stretch one's own ethnic background; learning to speak other languages and to use them in outreach; being intentional about face-to-face and heart-to-heart meetings between people of different ethnic origins; and affirming the unifying identity that is shared by our common faith in Jesus Christ. This entails the readiness to be changed by the encounter with those who are ethnically different from us.

If an evangelizing culture is to be resurrected after the death of evangelism, a third major obstacle that will need to be overcome is the maintenance of ethnic idolatries. We need to celebrate the gifts of God that are manifest in cultures and languages other than our own, while at the same time thanking God for our own particular culture. We need to chart new territory beyond the realm of ethnic idolatries. If this obstacle is to be overcome, we need to be changed by the gifts brought to the Lutheran church by people whose ethnic origins are different than those of the traditional Lutheran power base. These include the gifts of African American, Latino, and Asian Lutherans. To overcome the forces that lead to ethnic idolatries will require nothing less than a culture change.

WHAT LUTHERANS MUST LEARN FROM OTHERS

Confessing the sins and failures that block our evangelizing, Lutherans face the challenge of shaping a new evangelizing church culture in genuine humility. We have not shared the gospel with our neighbors as we ought. We have not even shared the gospel within our own households as we ought (see chapter five). Lutherans stand convicted of hoarding the treasure that God has entrusted to us in the gospel of Jesus Christ. We have treasured the gospel in our hearts and failed to open our mouths. When it comes to evangelizing, Lutherans are summoned to repentance. We need absolution for our sins and a new beginning.

While Lutheran theology holds to the centrality of the gospel of Jesus Christ, this theological conviction has not resulted in powerful evangelizing. We are in many ways novices in this field. It is only recently that Lutherans have begun to acknowledge their deficiency.[9] Yet within the body of Christ we are connected with other ecclesial traditions that have much to teach us about the art of evangelizing. What are some of the lessons we need to learn from other Christian traditions and even from those beyond the Christian fold?

From Evangelicals

There is much we need to learn from Evangelicals about the art of evangelizing. Too often Lutherans find themselves in a polemical relationship with Evangelicals because of the theological differences that separate us. Chief among these are our differing sensibilities about the role of the human will in the process of conversion. Lutherans have been quick to criticize the *decisional* theology in Evangelicalism and thereby overlook the genuine lessons that need to be learned.[10]

There are three lessons about evangelizing that Lutherans would do well to appropriate from the Evangelical tradition. The first is a deep and abiding passion for sharing the gospel.[11] Evangelicals understand in a profound way that the gospel is a message that needs to be shared. There is urgency about the Christian message that will not be stilled. Evangelicals are moved by a deep sense of gratitude for what God in Christ has done for them and thereby demonstrate passion that this precious gift needs to be given to others. As Lutherans seek to forge a new evangelizing culture, we must reclaim our own passion for sharing the gospel with others, both inside and outside the church.

A second gift from the Evangelical tradition is their intentionality about the practice of personal witnessing. It is simply expected within Evangelical culture that a Christian will personally witness in telling the story of what Christ means in one's life. Within Evangelicalism, formulas and models are taught by the church to help persons construct a personal testimony.[12] It is a normal practice within Evangelical culture to work at formulating testimony and to practice delivering it.[13] Older Christians encourage new Christians in the art of personal witnessing. Groups often meet for prayer and for sharing experiences in how the faith has been spoken to others. As Lutherans seek to forge a new evangelizing culture, we have much to learn from Evangelicals about the practice of personal witnessing.

A third gift to be received from Evangelicals is the practice of public testimony. Regularly at worship or in other group meetings, Evangelicals designate time for public testimony.[14] Such testimony is different than preaching. It is an occasion for a member to tell others what Christian faith means and to relate what God has been doing in his or her own experience.[15] Public testimony takes Christian faith out of the private sphere and into the public arena. It models a style of speaking the faith to others. Above all, it is a powerful means for the Holy Spirit to inspire faith in the hearer.

From Pentecostals

Like Evangelicals, Pentecostals have a strong passion for sharing the gospel. One lesson that Lutherans would do well to learn from Pentecostal churches is their vivid conviction about the present activity of the Holy Spirit. The work of God's Spirit is not confined to the distant past and faraway places. The Holy Spirit is God's living presence active in our world and in our lives today. This Spirit is dynamically at work in the evangelizing ministry of the church as Christians share the gospel throughout the world.

This conviction about the power of the Holy Spirit has contributed to the phenomenal worldwide growth of Pentecostalism, especially in the churches of the South.[16] While Luther's own theology was deeply influenced by his faith in the present activity of the Holy Spirit working through the means of grace,[17] this facet of his thought must be reclaimed for the renewal of the Lutheran church in its evangelizing today.[18] As Lutherans forge a new evangelizing culture, we must understand that the Holy Spirit accompanies us and works through us as we speak the faith to others.

From Historic Black Churches

Born of profound suffering in the trauma of slavery, the historic black churches are rooted in the faith in God's deliverance from all forms of oppression.[19] The words of Holy Scripture are a living story about God's ever new acts of deliverance from the forms of bondage that continue to oppress. As the word of God is preached today, it is the responsibility of the preacher to bring the word alive into the experience of the community and the responsibility of the hearers to appropriate that word into their own present life experience.[20] The *call and response* form of preaching, whereby listeners participate by speaking back to the preacher, makes the Bible a living address that meets the congregation in its existential struggles. The stories of God's activity in the past are full of lessons and promises about what God is continuing to accomplish today. As Lutherans seek to forge a new evangelizing culture, we need to learn from the historic black churches that the Bible is a living word that continues to claim our lives, especially our experiences of suffering.

The historic black churches also demonstrate in a powerful way the indivisible connection between speaking the faith and doing the faith. The black churches witness to the unity of telling the story of Jesus and risking one's life for the sake of justice. Mighty oration about God's purposes is to be matched by mighty deeds on behalf of God's cause. The heroic figures of the faith—Frederick Douglass, Sojourner Truth, Martin Luther King Jr.—each integrate powerful stories with courageous action in the cause of freedom. Speech and deeds are inseparable. Evangelizing entails the risk of political critique of the status quo. As Lutherans seek to forge a new evangelizing culture, we have much to learn from the historic black churches about backing up our rhetoric with lives of integrity in the pursuit of justice for all.

From Roman Catholics

The Second Vatican Council was a watershed event in modern Roman Catholic history. Following that event, a new term emerged to describe the process by which the Catholic faith was to interact with the many diverse cultures of the world: *evangelization*. The central document that articulates the Roman Catholic meaning of evangelization is the papal encyclical of Pope Paul VI, *On Evangelization in the Modern World*, issued in 1975.[21] Evangelization aims at the "renewal of humanity" through "the evangelization of cultures." The encyclical emphasizes "the primary importance of witness in life" and the "need of explicit proclamation" in the process of evangelization.[22]

In contrast to the imperialistic approaches of previous generations, evangelization today is to be characterized by a "generous attitude toward efforts at inculturation."[23] This entails deep respect for the integrity of the cultural reception of the Christian faith and a new recognition of the plasticity of the cultural forms in which the gospel message becomes incarnate. While affirming the universality of the Christian message, evangelization takes seriously the diverse ways that the one faith becomes manifest in particular times, places, and cultures. Evangelization involves a mutual exchange and interpenetration between the content of the faith already embedded in certain cultural forms and the content of the faith as it becomes incarnate in new cultural forms. As Lutherans seek to forge a new evangelizing culture, we need to demonstrate the same measure of respect to other cultures as does the Roman Catholic tradition in its efforts at evangelization.

From the Global Church

The most rapid growth of Christianity in recent decades has been occurring in the churches of the southern hemisphere. Philip Jenkins has analyzed the projections for the twenty-first century and declared that the future of Christianity, "the next Christendom," will be largely determined by the defining characteristics of the churches of the South.[24] One of the most impressive marks of the emerging global church is its fervor for spreading the gospel.[25] What do Lutherans have to learn from the experiences of these rapidly growing churches?

Those who have traveled to Africa and studied the phenomenal growth of the Lutheran church in places like Tanzania note that one striking characteristic of ecclesial life is the expectancy that God is acting in their lives today. God is not someone who once was active but now has retired from the scene. Instead, there is a vivid expectancy that God is alive and working in the life of the people in the present moment. Jesus Christ is alive to meet people with grace, forgiveness, and assistance as they face the challenges of their existence. The Holy Spirit is dynamically present to bring people to faith and to work signs of God's blessing. The Tanzanian Lutherans understand that God is accompanying their journey as a living partner as they share their faith with others. Expectancy of God's activity in their lives lends energy and enthusiasm for evangelizing. As Lutherans seek to forge a new evangelizing culture, we must draw upon the fervor of the southern hemisphere churches whose vivid sense of the living God leads them into expectant evangelizing.

Another common characteristic of the global church is the focus on the ministry of all the baptized.[26] There is a dramatic shift from a clergy-centered to a laity-centered understanding of Christian ministry. In many contexts this leadership is formed through the preparation of those who will guide the life of church members in cell groups. Those with the proper gifts among the baptized are trained as leaders to facilitate sharing, Bible study, prayer, and singing in the cell groups. Cell groups are proactive in addressing needs, and within the cell groups baptized lay leaders guide the other members in learning to witness to their faith, first with one another, then to those beyond the church.

The role of clergy in this process is the equipping of the baptized for leadership. The baptized are empowered as leaders to carry out ministry with authority among the members, and members are empowered to carry out their ministry in their daily lives. One of the key teachings in this model is the importance of evangelizing. Evangelizing permeates the life of the church and is the responsibility of all the members. To be a Christian is to be an evangelist. The priesthood of all believers is involved in the work of evangelizing. As Lutherans seek to forge a new evangelizing culture, we must focus on the revival of the universal priesthood of evangelizers by empowering the baptized for leadership.

From Other Religions

There are also lessons that Lutherans need to learn about evangelizing from faithful representatives of the other great religious traditions of the world. The following is only suggestive of what can be learned through the careful process of interreligious dialogue described in the previous chapter.

JUDAISM. In Judaism the prophet waited upon the Spirit to give utterance to a word of the Lord that worked weal or woe in the lives of the people. In what ways do we need to pray for and depend upon the Spirit to empower our own speaking the faith?

ISLAM. In Islam the first of the five pillars is confession of the faith. Muslims are expected several times a day to confess their faith in Allah and the messenger of God, Muhammad. Moreover, the other four pillars of Islam direct Muslims to give public witness to their faith by observing the hours of prayer five times each day, by fasting during the month of Ramadan, by the giving of alms, and by making pilgrimage to the holy city of Mecca. In what ways do we need to become more deeply grounded in our confession of faith and give public witness to our God?

HINDUISM. In Hinduism, the distinct branches of the religion each in their own way—through sacrifice, meditation, duty, or devotion—provide a path to the attainment of the ultimate unity of all things. Proper awareness leads the believer to the apprehension of the sacredness of all that exists. In what ways do we need to apprehend the sacredness of the other, as someone made in the very image of God, in order to demonstrate utmost respect to the ones with whom we speak?

BUDDHISM. In Buddhism, the Four Noble Truths provide a path out of the inherent suffering of the world into the bliss of enlightenment. Mahayana Buddhism evolved as the vehicle to bring this enlightenment to all creatures out of the motive of deep compassion. In what ways do we need to be moved by the compassionate love of God to bring to all creatures the blissful gospel of our Lord?

An incarnational approach to evangelizing is convinced that wherever we go in the world, among people of whatever religion, the living Christ has already gone before us. Therefore we anticipate meeting the presence of the living Christ even in our encounter with Jews, Muslims, Hindus, Buddhists, or people of other religions. As we respectfully learn from representatives of other religious traditions and experience their lives of integrity, we also discover lessons about the meaning of evangelizing. As Lutherans seek to forge a new evangelizing culture, we need to approach people of other faiths with respect, expecting that we will be changed by the encounter.

THE HOLY TRINITY: AN EVANGELIZING GOD

The formation of an evangelizing church culture begins with the activity of the Triune God, who is an evangelizing God. As we have mined the Scripture and the Christian tradition in this book, we have laid the groundwork for a trinitarian theology of our evangelizing God. Particularly in chapter four, we examined the biblical motifs that contribute to the interpretation of the Trinity as a missiological concept. We now make explicit the implications of understanding God as Trinity for the church in its evangelizing.

One of the most salutary developments in contemporary theology has been a recovery of the doctrine of the Trinity. Whereas the most significant nineteenth-century theologians relegated the Trinity to an afterthought in their systems, beginning with Karl Barth and consonant with the increasing influence of Orthodox theology, the twentieth century witnessed the revival of the Trinity as the foundation for a theology that is inherently evangelizing. For example, consultations of the Lutheran World Federation have explored the meaning of a trinitarian missiology.[27] This aspect of theology was never lost in Eastern Orthodoxy, so we turn first to that tradition in grounding an evangelizing church culture in the activity of a relating, evangelizing Triune God.

According to John Zizioulas, the being of God is essentially being in relation. "The being of God is a relational being: without the concept of communion it would not be possible to speak of the being of God."[28] The Trinity means that God is in essence a communion of three persons—Father, Son, and Holy Spirit. The persons of the Trinity exist with one another in a communion of mutual love, "existing in and for one another through an unceasing movement of interchange."[29] The persons of the Trinity relate to one another through what John of Damascus termed "*perichoresis*." "*Perichoresis* expressed the idea that the three divine persons mutually inhere in one another, draw life from one another, and are what they are by relation to one another. *Perichoresis* means being-in-one-another, permeation without confusion."[30] A prominent image used to depict *perichoresis* is that of a divine dance. Each person of the Trinity moves uniquely in the dance but always entirely in relationship to the other dancers. God begets and is begotten; God proceeds and is source of the procession. The persons of the Trinity relate to one another within the unity of the Godhead in a dancing communion of mutual love.

Human beings were created in the image of God. This means that human beings were created for relationship with the Triune God and for relationship with one another. As is true for the Trinity, human beings are created to live in relation. We are created to join in the dance of the three persons of the Trinity. Just as the "being of God is a relational being: so also is the being of humans. God is self-giving, sharing, response: so also are humans in the divine image."[31] Humanity was created to join in the mutual communion of the three persons of the Trinity, to partake of the mutual communion of love. This is the created intention of ecclesial existence, the church as eternal participation in the loving relations of the three persons of the Trinity.

The fall into sin can be understood as the rupture of the dance of humanity with the Triune God. Humans become estranged from the relationships of love shared freely in communion with the divine persons. Thereby, humans also become estranged from one another. Instead of existing in life-giving relation with the Trinity, we seek to live for ourselves, as isolated individuals. Humans assert their own *being* rather than dwelling in the truth that their ultimate being exists only in *communion* with God. "The fall consists in *the refusal to make being dependent on communion*."[32] Humans no longer recognize that their very being is constituted for relationship with the Holy Trinity.

Enter the mission of the evangelizing God. The Triune God has infinite passionate love to restore humans into life-giving relationship. The sending of the Son to become incarnate reveals the divine mission of restoring communion with estranged humanity.[33] The fullness of the Triune God's love is poured out in the Son's death on the cross. The eternity of the Triune God's love is verified in the Son's resurrection from the dead on Easter. The Holy Spirit restores humans to relationship with the Trinity by actualizing Christ's reconciling work. This takes place as humans are incorporated into the church, the body of Christ. "The Holy Spirit, in making real the Christ-event in history, makes real *at the same time* Christ's personal existence as a body in community."[34] Ecclesial life is the restoration of life-giving relationships among the members of Christ's body and the Holy Trinity. The Triune God is an evangelizing God who restores relationship with humanity through the mission of the Son and by the power of the Spirit.

Notice that the church is nothing other than a community that is defined by life-giving relationships—with the three persons of the Trinity, and thereby among the members of the body of Christ. The church is constituted by relating. Church is a culture of relating in loving communion with the triune persons. Church is a culture of relating to one another in the same Spirit that the triune persons relate to each another.

The primary way that this relating is expressed within the church is through the word. In this context, we will consider the sacraments as manifestations of a visible word (Augustine).[35] Through the word, the Triune evangelizing God works to bring us into life-giving relationship. This word certainly includes what we celebrate at worship—the proclamation of the word in a sermon and the encounter with the visible word in baptism and Holy Communion. God indeed promises to relate to us through the proclaimed and sacramental word. But if the church is a way of relating, a culture of relating in loving communion with the triune persons, then every relationship and every word that is spoken in the church is truly a reflection of the divine communion.

This is the full significance of the Lutheran affirmation that Christ is really present in the mutual conversation and consolation of the brothers and sisters (Smalcald Articles, Part III, Article 4). As was expressed in chapter four, "Redeemed persons are to be in relation with one another just as they are now in relation to God."[36] In the words spoken between the members of the church, the Triune evangelizing God draws us deeply into the divine communion of love. As we relate to one another, God's own evangelizing mission is extended in, with, and through our words. The church is a culture that has been created to participate in the Trinity's evangelizing mission in the world. In its essence the church exists through the way its members relate to one another in communion with the Triune God. This communion comes to expression through the evangelizing power of God's word made manifest through the words the members speak.

The theological foundation for the church's evangelizing is nothing other than God's own triune existence. The Trinity longs for communion with humanity, sends the Son into the world to restore us to relationship, and by the power of the Spirit draws us into communion in the church. As members of the church, we relate to one another through evangelizing words that are expressions of God's own relation-building, evangelizing word. The church is a culture that comes to expression through words spoken between members that ground us in life-giving relationship with each other and in communion with the Triune God. Our relations with one another and with the divine persons are mediated through our speech—*evangelizing words*.

The church that the Trinity has called into existence by the power of the evangelizing word has a mission. Even as the Triune God is restless for the restoration of relationship with all of estranged humanity, so the church remains restless for the restoration of all humanity into communion with God. The full communion of the Trinity attains its eschatological destiny only in the kingdom of God, when God will "be all in all" (1 Cor. 15:28). Until that day, the church's mission is to serve by reestablishing life-giving relationships with all humanity.

The church is to speak evangelizing words that restore human persons into relationship with the loving communion of the Triune God. The members of the church are sent to be speakers of evangelizing words that create relationship between every human person and three persons of the Holy God—Father, Son, and Holy Spirit. As members of the church, it is our mission to speak evangelizing words that draw others into the communion of the Trinity. Our own lives only have meaning by virtue of our having been restored to relationship with the church and the triune persons. Evangelizing is not something that we do; evangelizing is what we are. Our being is only in communion.

THE RESURRECTION OF
AN EVANGELIZING CHURCH CULTURE

What is meant by *culture*? We add this to our earlier definition: "Insofar as it is specific to a particular group of people, *a culture tends to be conceived as their entire way of life*, everything about the group that distinguishes it from others, including social habits and institutions, rituals, artifacts, categorical schemes, beliefs and values."[37] A culture is an entire way of life. Peter Stromberg stresses that a congregational culture is a *commitment system*.[38] Congregational culture is disclosed through the particular set of commitments made by a church. This emphasis has fruitfulness also for thinking about the commitment system of a church body like the Evangelical Lutheran Church in America. A culture comes to expression through every aspect of a people's life, including its ways of relating and speaking. A culture is not something a people does; a culture is something that inhabits a people. A culture is something a people is. A culture is what we as a church are committed to.

Even as we call for the *death of evangelism*, we do so for the sake of resurrecting *evangelizing* as integral to what it means to *be* church culture. Harbingers of this resurrection are to be found scattered on the landscape if we have the eyes to see. Jan Linn, for example, has written: "Far from being something we do, evangelism is something we are."[39] His proposal outlines practical steps for "*becoming* a witness evangelism church." "Intentional witnessing depends on the church being the church, living out of a deep center of spiritual power, functioning as the body of Christ engaged in ministries that witness to the One who is the head."[40]

George Hunter summons the church to take up "the Celtic way of evangelism."[41] Hunter holds up the ancient model of the Celts who sought to inculturate Christian faith by the establishing of "a monastic community welcoming seekers as guests and teams from the monastic community visiting settlements for weeks or months."[42] According to this approach, the evangelizers dwell with the seekers for an extended period of time, until the *way* becomes part of their own being. Key practices for this culture are ministries of hospitality (including cell groups), a conversational approach, and sending teams who set up "colonies" among a foreign people.[43]

Mark Hanson, presiding bishop of the Evangelical Lutheran Church in America, envisions an ELCA that is "a witnessing church" and "an inviting church." "Being an inviting church means inviting your neighbors, colleagues, and family members to come and hear the story of God's love in Christ. Most of us have come to the faith because someone else has brought us."[44] Hanson invites congregations to take an inventory of the first impressions people have of them. How does a congregation exude hospitality and a welcome for all?

The authors of this book propose that *nothing short of a change of culture is necessary for the Lutheran church to become an evangelizing church*. We need to reconfigure our fundamental *commitment system*. To change a culture (an entire way of life), including the social habits, rituals, beliefs, and values of the institution, will require *intentionality*, especially by the leadership of the church. We will need to abandon our present comfort zone. Cultures only change by sustained attention over an extended period of time. If the Lutheran church is to become an evangelizing church, there needs to be ongoing commitment to changing our existing church culture. Do we have the collective will for such an undertaking?

What needs to change in Lutheran church culture has to do with *both the style and substance of our relating to one another and to the world around us*. The culture of our Triune God is a culture bringing us and all people into life-giving relationships. The Christian God is an evangelizing God who relates to all human persons through the gospel of Jesus Christ. This occurs as we meet Jesus Christ in community with each other. If the Lutheran church is to become an evangelizing church, then we need to take stock of the way that we live out our common life in community, the quality of our ways of relating. Such an inventory will reveal that we are a church that has a deep and rich theological and worship tradition, but that we are also a church that has failed to learn how to speak the Christian faith either to each other or to the world around us.

Lutheran church culture needs to cultivate *intentional speaking of the faith*.[45] The key aspect of Lutheran church culture that must change involves how we speak the faith both among ourselves within the church and especially to those outside the church. If a new manner of speaking the faith is to emerge at the magnitude of a culture change, then everything about our way of relating needs to be reconsidered: how we employ Scripture, how we worship, how we do catechesis, how we relate to one another in community, and how we encounter others. The particular focus of our efforts in all of these areas must be our capacity to speak the faith. What strategies might be employed in a church that is intent on developing an evangelizing culture?

Throughout this book the authors have stressed the importance of *Scripture* for grounding the church's evangelizing. In an evangelizing church culture, Scripture is not only something that members hear in readings and sermons at worship. Nor is Scripture only something members read and study in classes. In an evangelizing church culture, *Scripture is something the baptized learn to speak and tell to others*. The baptized not only hear Bible stories and learn Bible stories and study Bible stories. Rather, the baptized from an early age and into adulthood begin to tell Bible stories and speak Bible stories to each other. The language of the congregation becomes permeated with scriptural references and allusions. The stories of Scripture become an indispensable vehicle for telling the stories of our own lives.[46]

In this book the authors have stressed the centrality of worship in the life of the church and argued for a dynamic connection between *worship* and evangelizing. Specifically, what needs to be highlighted is how *worship brings our faith to speech and sends us forth to be speakers of this faith to others.* At worship we become speakers of the Christian faith. Through our singing, our confessing, our praying, and our sharing of the peace, we practice speaking the faith as members of the worshiping community. Those who worship are not passive recipients of the service, but are immersed in the culture of God's kingdom and become speakers of that kingdom. The personal experiences of Lutherans as they encounter the presence of God at worship are a tremendous resource that needs to be tapped on behalf of the church's evangelizing. How can leaders intentionally build a church culture where the baptized learn to articulate the experiences of what God has done for them at worship—in word, sacrament, and community?[47] As the people of God sent from worship into the world, how can the experiences of God's forgiveness, mercy, and grace that become real in our lives at worship become the basis for our testimony in daily life?

In chapters three and five the authors stressed the recovery of a *catechesis* that serves evangelizing. In most conventional catechesis, students learn the content of the faith by study of the Scriptures and the catechism. Traditionally, this has even meant memorization of Scripture and catechism. Where our catechesis has failed miserably is in instilling the capacity to speak the faith, either to one another within the church or to those outside the faith community. In fact, learning to speak the faith has not even been seriously contemplated as a desired outcome of the catechetical process. We have focused intently on mastering content, a set of beliefs. But we have not been intent that catechumens become practitioners of the faith, including masterful speakers of their faith. How can teachers of confirmation and adult catechesis become intentional about equipping the members of the church to speak our faith questions and faith stories to one another? How can an evangelizing articulation of the faith become a normal and desired outcome in the Lutheran catechetical process?[48]

The purpose of this book is to promote a Lutheran church culture in which evangelizing is an ordinary and not an extraordinary phenomenon. To nurture such an evangelizing culture involves intentionality about how we relate to one another within the Christian church and especially how we relate to those beyond the Christian community. We propose that particular attention must be devoted in every area of church life to the practice of speaking the faith. We must become proficient in speaking the name of Jesus Christ in ways that resonate with our own faith experience. We must become proficient in speaking our stories of the faith in ways that connect with the longings of those beyond the Christian community.[49] *We must become proficient speakers of the faith in the way we relate.* This is what it would mean to develop an evangelizing church culture in communion with the Triune God.

What might an evangelizing church culture look like in practice? What are some of the practices that we might implement on the way to an evangelizing church culture among Lutherans?[50] We propose four practices that can assist Lutheran congregations in the development of an evangelizing church culture. Where practices like these have been implemented, amazing transformation in evangelizing begins to take place. These are practices that can transform a congregation from the inside out.

Modeling of Speaking the Faith by Leaders

We cannot expect to develop an evangelizing church culture unless the leaders of the church are practitioners of that culture. This means that both ordained and lay leaders of the church need to practice a new way of speaking the faith within and beyond the Christian community.[51] Not only must leaders be speakers of the faith in formal settings like worship, Bible study, or confirmation classes; leaders must be speakers of Scripture and their own faith stories as they relate to others, whether in the congregation or beyond. Leaders must move beyond the bifurcation of their lives between what is churched and what is not churched. In a new evangelizing church culture, speaking the faith will be integrated into normal conversation with others. Learning the art of speaking the faith will become an integral dimension in forming new leaders of the church throughout the theological education system, including seminaries.

Mentoring in Speaking the Faith

One of the most encouraging trends in Christian education has been the introduction of mentoring relationships between adults and young people. Mentoring typically involves a formal relationship between a particular adult and a younger member of the congregation, for example, as a part of confirmation instruction. The kind of mentoring needed for the development of an evangelizing church culture is very specific, however. It is a mentoring that concentrates on the sharing of one's faith story and telling about how God in Christ continues to be active in one's life. Such mentoring certainly can have good effect as part of the process leading to confirmation.

There are many other situations, however, in which mentoring can also be very constructive: a mentor for each new member of the church, a mentor for parents at the birth of a child, a mentor for those traversing a life crisis, or a mentor for those moving into skilled care in their elderly years. In order for mentoring to be effective in accomplishing its purpose, there needs to be training for mentors and opportunities for mentors to meet together. On these occasions, the focus would be on the importance of articulating the faith verbally and there would be opportunity to share how this has been done. This form of mentoring has a very specific intent: the speaking of one's faith for the evangelizing of another.

Small-Group Conversation in Order to Learn to Speak the Faith

This chapter has already made reference to the usefulness of cell groups in the process of evangelizing. The entire small-group movement provides a backdrop for this aspect of congregational life.[52] Small groups are always most useful when they engage participants in a deeper encounter with God's word in Bible study. In this case, however, we are talking about small groups that study the Bible for a specific purpose: to engage in conversation about the faith for the sake of evangelizing. Small groups can provide a safe and trusting environment for church members to tell the stories of their lives to one another, including specifically the stories of their faith journeys. For many people, a small group might be the first setting in which they will venture to talk with others in a personal way about their faith in God.

In order for small groups to serve the purpose of fostering evangelizing conversation, however, there will need to be intentionality about the format of the group and the agenda that it follows. Members of the group will need to be guided to tell their spiritual autobiographies and to speak about how they understand what God in Christ is currently doing in their lives. Small-group members might even be encouraged to practice speaking the faith to those outside the church and to report to one another how those conversations went. To learn to speak the faith in the trusted climate of a small group has much promise for contributing to a culture change in the entire congregation.

Speaking the Faith as Public Testimony

When Lutherans gather for worship, we are accustomed to one particular form of public testimony in the form of preaching. However, preaching does not usually afford the possibility for very many members of the church to witness publicly to their faith. If the Lutheran church is to transform its culture toward evangelizing, one practice that could dramatically alter our life together would be public testimony. Because worship is the most well-attended, formative event in the life of a congregation, it is extremely valuable for the sake of evangelizing to introduce a time for testimony on a regular basis. Perhaps located within the worship service in proximity to the reading of the lessons and the sermon, particular members can be invited to speak on the theme "What my faith means to me." Congregations that have experimented with such public testimony have discovered its power. Testimony by members connects with the life experience of the entire congregation to deepen faith and encourages others to render an account of what they themselves believe. Over a period of time, regular public testimony promises to dramatically change church culture. We cannot help but be changed by the testimony of our fellow believers. We will develop a new language for speaking the faith not only among ourselves but also to those outside the church.

These are four exemplary practices that can contribute to the emergence of an evangelizing church culture. Already congregations that are employing such practices are experiencing transformation. Practices like these can begin to infuse the Lutheran church with a new evangelizing spirit. We must be emboldened to develop ever new practices of speaking the faith to one another and to the world!

What other practices can we together imagine that could help transform our church into a culture of speaking the gospel to one another and to the world?

Summary

After the death of evangelism, we look for the resurrection of an evangelizing church culture that draws upon the passion of our Triune God in equipping the saints for speaking the faith with integrity and boldness. The Lutheran tradition must repent of its failings, and it has many valuable lessons to learn from others about the call to evangelize. We conclude with an epilogue that highlights a Lutheran contribution to the future of an evangelizing church.

A LUTHERAN CONTRIBUTION TO AN EVANGELIZING CHURCH

Throughout this book the authors have pointed out the failure of the Lutheran tradition to seriously engage in evangelizing. The previous chapter proposed that *evangelism*, in the conventional sense of being a program, needs to die. It needs to die along with vestiges of an *evangelism culture*, which includes clericalism, the privatization of faith, and ethnic idolatries. This book is written in the hope that after the death of evangelism, a renewed and reformed Lutheran church will be resurrected that takes seriously the evangelizing mission of the Triune God.

As we imagine the future shape of an *evangelizing* Evangelical Lutheran Church in America, what does the Lutheran tradition have to offer? We believe that, more than anything else, the Lutheran tradition offers us a deep and abiding conviction about the centrality of Jesus Christ and the gospel that Jesus brings! In conclusion, we set forth twelve commitments that we believe are the foundation for the formation of an evangelizing church. These are based on the arguments developed in the chapters of this book and are grounded in the wisdom of the Lutheran theological tradition.

1. LUTHERAN EVANGELIZING IS REALISTIC ABOUT THE HUMAN CONDITION. Lutheran theology understands the human condition. We are in bondage to sin and cannot free ourselves. For Lutherans, sin is not something we dispense with once we have become Christians. We remain totally sinners, even as we receive the gift of the forgiveness of our sins by the power of the gospel of Jesus Christ (*simul justus et peccator*). Whereas some Christian traditions stress the newness of life that comes to the convert, Lutherans are more sanguine. Yes, there is a newness that comes through the power of Jesus Christ—forgiveness of sins, deliverance from evil, and eternal life. But at the same time we know the truth of our condition—that sin continues to cling to our lives and that we succumb to ever new forms of idolatry. The sin of the human condition not only negatively affects our lives as individuals but also influences our social reality, leading to many forms

of deprivation and oppression (see chapter six). Lutheran theology can assist the whole catholic church in being realistic about the human condition and thereby recognizing our desperate need for the gift of the gospel (second use of the law). We need the power of the evangelizing gospel of God every moment of our lives!

2. LUTHERAN EVANGELIZING CENTERS ON THE SOLAS. Lutherans begin with some core commitments about God and what God has done for us. The Lutheran *sola*s express these central convictions in order to put *God and God's saving activity* at the center of our evangelizing as a church. Therefore Lutherans boldly assert that our salvation is in Christ alone (*solus Christus*), by grace alone (*sola gratia*), and through faith alone (*sola fide*) (see chapter six)! Evangelizing belongs to the very essence of the Triune God, who desires to draw all persons into communion. Among the *sola*s, priority is granted to the Bible as the source of authority for all the other teachings of the church. For this reason, the authors of this book have given special attention to word alone (*sola Scriptura*), particularly through the discussion in chapter four. The Lutheran insistence on the *sola*s can help center the whole catholic church on the Triune God as the chief actor in all our evangelizing efforts.

3. LUTHERAN EVANGELIZING CONNECTS WITH THE HUMAN CONDITION THROUGH THE SIMULS. Whereas the *sola*s insist on the centrality of God's activity in bringing about human salvation, the *simul*s remind us of how God is at work in the world among all peoples apart from particular knowledge of Jesus Christ (see chapter six). For example, Lutherans speak of a "general knowledge of God" that belongs to all people through creation (Romans 1). All people can know the existence of a Creator God through the things that God has made. There are simultaneously two ways of knowing God: through general knowledge of God known by way of the creation (law) and through special knowledge of God known in Jesus Christ (gospel). This recognition of the knowledge of God that belongs to others makes us appreciate their insights in interreligious conversation. Another *simul* that has importance for evangelizing is the Lutheran insistence that we are justified and sinful at the same time, *simul justus et peccator*. This conviction means that Christians share with all humanity the condition of sinfulness, even after we have come to faith in Jesus Christ. This recognition makes us humble as we go about the work of evangelizing, helps us identify with the fallibility of others, and provides a connecting point for speaking the gospel to them.

4. LUTHERAN EVANGELIZING IS ALL ABOUT THE GOSPEL. The gospel is God's free act of mercy toward sinners in Jesus Christ. The gospel is based entirely on God's promise; it is a free gift. There is no condition that human beings must fulfill in order to make the gospel true or efficacious. The gospel of Jesus Christ is entirely God's decision about us, the fulfillment of God's plan, and an event at God's own initiative. Lutheran theology insists on the promise character of the gospel of Jesus Christ. God in Christ is the actor, the missionary, and the evangelizer who gifts us with forgiveness, love, and grace even though we do not deserve it. The authors of this book stress that Jesus Christ is a living person who meets us in our lives (see chapter three). This is the message that the church has to communicate through its evangelizing: "Jesus Christ died and was raised for you! You are made God's child in baptism. For Christ's sake you will inherit eternal life." This is nothing other than the central Lutheran conviction that we are saved by grace alone through faith alone in Christ alone, the doctrine of justification by grace through faith. Sheer promise!

5. LUTHERAN EVANGELIZING STRESSES WORD, SACRAMENT, AND CHRISTIAN COMMUNITY AS THE MEANS OF GRACE. This book proposes a corrective to the formulaic use of the term "Word and Sacrament" in Lutheran theological parlance. Yes, Christ comes to us in the proclaimed word of a sermon. Yes, Christ meets us as the living Son of God in baptism and Holy Communion. But when we speak about Word and Sacrament, the divine action through the means of grace always occurs within and through the gathered assembly (Augsburg Confession, Articles VII and VIII). For the sake of an evangelizing Lutheran church, we insist that the members of the Christian community are a means of grace for one another and to the world. We take with utmost seriousness Luther's claim that "the mutual conversation and consolation of the brothers and sisters" is itself a means of grace (Smalcald Articles, Part III, Article 4). If we are to be transformed into an evangelizing church, Lutherans urgently need to claim the truth that they themselves, as members of the Christian community, are a means by which God brings the gospel to the world!

6. LUTHERAN EVANGELIZING UNDERSTANDS THE MISSIONAL CHARACTER OF CHRISTIAN WORSHIP. When Lutheran Christians gather for worship and invite others to join them, they assemble in the attitude of expectancy that God will meet them. Worship is an evangelizing activity because the evangelizing Triune God promises to encounter us there and establish life-giving relationship with us. The primary actors at worship are not the members of the gathered assembly, as indispensable as their participation might be. Rather, the primary actor at worship is our missional God who is seeking to do something with us (see chapter four). God seeks to do nothing less than bring us into the *culture* (kingdom) of God. Everything we do at worship is an expression of what it means to live in accordance with God's kingdom. We become forgiven and forgiving people, people who live to sing God's praises, people who attend to God's word, people who confess their faith, people who pray, people who make peace, and people who share their bread with others. At worship God evangelizes us in order that we might be set free for an alternative culture—a culture in which we become speakers of an evangelizing word to others.

7. LUTHERAN EVANGELIZING IS PROPELLED BY THE GIFT OF CHRISTIAN FREEDOM. Chapter two highlighted this fundamental feature of Lutheran theology. The gospel of Jesus Christ not only sets us free *from* our sin, but even more sets us free *for* our neighbors. We are set free for our call to evangelize. The Lutheran tradition is grounded deeply in an attitude of thanksgiving for what God has done for us and for the world in Jesus Christ. We are profoundly grateful as a people for the gift of the gospel that changes our lives, grants us a true home, and establishes us in life-giving relationship with God and with others. Christian freedom, as Luther wrote, is not only freedom *from* all that holds us captive. Christian freedom is *for* all that our evangelizing God was for on the cross. Christian freedom is freedom for my neighbor, freedom to love my neighbor so much that I share with my neighbor the greatest of all gifts, telling the story of what God in Christ has done for me.

8. LUTHERAN EVANGELIZING INSISTS ON THE MINISTRY OF ALL THE BAPTIZED. The primary agents in God's evangelizing mission in the world today are the baptized. It is critical that the Lutheran church at last put into practice what it has long professed about the priesthood of all believers. All the baptized are God's vanguard for speaking the evangelizing message of the kingdom in every arena where they live their lives. The baptized must be liberated from the suffocating grasp of clericalism and become the church's frontline evangelizers as they take up their calling as speakers of the Christian faith to others. This does not mean that the ministry of the ordained is no longer necessary. Rather, we propose that the office of pastor be reconceived as an office of evangelizing (see chapter three). This means that pastors preach and proclaim the gospel with power in order that the baptized are set free from all that constrains them and that they are sent out to serve God's evangelizing mission in local communities and worldwide. The ministry of pastors assists the baptized to discern their gifts and equips them for speaking the gospel with integrity.

9. LUTHERAN EVANGELIZING KNOWS THE PAIN OF THE CROSS AND THE POWER OF THE RESURRECTION. The Christian gospel is costly. We confess that God became incarnate in the humanity of Jesus Christ and that it cost Jesus' death on the cross to accomplish our reconciliation. As we saw in chapter six, the Lutheran tradition is rooted in a theology of the cross. This means, first, that knowledge of God is mysteriously revealed on the cross. God identifies completely with the human condition, even in its experience of negativity, sin, estrangement, idolatry, and death. Jesus entered totally into our experience of negativity. This is the message that we carry into the world through evangelizing. The theology of the cross means, second, that Lutherans expect God to be present and active still today in the experiences of suffering, loss, and even death. Lutheran evangelizing ought not to shy away from entering into what appear to be the most godforsaken places in human experience. For the sake of Christ's resurrection from the dead, we hope against hope that God in Christ is present even there!

10. LUTHERAN EVANGELIZING DEPENDS ON THE HOLY SPIRIT. The Holy Spirit is God's vital presence in the world and is active in drawing us into divine communion. We were created for life-giving relationships with God and with one another. Chapters four and five emphasize how the Holy Spirit was the living reality of God in biblical times and how this same Spirit continues to blow through the church today. The Holy Spirit promises to be present through Word, Sacrament, and Christian community to bring people to faith and to incorporate them into communion with the Triune God. The Holy Spirit guides the Christian community in its process of listening and discerning (see chapter five). The Holy Spirit summons the members of the church to be vehicles of God's grace to a hungry and dying world. And the Holy Spirit sends the church into the world. As we engage

in evangelizing, we depend on the Holy Spirit to be with us in accomplishing this great work of calling, gathering, enlightening, sanctifying, and *sending* (see chapter four). All glory to God!

11. *Lutheran Evangelizing Invites Adults into Catechesis toward Baptism and Holy Communion.* For centuries the normal process has been baptism of infants and confirmation of adolescents. Lutherans have been assertive in stressing the priority of God's grace that is demonstrated through the baptism of a little child. While the revitalization of baptismal and confirmation ministry with youth will be of continuing importance, it becomes an increasingly urgent priority that we normalize a catechetical process for adult inquirers leading to baptism and Holy Communion (see chapters three and five). There are millions of adults who have never come under the sway of the gospel of Jesus Christ. The mission of the church in our context must become very intentional in its evangelizing outreach to these persons. Lutheran congregations need to normalize adult inquiry classes and the procedures for welcoming adults into the church through baptism. The baptized members of Christ's body must find the words to speak the faith in a way that invites these adults as inquirers into the catechetical process, with serious attention being given to preparation for baptism.

12. *Lutheran Evangelizing Receives the Gift as a Call.* Lutheran theology is nothing if not emphatic about the gospel of Jesus Christ as God's gift of forgiveness, love, and grace. The gift-character of what our Triune God has done for us in Christ is the solid center of Lutheran teaching. What Lutherans have not always understood is that this gift is a person named Jesus Christ. Bonhoeffer, among others, warned the church of the deadly error of making grace cheap. This means that we have too often tried to take the blessings offered by Christ without entering into a living relationship with him. Because the gospel is a person named Jesus Christ, whenever we receive the gifts of the gospel, at the same time we receive the call from Christ: "Come, follow me!" This is the very point of the Lutheran confessional emphasis on "new obedience" and "good works" (Augsburg Confession, Article VI). Jesus Christ is calling the church to the good work of evangelizing in his name—speaking the good news and inviting all people into communion with our Triune God. The gift of Christ is always a call to evangelize (see chapter two).

Crucial to the very name of being the Evangelical Lutheran Church in America is the term "evangelical." In the heritage of the Reformation, we are a church that is always to be in a process of reforming (*ecclesia semper reformanda*). One of the most pressing reforms of our time is the discovery of what it means to be an evangelizing church. As we have seen in this book, there is much about the existing evangelism paradigm that simply has to die. Yet we confess our faith in a Triune God who is passionately in love with the world and who desires to be in communion with all people. It is for the sake of this world that God loves that we must learn to speak the faith with unprecedented boldness, conviction, and integrity. After the death of evangelism, may God raise up a new Lutheran church, one that is grounded in its rich theological tradition and alive with a new culture of evangelizing!

STUDY GUIDE

Study Guide Format

This study guide provides the following information for each chapter:
a. Overview of Chapter—a brief summary of the chapter's content
b. Bible Passages for Further Study
c. Questions for Discussion—questions that relate the content of the chapter to a specific congregation and ministry context
d. Additional Readings to Consider—several suggested chapters from books in the annotated bibliography that might be considered as supplemental readings for discussion of the chapter

Suggested Study Method

Persons are encouraged to use this study guide for a group discussion of the book, if possible. However, the guide can also be helpful to an individual for thinking about how to relate the book's content to one's own congregation and its ministry.

1. A LUTHERAN CONFESSION[1]

Overview of Chapter

Lutherans have a double confession to make. They must confess that they are not particularly good at evangelism. Lutherans tend to be either skeptical or overly pragmatic, or to view everything we do as evangelism. Yet Lutherans possess an incredible theological heritage to draw on that can help shape an evangelizing church. To become such, it is necessary to keep our confessional heritage in conversation with a missional understanding of the church and God's mission in the world. This book invites the Evangelical Lutheran Church in America, along with other Lutheran bodies and the larger church, to consider anew the rich resources within a Lutheran understanding of the Bible and God's work in the world and the church. The key issue is, "What does it mean to be the church, an evangelical church that lives for the sake of the world?"

Bible Passages for Further Study

Compare and contrast the two types of confession by Peter in Matthew 16:13-20 and Acts 10 (see especially verses 30-43). How are they different?

Questions for Discussion

1. The authors make a distinction between "evangelism" and "evangelizing." What is your initial understanding of how these are being defined, used, and contrasted in this book?
2. Review the three approaches Lutherans often take to evangelism—skeptical, overly pragmatic, or viewing everything the church does as "evangelism." Which of these approaches, if any, are most typical of your congregation at present? What are some things that have contributed to this being the case?
3. To what extent are the influences of the Lutheran immigration story and the approaches of early Lutheran leaders present in your congregation in terms of its views of our confessional heritage and its approach to evangelism?
4. How do traditional Lutheran theological understandings of human nature and divine grace inform a Lutheran approach to evangelizing? How does your congregation's theological understanding compare to these views? What implications might this have for how your congregation approaches evangelizing?
5. What is the most helpful insight or idea that you took away from this introductory chapter? How does this insight or idea affect your understanding of evangelizing?

Additional Readings to Consider

Guder, Darrell, et al. *Missional Church*, chapter 1, pp. 1–17.
Van Gelder, Craig. *Essence of the Church*, chapters 1 and 2, pp. 13–44.

2. The Gift Is a Call

Overview of Chapter

There is an evangelizing impulse within Lutheranism. Having heard and believed the gospel message himself, Luther risked everything so that everyone could hear it. But that impulse weakened in following centuries. Though various Lutheran leaders have reclaimed this impulse through the centuries, today it is barely discernable in most Lutheran congregations in the United States. Several hurdles must be overcome to recover Lutheranism's evangelizing character. The trickiest is a theological one. We have tended to use our most cherished doctrine—justification by grace—as an excuse to do nothing.

But Lutheran voices across the centuries call us back to this truth, that the gift of salvation is also a call to follow Jesus. The gift is a call.

Bible Passages for Further Study

Note the idea of "sending" in John 8 (especially v. 16); 15 (especially v. 26); 17 (especially v. 18); and 20 (especially v. 21). How are they related?

Questions for Discussion

1. Recent studies show that the average Lutheran congregation is in steady decline both in numbers and in members' willingness to share their faith. How average is your congregation? If so, how do you explain your congregation's decline? If not, how do you explain your congregation's vitality?

2. The author argues that the gift we are given through Jesus Christ is also a call to follow him. In what way do you, personally, experience this "call" to follow Jesus as a "gift"? Jesus also calls a congregation to be a part of God's mission in the world. How does the author describe God's mission? How is your congregation presently participating in that mission? If not, why not?

3. The author describes four hurdles we face in becoming an evangelizing church. What are these hurdles? Which of them do you recognize in your congregation? From your perspective, which one is most problematic?

4. There has been a powerful urge in Lutheranism to break the gospel free from whatever held it captive. Martin Luther, the Pietists, Søren Kierkegaard, and Dietrich Bonhoeffer are all examples of leaders who reconnected the gift of grace with the call to follow Jesus. Which do you find the most compelling? Why?

5. The call of Jesus is a costly one. Answering it will lead us out of our comfort zone, where we will need to leave behind some of the things we love the most about our church. What might your congregation have to leave behind in order to answer this call? What might you personally have to leave behind? How might we help one another to respond to the call, regardless of the cost?

Additional Readings to Consider

Bonhoeffer, Dietrich. *Discipleship*, chapters 1 and 2, pp. 43–76.
Luther, Martin. *A Treatise on Christian Liberty*.

3. ADDRESSING CAPTIVES IN BABYLON

Overview of Chapter

How does one address Christians in Babylon? First, we name the chains that hold us captive, and then we look to the door of freedom. There is a way out! The great need in the Lutheran church today is to recognize and address the Babylonian Captivity in which it is caught. It must break the chains that hold Word and

Sacrament ministry captive; and it must renew its theological vision for becoming an evangelizing church. This vision centers on the means of grace as Word, Sacrament, and Christian community. A fresh wave of programmatic evangelism among clergy and laity, although praiseworthy up to a point, does not address the real issue. There is a need for a renewed vision about evangelizing that is, finally, not about doing something for God. Rather, it is a vision about God's activity in the world through Jesus Christ and our own participation in that activity. This is God's gift that is also our call to become an evangelizing church.

Bible Passages for Further Study

Read through the Gospel of Luke, and note all the ways that "Jesus comes to people" in this Gospel. Study especially Luke 24:13-35.

Questions for Discussion

1. The image of the "Babylonian Captivity" is found in the biblical narrative and is also part of Luther's description of the church in his day. Would you agree with our use of this image to describe many Lutheran congregations today? To what extent is your congregation a part of this captivity in its approach to ministry?
2. This chapter identifies a sevenfold captivity of Word and Sacrament ministry that characterizes much of Lutheranism in the United States. Which of these captivities most applies to your congregation? How? Why?
3. This chapter defines "evangelizing" simply as "Jesus coming to people." In what ways has Jesus come to you personally? To your congregation? How might this definition be used to reimagine your congregation's outreach in its community?
4. The key to expressing the death of evangelism and the resurrection of an evangelizing church culture is freeing all the baptized for ministry. To what extent are all the baptized in your congregation participating in God's mission within your context? What else might be done in inviting them into this call?
5. To what extent does your congregation need to move from doing "evangelism programs" to developing an evangelizing culture? What ideas did you find helpful in this chapter for a "resurrection of evangelizing church" to become true of your congregation (see especially the seven theses)?

Additional Readings to Consider

Bonhoeffer, Dietrich. *Christ the Center*, part 1, pp. 43–68.
Kolb, Robert. *Speaking the Gospel Today*, introduction, pp. 9–20.

4. For the Sake of the World

Overview of Chapter

God has a passion for the world. This is the location where the mission of God (the *missio Dei*) takes place. The entire biblical story conveys the essential message about God's passion for the world and God's desire to bring salvation to it. The church participates in God's mission in light of the redemptive work of God accomplished in Christ. This was announced by Jesus as the presence of the kingdom of God in the world, a presence that Jesus declared as being both "now" and "not yet." The church is to bring to the world the good news that salvation is about *everything*, and share this message with *everyone everywhere*. When read from the perspective of the world, the Lutheran confessional tradition is seen to contain an abundance of resources that undergird and support an evangelizing church. Because God's mission focuses on the world, an evangelizing church is careful to read its context, even as it is also read by that context.

Bible Passages for Further Study

Read through the Acts of the Apostles and note each time the "Spirit" or "Holy Spirit" is mentioned. In how many different ways does the Spirit lead the church?

Questions for Discussion

1. This chapter relates the mission of God in the world (*missio Dei*) to the kingdom of God as announced by Jesus. How are these two ideas related? What implications does this have for understanding the mission of the church?
2. What is the role of the Spirit in leading the church to bring to the world the good news that salvation is about everything and is to be shared with everyone everywhere? How does the Spirit's presence in the book of Acts inform this? How has the Spirit led your congregation in the past, and how is the Spirit leading your congregation in the present in relationship to participation in God's mission?
3. This chapter reread five Lutheran confessional themes from the perspective of God's mission in the world. Which of these rereadings would be most useful in helping your congregation develop a passion for becoming an evangelizing church? How would you apply it to your situation?
4. An argument was made that Luther's inclusion of "mutual conversation and consolation" in the Smalcald Articles leads to regarding the Christian community as a sign or foretaste, an instrument in the world. What kind of sign is your congregation at present? What foretaste is available in your congregation of God's planned future? In what ways is your congregation an instrument within your context?
5. Four ways are mentioned of how our context often reads the church. Which one(s) most applies to your congregation? In what way? What might be done to overcome this limited understanding of your congregation by your context?

Additional Readings to Consider

Fryer, Kelly A. *Reclaiming the "L" Word*, chapters 2 and 3, pp. 27–50.
Guder, Darrell. *The Continuing Conversion of the Church*, chapter 2, pp. 28–48.

5. CALLED OUT OF OUR COMFORT ZONE

Overview of Chapter

A congregation's purpose is to tell the story of God's reconciling gift revealed in Jesus Christ. Congregations are called out communities (*ekklesia*), sent by God to participate in God's reconciling activity in the world. When we understand that our gift is a call, it leads to our becoming an evangelizing church. Evangelizing is more about what a congregation *is* than what it *does*. It expresses a congregation's passion for Christ and its compassion for the world. Congregations are called out of their comfort zones of race, ethnicity, class, doctrinal captivity, and indifference to live instead for the sake of the world. This chapter explores how congregations as missional communities can develop an evangelizing culture by use of four core activities—they *listen, discern, speak,* and *act.* It presents the ministry of reconciliation as the primary reason for evangelizing, and suggests a self-organizing systems approach for shaping an evangelizing congregation.

Bible Passages for Further Study

Read 2 Corinthians 5:11-21. What is our role in God's mission in the world?
Read John 4. Study this chapter for patterns of "listen, discern, speak, act."

Questions for Discussion

1. Does your congregation have a mission or purpose statement? If so, what is it? If not, what seems to be the "understood" purpose of your congregation? How does this current statement or understanding compare to this chapter's presentation of a congregation as a missional community?

2. This chapter identified a number of comfort zones from which the church needs to be called. Which, if any of these, is most evident in your congregation? How does this hinder the congregation from sharing the gospel with persons in your context and beyond? What would your congregation have to risk if it responded to being called out of this comfort zone to participate in God's mission in your context?

3. The activities of listen, discern, speak, and act were presented as foundational for helping congregations become evangelizing communities. What is meant by each of these words? How are these activities presently functioning in your congregation? What might be done to strengthen their use?

4. This chapter presents the gospel as being about the ministry of reconciliation. What signs are evident within your congregation that this ministry of reconciliation is presently taking place? What signs of this ministry of

reconciliation are visible within the context in which your congregation is ministering?

5. A congregation is presented in this chapter as being a self-organizing system that can help us better understand how to nurture an evangelizing culture. How might these characteristics assist your congregation to be open to change?

Additional Readings to Consider

Bowen, John P. *Evangelism for Normal People*, chapter 3 and 4, pp. 39–64.
Nessan, Craig L. *Beyond Maintenance to Mission*, chapters 2 and 3, pp. 13–33.

6. Navigating Difficult Questions

Overview of Chapter

The church's task of evangelizing can neither be oblivious to, nor feel paralyzed by, difficult and challenging questions. Today there are a number of pressing issues that need to be addressed. We now live in the midst of a growing religious plurality and interreligious encounter. All around us in the broader world and within our own context we are painfully aware of the reality of suffering and the brokenness of many people. The pervasiveness of the emerging postmodern worldview is now becoming like the air that we breathe. This chapter critically and constructively explores Lutheran theological resources for addressing such issues in relation to the theology of an evangelizing church. The Lutheran dialectic of *solas* and *simuls* along with the theology of the cross of the risen Christ are developed as foundations for such a theology. Some directions are proposed to help an evangelizing church address the postmodern generation.

Bible Passages for Further Study

Read John 14 and note the argument Jesus is making in relation to his claim that appears in verse 6. Also read Acts 4 and note the context within which Peter makes the claim that appears in verse 12.

Questions for Discussion

1. Today we live in a culture where most people hold that faith is a matter of personal preference, where persons are not supposed to push their faith preference on another. How does this chapter address the issue of taking responsibility to share one's faith preference with others?

2. What other religions are now present in your ministry context? How can we authentically profess our faith as Christians in the midst of these other religions while acknowledging the positive values of these faiths and their beliefs?

3. The texts of John 14:6 and Acts 4:12 are often used to develop the exclusiveness of Jesus Christ. How does your congregation use or understand these

texts? How does this chapter use these texts for better understanding how to live within a religiously plural society?

4. Today there are many "crucified people" in our world, as well as in our local contexts. What does the good news of Jesus Christ mean to the "Saturday people"? What is your congregation doing to reach out to such persons? In what other ways might it reach out?

5. How does the worldview of your congregation compare at present to that of the emerging postmodern worldview? What are some ways in which your congregation might embody the message of Jesus Christ to a postmodern generation in becoming an evangelizing church?

Additional Readings to Consider

Ariarajah, Wesley. *The Bible and People of Other Faiths.*
Kallenberg, Brad J. *Live to Tell: Evangelism for a Postmodern Age.*
Thomsen, Mark W. *Christ Crucified*, chapters 4 and 5, pp. 75–103.

7. After the Death of Evangelism—
the Resurrection of an Evangelizing Church

Overview of Chapter

Evangelism, as one church program among others, must die in order for an evangelizing church to be resurrected. However, if the evangelizing potential of the Lutheran tradition is to come alive, then a number of obstacles must be overcome. These include especially the obstacles of clericalism, privatization of religion, and ethnic idolatries. It is important that Lutherans, in seeking to become an evangelizing church, draw on lessons that can be learned from others, including Evangelicals, Pentecostals, historic black churches, Roman Catholics, the global church, and even other religions. A Lutheran paradigm for an evangelizing church is best grounded in the evangelizing character of the Triune God, who desires to bring all persons into reconciled and life-giving relationships. This grounding leads to the resurrection of an evangelizing culture where speaking the faith belongs to the church's core identity and reason for existence, and is promoted by the implementation of intentional ministry practices.

Bible Passages for Further Study

Read Ephesians 4:7-16. What is the role of leadership in the church?
Read 1 Corinthians 12. How is the church to function in doing ministry?

Questions for Discussion

1. This chapter notes how an understanding of evangelism as being primarily a program has been pervasive throughout most Lutheran congregations. To

what extent has this been true in your congregation? Which programmatic approaches has your congregation tried in the past or using at present?

2. What is meant by the "death of evangelism" as presented in this chapter? How would taking this approach apply to your congregation, especially in light of its seeking to become an evangelizing church?

3. Every congregation faces some obstacles in trying to become an evangelizing church. This chapter identified three—clericalism, the privatization of faith, and ethnic idolatries. To what extent are any of these obstacles present in your congregation? What might be done to remove them?

4. There are many lessons for Lutherans to learn from other Christian faith traditions and even other religions. Of the lessons mentioned in this chapter, which applies most helpfully to your congregation? How might this be applied to your context?

5. How is our speaking the faith to others an expression of the Triune God's evangelizing efforts? How do you see speaking the faith practiced by the members of your congregation? What practices of learning to speak the faith might be introduced into your congregation?

Additional Readings to Consider

Hunter, George G. *The Celtic Way of Evangelism*, chapter 4 and 5, pp. 47–75.
Olson, Mark A. *Moving beyond Church Growth*, chapter 4, pp. 49–54

Epilogue: A Lutheran Contribution

Overview of Epilogue

There are twelve commitments that the authors offer as the foundation for forming an evangelizing church.

1. Lutheran evangelizing is realistic about the human condition.
2. Lutheran evangelizing centers on the *solas*.
3. Lutheran evangelizing connects with the human condition through the *simuls*.
4. Lutheran evangelizing is all about the gospel.
5. Lutheran evangelizing stresses Word, Sacrament, and Christian community as means of grace.
6. Lutheran evangelizing understands the missional character of Christian worship.
7. Lutheran evangelizing is propelled by the gift of Christian freedom.
8. Lutheran evangelizing insists on the ministry of all the baptized.
9. Lutheran evangelizing knows the pain of the cross and the power of the resurrection.
10. Lutheran evangelizing depends on the Holy Spirit.
11. Lutheran evangelizing invites adults into catechesis toward baptism and Holy Communion.
12. Lutheran evangelizing receives the gift as a call.

Questions for Discussion

1. Which of these commitments are most representative at present of the life and ministry of your congregation? What are some evidences of this in the current practices of the congregation and behaviors of the members?

2. Which ones of these commitments are least representative at present of the life and ministry of your congregation? What are some evidences of this in the current practices of the congregation and behaviors of the members?

3. Develop a plan for helping your congregation to become an evangelizing church. What theological understandings need to be formed? What issues and/ or obstacles need to be addressed? What shared practices need to be cultivated? What action steps need to be taken to address all three of these dimensions?

Additional Readings to Consider

Briese, Russell John. *Foundations of a Lutheran Theology of Evangelism*, chapter 7, pp. 267–88.

Linn, Jan. *Reclaiming Evangelism*, chapter 5, pp. 57–102.

ANNOTATED BIBLIOGRAPHY

Ariarajah, S. Wesley. *The Bible and People of Other Faiths*. Rei ed. Maryknoll, NY: Orbis, 1989.

> This book explores the premise that Jesus is not only unique, but is also available to people of other faiths. Ariarajah addresses problematic texts of Scripture relating to the person and work of Christ, especially those that have implications for people of other faiths. The author provides a helpful understanding of an incarnational approach to mission and also offers a meaningful analysis of how followers of Christ should relate to people of other faiths along the continuum of witness and dialogue.

Bonhoeffer, Dietrich. *Christ the Center*. Translated by Edwin H. Robertson. San Francisco: HarperSanFrancisco, 1978.

> This volume by Bonhoeffer reveals his deep commitment to the importance of Christian doctrine, especially the person and work of Jesus Christ. He draws on historical understandings but carefully and critically relates their meaning to the church in his day. The clear christological teaching in this book is foundational to understanding the genius of the Lutheran faith as developed and presented by Bonhoeffer.

Bonhoeffer, Dietrich. *Discipleship*. Edited by Geffrey B. Kelly and John D. Godsey. *Dietrich Bonhoeffer Works*, vol. 4. Minneapolis: Fortress Press, 2001.

> This volume serves as the newest translation of the Bonhoeffer classic, published in 1937, originally titled *The Cost of Discipleship*. Living amid the chaos and horror of Nazism, Bonhoeffer tells us what it means to follow Christ. Drawing on the Sermon on the Mount, Bonhoeffer differentiates between cheap grace and costly grace. This foundational insight continues to call each generation to a fresh understanding of what it means to be a disciple of Jesus.

Bowen, John P. *Evangelism for Normal People*. Minneapolis: Augsburg Fortress, 2002.

> This book serves as a great introductory text in evangelism for Christians who think that evangelism is done only by weird people, not by "normal" people like themselves. Many, Bowen says, have been put off by modern-day expressions of evangelism but still feel they have something to share. The book is divided into two parts. The first half traces the story of evangelism in the Bible from Genesis to Revelation. For Bowen, evangelism is God's work that we are invited to participate in. The second half looks at the implications of the evangelism story and addresses the difficult questions one faces when discussing evangelism.

Braaten, Carl E., and Robert W. Jenson. *The Strange New Word of the Gospel: Re-Evangelizing in the Postmodern World*. Grand Rapids: Eerdmans, 2002.

> Braaten and Jenson have edited a volume of essays that delve into the necessity of "reawakening" faith through the "strange new word of the Gospel" in this postmodern culture in which we find ourselves. It offers suggestions as to how the church can be effective in this new culture. While many people are returning to religion, they claim, few are returning to the church culture in which they were brought up. Essay topics include a reexamination of postmodernism, a critique of seeker services and the need for a return to liturgy, and reclaiming the "full power" of the church's missionary calling. The various authors represent scholarship in the Catholic, Protestant, and Orthodox traditions.

Briese, Russell John. *Foundations of a Lutheran Theology of Evangelism*. Frankfurt: Peter Lang, 1994.

> After an introduction including an overview of the contemporary situation in which we currently exist, and clarifying the terminology used within the book, Briese lays out a clear case as to whether or not Lutheran theology provides a basis for evangelism. He starts his journey by exploring the emphases in mission theology emerging throughout the history of the International Mission Council, the Ecumenicals, and the Evangelicals. He then gives us a broad understanding of the Lutheran theological view of evangelism from Luther to the present day. Briese ends his book by laying out ten theses for a Lutheran theology of evangelism.

Fryer, Kelly A. *Reclaiming the "L" Word: Renewing the Church from Its Lutheran Core, Lutheran Voices*. Minneapolis: Augsburg Fortress, 2003.

> Kelly Fryer has written a great, easily readable book that serves to rejuvenate congregations by going back to the basics. Through her stories and illustrations, she helps her readers understand what it means to be Lutheran all over again. The book is arranged around her five guiding principles: Jesus is Lord, everyone is welcome, love changes people,

everybody has something to offer, and the world needs what we have. These principles, according to Fryer, are what make us uniquely Lutheran.

Guder, Darrell L. *The Continuing Conversion of the Church*. Grand Rapids: Eerdmans, 2000.

> In this book, Guder shows how the church can more effectively carry out its missionary calling by building a new theology of evangelism for the world in which we now find ourselves. In the first part of the book, Guder shows us how the church moved away from a biblical understanding of evangelism. He then discusses the contemporary challenges the church is facing that illustrate the need for conversion. Part three then paints a picture of what a missional theology will look like with regard to the current institutional structures and practices of the church. Both the theology and practice of evangelism in churches today must be redesigned in order for the church to carry out its faithful witness to the world.

Guder, Darrell L., et al. *Missional Church: A Vision for the Sending of the Church in North America*. Grand Rapids: Eerdmans, 1998.

> Following a two-year study conducted by the Gospel in Our Culture Network, six ecumenical authors published this volume, issuing a challenge for churches today to recover their missional vocation within the North American mission field. Within this context, the authors address the biblical, theological, and cultural issues the church faces as it strives to live out its calling in participating in God's activity in the world. This book helps redefine the missionary nature of the church within that context and offers tools to live out that calling. Though each chapter was written by a different author, the book reads coherently as one volume. This is an important book for any congregation or congregational leader seeking to develop a missional identity in today's world.

Hunter, George G. *The Celtic Way of Evangelism: How Christianity Can Reach the West—Again*. Nashville: Abingdon, 2000.

> George Hunter takes us back to one of the most successful evangelical periods in church history: Celtic Christianity. In this book he shares their story, their practices, and their ability to adapt, convert, and send missionaries out, as a model for Christians today. Hunter argues that North America is not unlike the situation in which the early Celtic preachers found themselves: people hungry for spirituality and unfamiliar with the Christian faith. In order for us to succeed, he argues, we must learn from the Celts.

Kallenberg, Brad J. *Live to Tell: Evangelism for a Postmodern Age*. Grand Rapids: Brazos, 2002.

> Kallenberg brings a combination of wit, intellectual insight, and passion to helping the church understand the gospel and use it for engaging

the postmodern world. He takes the position that postmodern philosophy can help us think about what it means to become a Christian. He is steeped in both philosophy and evangelism, understands their intersections, and offers a radically different and compelling account of conversion. Kallenberg weaves real stories of witness and corporate evangelizing into his argument and makes key philosophical concepts understandable for the reader.

Kolb, Robert. *Speaking the Gospel Today: A Theology for Evangelism.* Rev. ed. St. Louis: Concordia, 1995.
> *Speaking the Gospel Today* offers a theology of evangelism that connects doctrine and everyday conversation. This is a practical textbook demonstrating how to become a "bridge-builder" who takes the word of God to the world. *Speaking the Gospel Today* offers a plan that consistently uses the law-gospel distinction, a sound presentation of God the Creator, and an extensive examination of evil. This book will challenge, motivate, and equip believers for a clear, effective, and powerful Christian witness.

Linn, Jan. *Reclaiming Evangelism: A Practical Guide for Mainline Churches.* St. Louis: Chalice, 1998.
> Many mainline churches today are in the midst of deep change and are struggling with their identity. Linn relates this struggle to the issue of evangelism, arguing that evangelism is not a numbers game. Rather, evangelism is an unbridled spirituality that finds its expression in ministries that intentionally witness to Jesus Christ as Savior and Lord. Included in this book are detailed practical steps for reclaiming this essential ministry, plus a model for restructuring congregational life to implement these steps. The author's approach to evangelism is creative and fresh. He helpfully critiques and reframes many of the current popular approaches that churches attempt to use to foster evangelism. His practical suggestions for developing evangelism as a Christ-centered practice are quite helpful.

Luther, Martin. *A Treatise on Christian Liberty (Also Called the Freedom of a Christian).* Translated by W. A. Lambert and revised by Harold J. Grimm. Philadelphia: Fortress Press, 1957.
> *A Treatise on Christian Liberty* was written by Martin Luther in an attempt to explain his ideas to Pope Leo, which resulted in Luther's excommunication from the church. In this letter, Luther provides the core of his theological thinking. His discussion on freedom has led subsequent generations to explore the issues of individual freedom and liberty while exercising the responsibility of being a slave to all. Luther presents his view of the twofold nature of man, the spiritual and the bodily. No outward (bodily) work of man, Luther claims, can justify the inward. We are

justified by faith alone. Only when work is done out of joy and love can we be truly free to serve.

Nessan, Craig L. *Beyond Maintenance to Mission: A Theology of the Congregation.* Minneapolis: Fortress Press, 1999.

This book argues compellingly for the centrality of mission in understanding the church and provides a model for congregational leadership that will help move congregations beyond a maintenance mentality to vital engagement with the world God loves. Nessan's model of congregational leadership is strongly centered on the worship life of a congregation and the entirety of the church's ministry. The chapters provide solid theological and practical direction on the themes of worship, education, fellowship, stewardship, evangelism, global connections, ecumenism, and social ministry. It is a book that will find a home in both the academy and the parish—a textbook for seminarians and a guide and resource for pastors and lay congregational leaders.

Olson, Mark A. *Moving beyond Church Growth: An Alternative Vision for Congregations.* Minneapolis: Fortress Press, 2002.

With twenty-plus years of ministry experience to back him up, Olson makes the claim that church-growth models set pastors up for failure and disappointment, trapping them in models from the Constantinian church and modernity. Instead, he calls church leaders to a faithful, bold, and courageous rethinking of congregational life and witness in substance, purpose, and style. In this model, pastors' primary responsibilities are not to fix everything and everybody, but to enable people to be present to each other and to provide hope.

Schreiter, Robert J. *The Ministry of Reconciliation: Spirituality and Strategies.* Maryknoll, N.Y.: Orbis, 1998.

The author stresses the importance of the ministry of reconciliation in our present world of brokenness and conflict. Drawing upon the post-resurrection appearances of Jesus, he constructs a theological framework for understanding how reconciliation works within different contexts to address different issues. A set of strategies is offered at the end of the book that addresses contemporary challenges related to the ministry of reconciliation, such as the individual and social reconciliation, truth and justice, and amnesty and pardon.

Thomsen, Mark W. *Christ Crucified: A 21st Century Missiology of the Cross.* Minneapolis: Lutheran University Press, 2004.

Thomsen uses his background in mission and interfaith relations to affirm Luther's theology of the cross, while freeing it from a variety of traditions that have distorted it. The church in a global world must learn to use the theology of the cross to respond to the diverse needs of Christians throughout the world, especially in relation to dialogue with other religions. Thomsen's understanding is that the only God who exists is the one that is embodied and identified in the Crucified. God's love through the suffering Christ embraces the whole world. This understanding of Christ opens us up to each other and to all people. It is a helpful missiological understanding for those seeking to be in witness, dialogue, and service with persons who profess other religious commitments.

Van Gelder, Craig. *The Essence of the Church: A Community Created by the Spirit.* Grand Rapids: Baker, 2000.

> *The Essence of the Church* gives you a peek into the thirty-year journey Van Gelder has traversed in working in ministry. He argues for a rediscovery of the church in the twenty-first century as a social community led by the Holy Spirit. By reconnecting ecclesiology and missiology as a missiological ecclesiology (missional church), we are given an opportunity to rethink the very nature of the church. The church does not exist for itself but belongs to God and is involved in the redemptive work of God in the world. This is an insightful, readable book that integrates biblical, theological, and theoretical principles.

NOTES

1. A Lutheran Confession

1. Mark Noll, "American Lutherans Yesterday and Today," in *Lutherans Today: American Identity in the 21st Century*, ed. Richard Cimino (Grand Rapids: Eerdmans, 2003), 20. This chapter has provided a helpful framework for some of the substance of this chapter's analysis as well as the framing of the question about Lutherans in mission.

2. Richard Bliese, "Lutheran Missiology: Struggling to Move from Reactive Reform to Innovative Initiative," in *The Role of Mission in the Future of Lutheran Theology*, ed. Viggo Mortensen (Aarhus: The Centre for Multireligious Studies, University of Aarhus, 2003), 11f.

3. These popular labels are only partial and imprecise descriptions of the differences that separated these two groups. Old Lutherans were willing to adjust to the American scene to some degree, and the American Lutherans were by no stretch of the imagination wholly opposed to the confessional writings or the theology of Luther. It might be more precise to refer to both groups as functioning along a similar polarity, where both groups lifted up issues of culturally relevant mission and faithful adherence to the confessions. "Strictness and moderation" should be evaluated along these two polarities of confession/mission. See Paul P. Kuenning, *The Rise and Fall of American Lutheran Pietism: The Rejection of an Activist Heritage* (Macon, Ga.: Mercer University Press, 1988).

4. This argument is ably made by James A. Scherer, *Gospel, Church, & Kingdom: Comparative Studies in World Mission Theology* (Minneapolis: Augsburg Books, 1987), 51–92.

5. Noll, "American Lutherans," 20.

6. The usual distinction between mission and evangelism is that mission refers to the larger mission of God in the world, what is often referred to as the *missio Dei*, and which locates the redemptive activity of the kingdom of God as announced by Jesus in all the world. The church participates in this mission, which is focused on bringing redemption to bear on every dimension of life. Within this mission, there is a more focused activity of the church in announcing to the world the good news about Jesus Christ. This we understand to be the specific activity of evangelizing. While it often involves deeds as a dynamic part of the message that is announced, it always involves some word that clarifies that salvation is about being encountered by the living Christ.

7. See especially Dietrich Bonhoeffer, *Discipleship*, ed. Geffrey B. Kelly and John D. Godsey, *Dietrich Bonhoeffer Works*, vol. 4 (Minneapolis: Fortress Press, 2001).

8. A helpful discussion of this can be found in David J. Bosch, *Transforming Mission: Paradigm Shifts in Theology of Mission* (Maryknoll, N.Y.: Orbis, 1991), 327–41.

9. Noll, "American Lutherans," 20.

10. Ibid., 21.

11. Bosch, *Transforming Mission, 244–47.*

12. Dietrich Bonhoeffer, *The Communion of Saints: A Dogmatic Inquiry into the Sociology of the Church*, trans. R. Gregor Smith (New York: Harper & Row, 1963).

2. The Gift Is a Call

1. Martin Luther, *A Treatise on Christian Liberty (also called Freedom of a Christian)* trans. W. A. Lambert and rev. Harold J. Grimm (Philadelphia: Fortress Press, 1957), 8.

2. Ibid., 9.

3. Some Lutheran scholars have argued, in fact, that the priesthood of all believers is at the very heart of an authentic Lutheran understanding of evangelism and mission (see Russell John Briese, *Foundations of a Lutheran Theology of Evangelism* [Frankfurt: Peter Lang, 1994], and Robert Kolb, *Speaking the Gospel Today: A Theology for Evangelism*, rev. ed. [St. Louis: Concordia, 1995]).

4. This is James Scherer (*. . . That the Gospel May Be Sincerely Preached throughout the World: A Lutheran Perspective on Mission and Evangelism in the 20th Century* [Stuttgart, Germany: LWF/ Kreuz Verlag, 1982), referring to the conclusions drawn as far back as the nineteenth century by Lutheran mission commentator Gustav Leopold Plitt. Scherer agrees with Plitt but argues that Plitt didn't even go far enough. Plitt's evaluation "misses the radicality of Luther's missionary thinking" (p. 6), Scherer believes, and he spells out what he argues are the "lively impulses" latent in Luther's missionary thinking (pp. 12–13). Others, it must be noted, would take issue with both writers. The "father of missiology as a theological discipline," Gustav Warneck, has accused the Reformers (including Luther) of having "fundamental theological views" that "hindered them from giving their activity, and even their thoughts, a missionary direction" (David Bosch, *Transforming Mission: Paradigm Shifts in the Theology of Mission* [Maryknoll, N.Y.: Orbis, 1991], 244). Here Bosch is quoting Warneck from his book *Outline of a History of Protestant Missions*, 3rd ed., translated from the 8th German ed. [New York: Revell, 1906]). Bosch, himself the author of a classic mission text, has little regard for Luther's theology because of what he believes is a profound absence of missiological emphasis. The church that emerged as a result of Luther's influence was, Bosch believes, a church of "pure doctrine" but without mission (*Transforming Mission*, 249). Carl Braaten, likewise, has written that the Reformers—including Luther—left little in the way of inspiration or direction for the evangelical task: "The problem of a Protestant theology of mission is that its classical sources, the theology of the Reformers and the confessional writings, are totally devoid of any missionary consciousness" (Braaten, *The Flaming Center* [Philadelphia: Fortress Press, 1977], 15). He argues that the most helpful thing the Reformers left was a commitment to *sola scriptura*, which he believes obligates the church to "preach the gospel of the kingdom throughout the whole world." This debate about whether or not a missionary impulse can be found among the Reformers, including Luther, continues. It is helpful insofar as it continues to push contemporary Lutherans to mine the theological riches of the Reformation for missiological and evangelical resources. It is unhelpful when it convinces us to leave our legacy behind as irrelevant in a new day, on this new mission field.

5. Scherer, *That the Gospel May Be Sincerely Preached*, 37.

6. Mark Hanson, *Faithful Yet Changing: The Church in Challenging Times* (Minneapolis: Augsburg Books, 2002), 43.

7. Ken W. Inskeep, "An Evaluation of the 1991 Evangelism Strategy," Department for Research and Evaluation of the Evangelical Lutheran Church in America, October 3, 2000.

8. The concept of a *missio Dei* has roots that go back to the first part of the twentieth century, as Western Christians began to wrestle with the critique that their labors had been laced with ambiguous motives and goals; that they had been triumphalistic and imperialistic, in large part

due to their lack of self-awareness regarding the way in which their understanding of the faith was shaped by and bound up with their own Western context. Western Christians began to realize that God was up to something much bigger than they ever imagined. Karl Barth is sometimes credited with laying the theological foundations for this idea, as far back as the mid-1930s. But it was at a missionary conference (an ecumenical event including Christians from all over the world) held in Willingen, Germany, in 1952, that this new model of mission was really fleshed out. This conference "recognized that the church could be neither the starting point nor the goal of mission. God's salvific work precedes both church and mission. We should not subordinate mission to the church nor the church to mission; both should, rather, be taken up into the *missio Dei*, which now became the overarching concept. The *missio Dei* institutes the *missiones ecclesiae*. The church changes from being the sender to being the one sent" (Bosch, *Transforming Mission*, 370).

9. "[T]he human condition is marked by this power to imagine the otherness of the future in contrast to the 'alreadyness' of the world process. Our traditional dogmatic term for this is the *imago dei*. The image of God in man is this still unextinguished faculty to divine the Divine, to relate ourselves to the absolute future of our lives" (Braaten, *The Flaming Center*, 47).

10. John Bowen, *Evangelism for "Normal" People* (Minneapolis: Augsburg Fortress, 2002), 209. Bowen adds: "That would shed some light on why Jesus so often went to parties and used them as illustrations of the kingdom of God: they were rehearsals for the real thing."

11. Scherer quotes Luther here as a way of arguing that Luther's concept of—and commitment to— mission is placed firmly within his understanding of the kingdom of God. "For Luther, the church—along with God's word and the baptized believer—is a crucial driving instrument for mission, but nowhere does the Reformer make it the starting point or the final goal, as 19th century missiology tended to do. It is always God's own mission that dominates Luther's thought, and the coming of the kingdom of God represents its final culmination" (*That the Gospel May Be Sincerely Preached*, 7).

12. "Evangelism in the early church was rooted in the eschatological activity of God, which was inaugurated in the life, death, and resurrection of Jesus of Nazareth and continued in the acts of the Holy Spirit. Given what God had done in and through Christ and the Holy Spirit, it was only natural that Christians should proclaim the mighty acts of God in salvation and liberation, and that they should found communities committed to celebrating all that God had done. They were propelled by a wellspring of joy and love that was at once irrepressible and contagious." William J. Abraham, *The Logic of Evangelism* (Grand Rapids: Eerdmans, 1989), 92.

13. Scherer again quotes Luther as a way of grounding an authentic Lutheran missiology in the activity and initiative of a missionary God (*That the Gospel May Be Sincerely Preached*, 7).

14. Braaten, *The Flaming Center*, 43.

15. Carl Braaten and Robert W. Jenson, *The Strange New Word of the Gospel: Re-Evangelizing in the Postmodern World* (Grand Rapids: Eerdmans, 2002), 165.

16. This was, in fact, the cover story of the August 2003 issue of *The Lutheran*.

17. Ken Inskeep, "Religious Commitment in the Evangelical Lutheran Church in America," Findings from the *Faith Practices* Survey, 2001, Department for Research and Evaluation, ELCA.

18. Martin B. Copenhaver, Anthony B. Robinson, and William H. Willimon, *Good News In Exile* (Grand Rapids: Eerdmans, 1999), 2. These three authors do as good a job as any today of outlining and illustrating the dangers of philosophical liberalism within mainline Protestantism.

19. Braaten writes, "Our supposition has been that what lies at the root of the problem is not methodology but theology—confusion about the message, the medium, the gospel and the church" (Braaten and Jenson, *The Strange New Word of the Gospel*, 173).

20. Scherer, *That the Gospel May Be Sincerely Preached*, 250.

21. Here, Eric Gritsch is quoting the Gnesio-Lutheran Nicholas of Amsdorf, who battled the Philippist George Major in a controversy focused on the relationship between good works and salvation. It is worth reading Gritsch's treatment of the theological battles that emerged in

the early years of Lutheranism. Many of these battles continue today. Eric W. Gritsch, *A History of Lutheranism* (Minneapolis: Fortress Press, 2002), 89.

22. The Lutheran World Federation Revised Mission Document, Draft July 2002, 5.

23. Darrell Guder, a Reformed theologian writing in *The Continuing Conversion of the Church* (Grand Rapids: Eerdmans, 2000), describes the way in which the reduction of the gospel message is inevitable across Christian traditions. It is the risk God takes in the incarnation. People are given the job of translating the message; and people are sinful. We reduce the message of salvation to the forgiveness of *my* sins and the promise of heaven for *me*. We split it off from the call to follow every time. Guder calls for confession, repentance, and a vigilant commitment to recovering the fullness of the gospel in every generation.

24. According to Bernhard Lohse, *Martin Luther's Theology: Its Historical and Systematic Development* (trans. Roy A. Harrisville [Minneapolis: Fortress Press, 1999]), Luther's first effort at putting his own ideas into writing came in 1509/1510. In the first Psalms lecture, Luther was already clear about the very central role that Scripture would play and about what his hermeneutic would be for interpreting Scripture: "Jesus Christ is the sole key to understanding the Psalter." But his only ecclesiological statements appear "in the margin" (pp. 51–64).

25. From the introduction of Martin Luther, *A Treatise on Christian Liberty*, 5.

26. Ibid., 7.

27. Ibid.

28. Ibid., 22.

29. Ibid., 27.

30. Ibid., 28.

31. Ibid., 30.

32. Ibid., 33.

33. Ibid., 34.

34. Bosch, *Transforming Mission*, 248. In contrast to the "paralyzed" Reformers, Bosch offers a very positive view of the Anabaptists, who subscribed to the "Great Commission" and saw "the entire world, including Catholic and Protestant church leaders and rulers, consist[ing] exclusively of pagans. All of Christianity was apostate . . . Europe was once again a mission field" (247).

35. Ibid., 249.

36. Ibid., 250. The whole sorry story is told by Bosch, *Transforming Mission,* pp. 248–52. From my perspective, it is embarrassing to read the words of these forebears. Although I disagree with his decision to almost completely disregard the positive influence of the Reformation on mission, I can certainly understand his frustration with those who simply got it so wrong.

37. Briese, *Foundations of a Lutheran Theology of Evangelism*, 137–38.

38. Ibid., 141. Franke actually went "one step further than Spener in his plans for reform, since he wished not only to reform the church, which was Spener's interest, but to reform the world as well" (149).

39. Ibid., 152–53.

40. Philip Jenkins has narrated the remarkable growth of Christianity in the southern hemisphere. "The growth in Africa has been relentless. In 1900 Africa had just 10 million Christians out of a continental population of 107 million—about nine percent. Today the Christian total stands at 360 million out of 784 million, or 46 percent. And that percentage is likely to continue rising, because Christian African countries have some of the world's most dramatic rates of population growth. Meanwhile, the advanced industrial countries are experiencing a dramatic birth dearth. Within the next twenty-five years the population of the world's Christians is expected to grow to 2.6 billion (making Christianity by far the world's largest faith). By 2025, 50 percent of the Christian population will be in Africa and Latin America, and another 17 percent will be in Asia. Those proportions will grow steadily. By about 2050 the United States will still have the largest single contingent of Christians, but all the other leading nations will be Southern: Mexico,

Brazil, Nigeria, the Democratic Republic of the Congo, Ethiopia, and the Philippines. By then the proportion of non-Latino whites among the world's Christians will have fallen to perhaps one in five" ("The Next Christianity," *The Atlantic Monthly*, October 2002, 53–68).

41. Briese writes that the Pietists "insisted on conversion from unbelief to faith . . . on a response on the part of the one converted." This was no longer "evangelically-based, as in Luther, but based on the law. Luther was convinced that once the gospel was restored to the centre of church life, everything else would follow" (*Foundations of a Lutheran Theology of Evangelism*, 269).

42. "A research concerning the Danes' church attendance throughout the centuries and other questions on the relation between church and people is now under way lead by senior lecturer in practical theology at the University of Copenhagen, Hans Raun Iversen. He has already found out that the Danes have never been very keen on attending church. Nowadays it is lamented that countrywide merely two per cent of the members regularly come to church, and only one half per cent in Copenhagen. But this is not a new situation. Around 1900 no more than 10 per cent were churchgoers and back in the 18th century, when the king had made participation in the Divine Service compulsory, probably only 20 per cent obeyed his order. Hans Raun Iversen concludes that the Danes have the world record for low churchgoing! 'You cannot in the whole world find a people with so little regular attendance on religion as the Danes,' he says." *Church News from Denmark* 6/9 (September 2001), ed. Gunnar Martin Nielsen, Council on International Relations of the Editor: Evangelical Lutheran Church in Denmark, http://www.interchurch.dk/churchnews.htm.

43. Denzil G. M. Patrick, *Pascal and Kierkegaard: A Study in the Strategy of Evangelism* (London: Lutterworth, 1947), 148.

44. *Søren Kierkegaard's Journals and Papers*, ed. and trans. Howard V. and Edna H. Hong, vol. 3 (Bloomington: Indiana University Press, 1975), 204.

45. Ibid.

46. Søren Kierkegaard, *For Self-Examination/Judge for Yourselves*, ed. Howard V. and Edna H. Hong (Princeton, N.J.: Princeton University Press, 1990), 193–94.

47. Ibid.

48. Hong and Hong, *Kierkegaard's Journals and Papers*, 333.

49. Patrick, *Pascal and Kierkegaard*, 297.

50. Kierkegaard interpreting Luther (sermon on Luke 17:11-19, 14th Sunday after Trinity, translated by other editors as "Here you see what a living, powerful thing faith is . . ."), in *Self-Examination/Judge for Yourself*, 17.

51. Ibid., 102.

52. Patrick, *Pascal and Kierkegaard*, 111.

53. Kierkegaard's passion, clarity, and courage to stand against the church, for the church, went unappreciated in his day. His own brother, a pastor, used his funeral sermon to mock him, suggesting that Søren was a drunk and out of his mind who should have been "forcibly taken away by his friends until he recovered." Alastair Hannay and Gordon D. Marino, *The Cambridge Companion to Kierkegaard* (Cambridge, UK: Cambridge University Press, 1998), 37.

54. Dietrich Bonhoeffer, *Discipleship*, ed. Geffrey B. Kelly and John D. Godsey, *Dietrich Bonhoeffer Works*, vol. 4 (Minneapolis: Fortress Press, 2001), 55.

55. Ibid., 43.

56. Ibid., 44.

57. Ibid., 44–45.

58. Kolb, *Speaking the Gospel Today*, 7.

59. "The state of the church, 2000," *Barna Research On-Line* (Barna Research Group, Ltd., 5528 Everglades Street, Ventura, CA 93003), March 21, 2000. http://www.barna.org/cgi-bin/PagePressRelease.asp?PressReleaseID=49&Reference=B.

60. Braaten and Jenson, *The Strange New World of the Gospel*, 166.

61. "Just as the culture can be described in one sense as postmodern, and our approach to the Bible as postcritical, so also the relationship of the church to contemporary North American culture can be described as post-Christian. . . . we are experiencing the end of our particular version of Christendom. The post-Christian reality of contemporary culture means that the church no longer has a privileged position and can no longer expect to receive preferential treatment. It is becoming just one more truth claim in the midst of a plurality of alternative truth claims, all of which are seen as relative" (Craig Van Gelder, "Defining the Center—Finding the Boundaries," *The Church between Gospel and Culture: The Emerging Mission in North America,* ed. George R. Hunsberger and Craig Van Gelder [Grand Rapids: Eerdmans, 1996], 41).

62. *Global Mission in the Twenty-first Century* (Evangelical Lutheran Church in America, Division for Global Mission, 1999), 13

63. See *The Lutheran,* August 2003.

64. Briese, *Foundations of a Lutheran Theology of Evangelism,* 246.

65. Braaten and Jenson, *The Strange New World of the Gospel,* 163.

66. Ibid.

67. Ibid., 55.

68. In his little 40-page document, *The Freedom of a Christian,* Luther quotes 116 Bible verses. It was, unquestionably, Paul's writing that inspired Martin Luther the most. Fifty-six percent of the biblical verses he quotes are from Paul's writings. Fifty-five verses alone are from the authentic Pauline letters. Luther's notions about his major themes—including salvation and freedom—were unquestionably based, largely, on Paul's writings.

69. Karl Barth, *The Epistle to the Romans* (London: Oxford University Press, 1968), 234.

70. Ibid.

71. Edgar Krentz, "Freedom in Christ—Gift and Demand," *Concordia Theological Monthly* 40/6–7 (1969), 362.

72. Ibid., 364.

73. Donald Senior and Carroll Stuhlmueller, *The Biblical Foundations for Mission* (Maryknoll, N.Y.: Orbis, 1983), 181.

74. As a Pharisee, Paul would most likely have been strongly influenced by the law and the prophets of the Hebrew Bible (our "Old Testament"). And in the Old Testament, the authors of the book of Isaiah use this notion of salvation more than anyone else.

75. Bonhoeffer, *Discipleship,* 46.

76. Ibid.

77. This idea can be found, too, within the Lutheran concept of the priesthood of all believers: "More importantly, the Priesthood of All Believers is a gift and a task in the same breath. The general priesthood is an affirmation that forgiveness of man by God is possible without the ruling of a priest—and this precisely in the situation of a corrupted and abused sacramental system—and brings with it the task of forgiving and living in solidarity with others in the community of saints. That is, the Christian is forgiven, and now is free to forgive others" (Briese, *Foundations of a Lutheran Theology of Evangelism,* 122–23.

3. Addressing Captives in Babylon

1. For me, as a theologian working within a seminary, those mission/confession debates that have taken place within North American seminaries are particularly revealing. The nineteenth century witnessed the conflict between Samuel Schmucker and Henry Muhlenberg, leading to the historical rift between the Lutheran seminaries at Gettysburg and Philadelphia. The twentieth century saw a similar rift at Luther Seminary between George Aus and Herman Preus.

2. James Scherer, . . . *That the Gospel May Be Sincerely Preached throughout the World: A Lutheran Perspective on Mission and Evangelism in the 20th Century* (Stuttgart, Germany: LWF/Kreuz Verlag, 1982).

3. James Scherer, *Gospel, Church and Kingdom: Comparative Studies in World Mission Theology* (Minneapolis: Augsburg Books, 1987), 54.

4. See Rick Bliese, "What is God Up To?" in *A Story Worth Sharing: Engaging Evangelism*, ed. Kelly Fryer (Minneapolis: Augsburg Fortress, 2004), 27–28.

5. *An Evaluation of the 1991 Evangelism Strategy*, Ken W. Inskeep, October 3, 2000, www .elca.org/re/reports/evan 1991.pdf, and *Worship Attendance in the Evangelical Lutheran Church in America: Faith Communities Today*, Ken W. Inskeep and Jeffrey L. Drake, November 2000, www .elca.org/re/reports/ccspwrsp1.pdf.

6. As a rough average across the country, approximately forty percent of congregations appear stagnant within any given synod. An additional forty percent are experiencing decline. Given the vast number of congregations worshiping with less than 100 people on any given Sunday, these numbers point to serious trends for the future. In fact, the majority of ELCA congregations (5,738) have fewer than 350 baptized members. See the Inskeep studies in note 5.

7. Ken W. Inskeep, *An Evaluation of the 1991 Evangelism Strategy*, 11.

8. Darrell L. Guder, *The Continuing Conversion of the Church* (Grand Rapids: Eerdmans, 2000), 23. Also see David B. Barrett, *Evangelize: A Historical Survey of the Concept* (Birmingham, Ala.: New Hope, 1987). Barrett estimates that between 1850 and 1989, 9,280 (presumably Protestant) books on Christian evangelization appeared—3,725 of them in English (37). He further estimates that in the decade of the 1980s, at least 3,000 Roman Catholic books per year appeared on the subject, and from 1948 to 1987, 5,300 conferences on mission and evangelism had taken place (73–75).

9. "Christ himself is present to us in a very earthly way. Everywhere in the history of revelation God embodies himself for us. His Spirit came in the form of a dove and of the fiery tongues of Pentecost. And God still embodies himself for us. The Holy Spirit comes to us and brings Christ to us through the external, physical, sensible means of the word, of the human voice, and of the sacraments. All these words and sacraments are his veils and clothes, his masks and disguises with which he covers himself so that we may bear and comprehend him" (Paul Althaus, *The Theology of Martin Luther* [Philadelphia: Fortress Press, 1966], 22).

10. The Augsburg Confession, Article VII (Robert Kolb, Timothy J. Wengert, and Charles P. Arand, *The Book of Concord: The Confessions of the Evangelical Lutheran Church* [Minneapolis: Fortress Press, 2000], 32), and Calvin (*Institutes of the Christian Religion* [*Institutio* IV, 1, 9]) define the *notae ecclesiae*, or marks of the church, as the proper proclamation and hearing of the word, and the proper distribution and reception of the sacraments. These *notae ecclesiae* are signs by which the presence of the church is recognized.

11. "All this makes it clear that the theology of the cross results in a new understanding of what we call 'reality.' True reality is what the world and reason think it is. The true reality of God and of his salvation is 'paradoxical' and hidden under its opposite. Reason is able neither to understand nor experience it. Judged by standards of reason and experience, that is, by the standards of the world, true reality is unreal and its exact opposite is real. Only faith can comprehend that true and paradoxical reality" (Paul Althaus, *The Theology of Martin Luther*, 32f. [describing Luther's theology of the cross]).

12. Dietrich Bonhoeffer develops the topic of Christ coming as "the true image of the human 'sarx' [flesh]" in his 1933 lectures (*Dietrich Bonhoeffer Werke* 12:343–48 [Gesammelte Schriften 3:235–38]. These lectures have major implications for evangelizing in that Bonhoeffer discusses Christ as the humiliated God present today in Word and Sacrament, that is, in "the likeness of sinful flesh." See Dietrich Bonhoeffer, *Christ the Center* (San Francisco: Harper & Row, 1978), 106f.

13. Dietrich Bonhoeffer, *Discipleship* (Minneapolis: Fortress Press, 2003), 202.

14. For a standard description of the marks of the church, see Philip J. Hefner's chapter on "The Church" in *Christian Dogmatics*, ed. Carl Braaten and Robert Jenson (Philadelphia: Fortress

Press, 1984), 223f. In this chapter Hefner states: "Luther does not include mission among his seven marks of the church, but he does speak of other matters that imply it." Consequently, mission and the "marks" are often divorced in Lutheran theological discourse.

15. Gudina Tumsa, Ethiopian martyr, died in 1979. He is often considered the "African Bonheoffer." Born in the province of Wellega in 1929, Tumsa left home to attend a mission school in Nedjo. There he distinguished himself and often served as an interpreter for missionaries. Gudina received his basic theological training at the Nedjo Seminary and later attended Luther Seminary in the United States from 1963 to 1966. In 1974 the Ethiopian Revolution saw the overthrow of Emperor Haile Selassie. But with it came internal strife and regional rebellions. Tumsa was active in civil society's concerns. He opposed all forms of racism, the exploitation of farmers and domestic servants among his own people, and spoke out in favor of fundamental land reform. For many among the poor, oppressed, and disenfranchised in Ethiopia, Tumsa became a symbol of hope. In 1978, Tumsa was arrested for the first time. After his second arrest in 1979, the regime attempted to brand him a counterrevolutionary and political agent. Although given opportunities to leave Ethiopia, Tumsa was unwilling to leave the people he served. A few weeks after his second release, after attending church services, he was kidnapped by armed men in Addis Ababa and subsequently executed.

16. Martin Luther, *Babylonian Captivity of the Church* (1520) in *Luther's Works* 36:3. Luther also states here: "There are still a few other things which it might seem possible to regard as sacraments; namely, all those things to which a divine promise has been given, such as prayer, the Word, and the cross" (123). Likewise, Luther states at the beginning of the treatise: "To begin with, I must deny that there are seven sacraments, and for the present maintain that there are but three: baptism, penance, and the bread. . . . Yet, if I were to speak according to the usage of Scriptures, I should have only one single sacrament, but with three sacramental signs, of which I shall treat more fully at the proper time" (18).

17. For a brief discussion of the means of grace in relationship to evangelizing, see David J. Valleskey, *We Believe—Therefore We Speak; The Theology and Practice of Evangelism* (Milwaukee: Northwestern Publishing House, 1995), 94. Valleskey begins his section with a quote similar to Luther in *The Babylonian Captivity of the Church*. He writes: "Strictly speaking, there is only one means of grace: the gospel" (94). See also Robert Kolb, *Speaking the Gospel Today* (St. Louis: Concordia, 1995) and Russell John Briese, *Foundations of a Lutheran Theology of Evangelism* (Frankfurt: Peter Lang, 1994), 273f. Bonhoeffer is particularly helpful, using the term "form" instead of "means of grace" within his 1933 lectures on Christology, where he describes the real presence of Christ in three forms: Christ as Word, Christ as Sacrament, and Christ as Church (*Christ the Center*, 49f.). Thesis #2 builds upon Bonhoeffer's insight into Christ's presence. Evangelizing thus begins with a theology of Christ's presence and the "means of grace" that makes this presence possible "for you."

18. See the discussion on "confession" in Luther's Large Catechism. See also Smalcald Articles (Part III, Article 4).

19. James Nestingen, "Justification, Vocation, and Location in Luther's Reformation," in *Living Out Our Callings at Home* (Minneapolis: Centered Life Series, 2004), 5f.

20. The most famous dismissal of the Reformation as a paradigm for mission is David Bosch's monumental work on mission, *Transforming Mission* (Maryknoll, N.Y.: Orbis, 1991). See chapter 8, "The Missionary Paradigm of the Protestant Reformation." Bosch leans heavily on Lutheran sources (e.g., Gustav Warneck, the father of missiology as a theological discipline) for the judgment that "it has often been pointed out that the Reformers were indifferent, if not hostile to mission" (243–44). For a contrasting argument, see James Scherer, *Gospel, Church and Kingdom: Comparative Studies in World Mission Theology* (Minneapolis: Augsburg Books, 1987), 55f.

21. For a fuller description of St. Andrews's turnaround, see Richard H. Bliese, "Life on the Edge: A Small Church Redefines Its Mission," in *The Christian Century* 120/14 (July 12, 2003), 24–27.

22. This understanding of the nature of mission has come to be referred to as *missio Dei* (mission of God). Mission is thus derived from the very nature of God. During the twentieth century, the essentially missionary nature of the church became the dominant consensus of the worldwide community of Christian leaders and scholars. For those involved in the ecumenical missiological discussion, the "theology of mission" has become "missionary theology." Although much of the theological guild in North America remains unpersuaded, the new vocabulary of mission has established itself. It is formally endorsed by the Roman Catholic Church (see *Lumen Gentium, Ad Gentes,* and *Nostra Aetate*), in the World Council of Churches (*Mission and Evangelism: An Ecumenical Affirmation*—1982), and in many of the Evangelical documents (David Bosch, *Transforming Mission,* 535–62).

4. For the Sake of the World

1. This section draws primarily on materials from the Synoptic Gospels in an effort to develop a more holistic and synthetic understanding of the kingdom of God as announced by Jesus.

2. The book of Acts represents an important scriptural document for the church to reclaim in our day if we are to develop a sufficient understanding of: (a) the missionary nature of the church; (b) the importance of context and contextualization for engaging in evangelizing and mission; and (c) the person and work of the Spirit in the life of the church and the world.

3. This section offers a reading of key concepts in the Lutheran Confessions from the perspective of the missional hermeneutic that is laid out in the previous section regarding a biblical framework. While there are indications within Luther's understanding, and among many of those who followed in his path, that they shared such a missional hermeneutic, their context of Constantinian Christendom focused this hermeneutic primarily on the church that they were seeking to renew. It is helpful to read the Lutheran Confessions from the perspective of a missional hermeneutic that has the larger world as its horizon, which is being attempted here.

4. As translated by William R. Russell, *Luther's Theological Testament: The Schmalkald Articles* (Minneapolis: Fortress Press, 1995), 142.

5. Martin Luther, Small Catechism, The Third Article: "but instead the Holy Spirit has called me through the gospel, enlightened me with his gifts, made me holy and kept me in the true faith, just as he calls, gathers, enlightens, and makes holy the whole Christian Church on earth."

6. An example of this can be found in the Mission Statement recently developed by the Evangelical Lutheran Church in America, where it is stated: "Marked with the cross of Christ forever, we are claimed, gathered and sent for the sake of the world." The ELCA as a denomination found it important to place being *sent* as the movement that brings to fulfillment the work begun by the Spirit in *claiming* us.

7. "Nairobi Statement on Worship and Culture: Contemporary Challenges and Opportunities," published in S. Anita Stauffer, *Christian Worship: Unity in Cultural Diversity* (Geneva, Switzerland: Department for Theology and Studies, The Lutheran World Federation, 1996), Section 3—Worship as Contextual.

8. This point is ably argued by Lesslie Newbigin, *The Gospel in a Pluralist Society* (Grand Rapids: Eerdmans, 1989), see especially 80–115.

9. The concept of "translatability" is used here to describe the way in which the message of the gospel comes to expression within a specific culture, where it becomes embedded in and is expressed in relation to the language, worldview, and customs of that context. A helpful resource in understanding this point is Lamin Sanneh, *Translating the Message: The Missionary Impact on Culture* (Maryknoll, N.Y.: Orbis, 2002).

10. This point is developed by Craig Van Gelder, *The Essence of the Church: A Community Created by the Spirit* (Grand Rapids: Baker, 2002), 118–20.

11. William Rogers Brukaker, ed., *Immigration and the Politics of Citizenship in Europe and North America* (New York: University Press of America, 1989).

12. Steven Best and Douglas Kellner, *The Postmodern Turn* (New York: Guilford, 1997).

13. E. Franklin Frazier, *The Negro Church in America* (New York: Schocken, 1974), 35–51.

5. Called Out of Our Comfort Zone

1. Russell John Briese, *Foundations of a Lutheran Theology of Evangelism* (Frankfurt, Germany: Peter Lang, 1994), 15, quoting James Berquist, "Our Lutheran Heritage and a Theology of Evangelism," *Stavanger 1982: LWF Interregional Consultation on Mission and Evangelism*, LWF Report no. 13/14 (Stuttgart: Kreuz Verlag, 1983), 13.

2. John 3:16: "For God so loved the world that he gave his only Son, that everyone who believes in him may not perish but may have eternal life" (NRSV).

3. Kenn Inskeep, "*Congregations in the ELCA: An Overview,*" Department of Research and Evaluation, Evangelical Lutheran Church in America, September 2003.

4. *Toward a Vision for Evangelism in the Evangelical Lutheran Church in America*, 2001 Pre-Assembly Report: Evangelism Strategy, Section IV, 8.

5. Ibid., 14.

6. Martin Luther, The Small Catechism, The Creed, The Third Article.

7. *Use of the Means of Grace: A Statement of the Practice of Word and Sacrament* (Minneapolis: Augsburg Fortress, 1997), 18.

8. The formulation of "listen, discern, speak, and act" has been taken from the biblical material, mainly in Acts. "Listen, speak, and act" were extracted by the author, and "discern" was added through conversation with the book team. This formulation may also be seen other places in Scripture, such as Luke 24 and the Emmaus Road experience. Congregational ministry models and community organizing and development models may also include a version of some or all of these four functions.

9. Martin Luther, The Small Catechism, The Creed, The Third Article.

10. See chapter seven for a definition of culture, p. 114.

11. Evangelism Strategy Task Force, "Evangelism Strategy: Sharing Faith in a New Century," Chicago: ELCA, 2003, 10.

12. Robert J. Schreiter, "Theology in the Congregation: Discovering and Doing," in *Studying Congregations*, ed. Nancy T. Ammerman, Jackson W. Carroll, Carl S. Dudley, and William McKinney (Nashville: Abingdon, 1998), 23.

13. This phrase was shared by Dr. Paul Rajashekar during the discussions for this book. See Dr. Rajashekar's chapter, "Navigating Difficult Questions."

14. "And Jesus came and said to them, 'All authority in heaven and on earth has been given to me. Go therefore and make disciples of all the nations, baptizing them in the name of the Father and of the Son and of the Holy Spirit, and teaching them to obey everything that I commanded you. And remember, I am with you always, to the end of the age'" (Matt. 28:18-20 NRSV).

15. "Baptism was given to the Church by Jesus Christ in the 'great commission,' but also in his own baptism by John and in the baptism of the cross" (*Use of the Means of Grace*, 21).

16. Ibid., 25.

17 .Briese, *Foundations of a Lutheran Theology of Evangelism*, 122.

18. James Scherer, ". . . *That the Gospel May Be Sincerely Preached throughout the World: A Lutheran Perspective on Mission and Evangelism in the 20th Century* (Stuttgart: LWF/Kreuz Verlag, 1982).

19. Briese, *Foundations of a Lutheran Theology of Evangelism*, 127.

20. Ibid., 133.

21. "For creation waits with eager longing for the revealing of the children of God; for the creation was subjected to futility, not of its own will but by the will of the one who subjected it, in hope that the creation itself will be set free from its bondage to decay and will obtain the freedom of the glory of the children of God" (Rom. 8:19-21 NRSV).

22. In the gospel according to John 3:16, we are given the heart of the gospel message: "For God so loved the world that he gave his only Son, so that everyone who believes in him may not perish but may have eternal life." The apostle Paul expounds on this message in Romans 5:6-11: "For while we were still weak . . . Christ died . . . if while we were enemies, we were reconciled to God through the death of his Son, much more surely, having been reconciled, will we be saved by his life. But more than that, we ever boast in God through our Lord Jesus Christ, through whom we have now received reconciliation."

23. Johannes P. Louw and Eugene A. Nida, eds., *Greek-English Lexicon*, vol. 1, s.v. "reconciliation" (New York: United Bible Society, 1988), 502. The form used in Eph. 2:16 is *apokatallasso*. This form is stronger than *katallasso* and means to reconcile completely and leave no impediment to unity and peace.

24. Robert J. Schreiter, *The Ministry of Reconciliation: Spirituality and Strategies* (Maryknoll, N.Y.: Orbis, 1998), 29.

25. Ibid., 14.

26. Mark W. Thomsen, *Christ Crucified: A 21st Century Missiology of the Cross* (Minneapolis: Lutheran University Press, 2004).

27. Ibid., 13.

28. Evangelism Strategy Task Force, "*Toward a Vision of Evangelism in the ELCA: Evangelism Strategy Parts 1 and 2*," Evangelical Lutheran Church in America, 2001, 38.

29. *Demographic Report for Zip Code 60624*, Evangelical Lutheran Church in America, Department for Research and Evaluation (February 2003).

30. U.S. Census Data, 2000.

31. Ministry Area Profile 2002, based on Census 2000 data. "West Side African-American Ministries Lat=41.9 & Lon=87.7," Chicago, Illinois, Precept Group, Inc.

32. *Use of the Means of Grace*, 6. "Jesus Christ is the living and abiding Word of God. By the power of the Spirit, this very Word of God, which is Jesus Christ, is read in the Scriptures, proclaimed in preaching, announced in the forgiveness of sins, eaten and drunk in the Holy Communion, and encountered in the bodily presence of the Christian community. . . . The living heart of all these means is the presence of Jesus Christ through the power of the Spirit as the gift of the Father."

33. Margaret Wheatley, *Leadership and the New Science* (San Francisco: Berrett-Koehler, 1999), 78.

34. Ibid., 84.

35. Ibid., 75–90.

36. Ibid., 87.

6. Navigating Difficult Questions

1. This remark was made by Timothy Wengert, professor of church history and Lutheran Confessions at the Lutheran Theological Seminary at Philadelphia.

2. These are defined as all post-Reformation Christian groups—including the Mormon church, Pentecostals, and Jehovah's Witnesses.

3. "America's Protestant Majority Is Fading, University of Chicago Research Shows," *New York Times*, July 21, 2004. The NORC survey was conducted in 2002, the latest year for which statistical data are available. Interestingly, the survey found that the percentage of Roman Catholics has remained fairly steady at about twenty-five percent of the population between 1993 and 2002. During the same period, the number of people who said that they belong to other religions, including Eastern faiths, Islam, Orthodox Christians, and Native-American faiths increased from three to seven percent. See: http://www-news.uchicago.edu/releases/04/040720.protestant.shtml.

4. *The Lutheran*, July 2004, 47.

5. The terms *plurality* and *pluralism* are often used interchangeably in much of the current literature. In this essay, the term *plurality* is used to refer to the *fact* of religious diversity and *pluralism* refers to diversity as a *value* in itself.

6. Chaim Potok, *The Book of Lights* (New York: Knopf, 1981).

7. These views were expressed at a plenary session on "Proselytization and Religious Freedom" at the Fourth Parliament of the World's Religions held in Barcelona, Spain, July 2004.

8. For a Christian ecumenical discussion on the subject, see "Proselytism" by Nicolas Lossky, in *Dictionary of the Ecumenical Movement*, 2nd ed. (Geneva: WCC Publications, 2002), 940–41.

9. Elizabeth Hayes Alvarez, "Neighbors, Fences, and Religion in America," *Sightings*, Martin Marty Center at the University of Chicago, May 27, 2004 (electronic edition). The original story appeared in *New York Times*, May 5, 2004.

10. Martin E. Marty and Frederick E. Greenspahn, eds., *Pushing the Faith: Proselytism and Civility in a Pluralistic World* (New York: Crossroad, 1988), 158.

11. Carl E. Braaten, *The Apostolic Imperative* (Minneapolis: Augsburg Books, 1985).

12. For a thorough discussion of exegetical and hermeneutical issues pertaining to John 14:6, see Kenneth Cracknell, *Towards a New Relationship: Christians and People of Other Faiths* (London: Epworth, 1986).

13. For an overview of this issue, see Wesley Ariarajah, *The Bible and People of Other Faiths* (Geneva: WCC, 1985).

14. It has become popular, both in academic and ecumenical discussions, to analyze responses to religious plurality in terms of "Exclusivism," "Inclusivism" and "Pluralism." "Exclusivism" has been associated with the position that salvation can be found only through the person and work of Jesus Christ and that saving grace is not mediated through other religions. "Inclusivism" refers to the position that salvation extends beyond the boundaries of the church and that other religions play some positive role in God's plan for humanity. "Pluralism" refers to the position that all religions are culturally conditioned, yet valid or authentic, responses to the divine or ultimate Reality. The literature on this subject is enormous and growing. For a representative sample consult Gavin D'Costa, *The Meeting of Religions and the Trinity* (Maryknoll, N.Y.: Orbis 2000); M. Dhavamony, *Christian Theology of Religions: A Systematic Reflection on the Christian Understanding of World Religions* (Bern: Peter Lang, 1998); Paul F. Knitter, *Introducing Theologies of Religions* (Maryknoll, N.Y.: Orbis, 2002); John Hick, *A Christian Theology of Religions: The Rainbow of Faiths* (Louisville: Westminster John Knox, 1995); H Netland, *Encountering Religious Pluralism: The Challenge of Christian Faith and Mission* (Downers Grove, Ill.: InterVarsity, 2001).

15. The discussion on Lutheran understanding of other faiths is based on the studies initiated by the Lutheran World Federation. See *Religious Pluralism and Lutheran Theology*, ed. J. Paul Rajashekar, LWF Report 23/24 (Geneva: LWF, 1988). Essays by Paul Varo Martinson, Theodore M. Ludwig, and Carl Braaten in this volume focus on the issues of the dialectic of law and gospel in relation to a Lutheran theology of religions.

16. The insight was originally suggested by Theodore Ludwig, "Some Lutheran Reflections on Religious Pluralism," in *Religious Pluralism and Lutheran Theology*, ed. J. Paul Rajashekar. It was further developed in an unpublished paper, "Salvation and Religions: From *Sola* to *Simul*," by Paul Varo Martinson. The author of this essay is indebted to both these scholars and other Lutheran scholars who were part of an international study group between 1985 and 1992.

17. *The San Antonio Report, Your Will be Done: Mission in Christ's Way*, ed. Frederick R. Wilson (Geneva: WCC, 1990), 33.

18. There is a significant amount of literature on the theory and practice of interreligious dialogue. Most useful would be *Guidelines on Dialogue* (Geneva: WCC, 1977). A revised and enlarged version is available on the web: http://www.wcc-coe.org/wcc/what/interreligious/77glines-e.html.

19. For a good discussion on the subject from a Roman Catholic perspective, see "Dialogue and Proclamation," Joint Document of the Pontifical Council for Interreligious Dialogue and the Congregation for Evangelization of Peoples (June 21, 1991).

20. As quoted in "Periscope," *Newsweek*, May 19, 2003 (US Edition).

21. Derek Evans, "Making a Difference" in *In the Aftermath: What September 11 Is Teaching Us about Our World, Our Faith, and Ourselves*, ed. James Taylor (Kelowna, British Columbia: Northstone, 2002), 21.

22. This remark was made by President George W. Bush a few days after the terrorist attack on September 11, 2001. See *World Press Review* 48, no. 12 (Dec 2001); *Harper's Magazine*, September 25, 2001.

23. *Luther's Works*, 55 vols., ed. Jaroslav Pelikan and Helmut Lehmann (Philadelphia: Fortress Press; St. Louis: Concordia, 1955–1986), 31:39–58.

24. Walter von Loewenich, *Luther's Theology of the Cross* (Minneapolis: Augsburg Books, 1976).

25. See Jürgen Moltmann, *The Crucified God: The Cross of Christ as the Foundation and Criticism of Christian Theology* (New York: Harper & Row, 1974), 72. Also Mark W. Thomsen, *Christ Crucified: A 21st Century Missiology of the Cross* (Minneapolis: Lutheran University Press, 2004).

26. Douglas John Hall, *Confessing the Faith: Christian Theology in a North American Context* (Minneapolis: Fortress Press, 1996), 28.

27. *Luther's Works*, American Edition *(LW)* 31:40–41.

28. Elsa Tamez, *Amnesty of Grace: Justification by Faith from a Latin American Perspective* (Nashville: Abingdon, 1993).

29. The term comes from C. S. Song, *Jesus the Crucified People* (Minneapolis: Fortress Press, 1996).

30. The metaphor of the "Saturday people" comes from a meditation by the late Stanley J. Samratha, the former director of the Sub-Unit on Dialogue, World Council of Churches, Geneva.

31. Orlando E. Costas, *Liberating News: A Theology of Contextual Evangelization* (Grand Rapids: Eerdmans, 1989).

32. American Religious Identification Survey conducted by the City University of New York in 2001, *Philadelphia Inquirer*, March 27, 2002. See: http://www.gc.cuny.edu/studies/key_findings.htm.

33. For an overview of postmodernism, see Stanley J. Grenz, *A Primer on Postmodernism* (Grand Rapids: Eerdmans, 1996).

34. I have borrowed this analogy from Grenz, *A Primer on Postmodernism*, 1–10.

35. Brad J. Kallenberg, *Live to Tell: Evangelism in a Postmodern World* (Grand Rapids: Brazos, 2002), 50; Grenz, *A Primer on Postmodernism*, 167–68.

36. George A Lindbeck, "The Church's Mission to a Postmodern Culture," in *Postmodern Theology: Christian Faith in a Pluralist World*, ed. Frederic B. Burnham (San Francisco: Harper Collins, 1989), 51–52.

37. Kosuke Koyama, *Mount Fuji and Mount Sinai: A Critique of Idols* (London: SCM, 1984), 252.

7. After the Death of Evangelism—The Resurrection of the Evangelizing Church

1. Russell John Briese, *Foundations of a Lutheran Theology of Evangelism* (Frankfurt: Peter Lang, 1994), especially 273–87, and Robert Kolb, *Speaking the Gospel Today: A Theology for Evangelism* (St. Louis: Concordia, 1995). Briese writes: "Evangelism is the one ministry of the church, and both lay and ordained take part in it. Its instruments of evangelism, the word and the sacraments, are not only theory but practice. They are the means of grace: Whoever participates in them participates in the grace they bring. In participating in the gospel, the church will grasp its priestly task to the world and be equipped to perform it. Only in finding its identity in the gospel will the church naturally turn to those outside of its walls" (287).

2. Melvin Herskovitz, *Man and His Works* (New York: Alfred A. Knopf, 1948), 625, as quoted by Kathryn Tanner, *Theories of Culture: A New Agenda for Theology* (Minneapolis: Fortress Press, 1997), 27.

3. Sidney E. Mead, *The Lively Experiment: The Shaping of Christianity in America* (New York: Harper & Row, 1963), 66.

4. James A. Scherer, . . . *That the Gospel May Be Sincerely Preached throughout the World: A Lutheran Perspective on Mission and Evangelism in the 20th Century* (Stuttgart: Lutheran World Federation/Kreuz Verlag, 1982), 19–23.

5. See James A. Scherer, *Gospel, Church, and Kingdom: Comparative Studies in World Mission Theology* (Minneapolis: Augsburg Books, 1987), 70ff.

6. See David J. Bosch, *Transforming Mission: Paradigm Shifts in Theology of Mission* (Maryknoll, N.Y.: Orbis, 1991), 281–83.

7. Scherer, *That the Gospel May Be Sincerely Preached*, 30–32.

8. See Jean-François Lyotard, *The Postmodern Condition: A Report on Knowledge*, trans. Geoff Bennington and Brian Massumi (Minneapolis: University of Minnesota Press, 1984).

9. "Sharing Faith in a New Century: A Vision for Evangelism in the Evangelical Lutheran Church in America," Evangelism Strategy adopted at the 2003 Churchwide Assembly.

10. This critique is primarily based on the conviction that faith occurs as a gift of God worked by the power of the Holy Spirit, rather than as an act of human volition.

11. For example, Rick Warren, *The Purpose-Driven Church: Growth without Compromising Your Message and Mission* (Grand Rapids: Zondervan, 1995), chapter 9: "Who Is Your Target?" 155–72.

12. For example, John Wimber and Kevin Springer, *Power Evangelism* (London: Hodder & Stoughton, 1992).

13. For example, Bill Hybels and Mark Mittelberg, *Becoming a Contagious Christian* (Grand Rapids: Zondervan, 1994), chapter 10: "Starting Spiritual Conversations," 135–48.

14. See Ben Johnson, *An Evangelism Primer: Practical Principles for Congregations* (Atlanta: John Knox, 1983), 39–41.

15. See D. James Kennedy, *Evangelism Explosion* (Wheaton: Tyndale House, 1970), chapter 4: "The Proper Use of Testimony," 81–88.

16. For documentation of this growth in the context of Latin America, see David Martin, *Tongues of Fire: The Explosion of Protestantism in Latin America* (Oxford: Blackwell, 1990). This phenomenon has its parallel in Africa and Asia.

17. See Regin Prenter, *Spiritus Creator: Luther's Concept of the Holy Spirit* (Philadelphia: Fortress Press, 1953).

18. For a positive example of a Lutheran appropriation of Pentecostalism's focus on the Holy Spirit, see Richard A. Jensen, *Touched by the Spirit: One Man's Struggle to Understand His Experience of the Holy Spirit* (Minneapolis: Augsburg Books, 1975).

19. James H. Cone, *The Spirituals and the Blues* (New York: Seabury, 1972), 62–74.

20. Gayraud S. Wilmore, *Black Religion and Black Radicalism: An Interpretation of the Religious History of Afro-American People* (Maryknoll, N.Y.: Orbis, 1983), 236.

21. Apostolic Exhortation of Pope Paul VI, *On Evangelization in the Modern World/Evangelii Nuntiandi* (Boston: Pauline Books & Media, 1975).

22. See James A. Scherer and Stephen B. Bevans, eds., *New Directions in Mission and Evangelization: Basic Statements 1974–1991* (Maryknoll, N.Y.: Orbis, 1992), 89–200.

23. Robert J. Schreiter, *The New Catholicity: Theology between the Global and the Local* (Maryknoll, N.Y.: Orbis, 1997), 129.

24. Philip Jenkins, *The Next Christendom: The Coming of Global Christianity* (New York: Oxford, 2002).

25. For the significance of indigenous Bible translation in the spread of Christianity, especially in Africa, see Lamin Sanneh, *Whose Religion Is Christianity? The Gospel beyond the West* (Grand Rapids: Eerdmans, 2003).

26. Donald E. Miller, *Emergent Patterns of Congregational Life and Leadership in the Developing World: Personal Reflections from a Research Odyssey*, Pulpit and Pew Research Reports, No. 3 (Durham, N.C.: Duke Divinity School, 2003), 14–17.

27. Lutheran World Federation Consultation on Churches in Mission, *Into the Third Millennium: Together in God's Mission* (Geneva: The Lutheran World Federation, 1998).

28. John D. Zizioulas, *Being as Communion: Studies in Personhood and the Church* (Crestwood: St. Vladimir's Seminary Press, 1997), 17.

29. Kallistos Ware, "Seek First the Kingdom: Orthodox Monasticism and Its Service to the World," *Theology Today* 61 (April 2004): 14.

30. Catherine Mowry LaCugna, *God for Us: The Trinity and Christian Life* (San Francisco: Harper, 1991), 270–71.

31. Ware, "Seek First the Kingdom," 15.

32. Zizioulas, *Being as Communion*, 102.

33. See ibid., 108.

34. Ibid., 111.

35. See Robert W. Jenson, *Visible Words: The Interpretation and Practice of Christian Sacraments* (Philadelphia: Fortress Press, 1978).

36. Chapter four, p. 63.

37. Tanner, *Theories of Culture*, 27.

38. Peter G. Stromberg, *Symbols of Community: The Cultural System of a Swedish Church* (Tucson: University of Arizona Press, 1986), 3–14.

39. Jan G. Linn, *Reclaiming Evangelism: A Practical Guide for Mainline Churches* (St. Louis: Chalice, 1998), 57.

40. Ibid., 99.

41. George G. Hunter III, *The Celtic Way of Evangelism: How Christianity Can Reach the West . . . Again* (Nashville: Abingdon, 2000).

42. Ibid., 117.

43. Ibid., 117–21.

44. Mark S. Hanson, *Faithful yet Changing: The Church in Challenging Times* (Minneapolis: Augsburg Books, 2002), 43.

45. For a clear argument about the importance of addressing language patterns in the changing of culture, see the model from the business world in Robert Kegan and Lisa Laskow Lahey, *How the Way We Talk Can Change the Way We Work: Seven Languages for Transformation* (San Francisco: Jossey-Bass, 2001).

46. For a wonderful model that employs the weekly lectionary texts in this way, see Mark A. Olson, *Moving beyond Church Growth: An Alternative Vision for Congregations* (Minneapolis: Fortress Press, 2002), chapter 5: "Reclaiming the Sabbath: One Text at a Time," 56–62.

47. See Craig L. Nessan, *Beyond Maintenance to Mission: A Theology of the Congregation* (Minneapolis: Fortress Press, 1999), chapter 8: "Evangelism: Telling the Kingdom," 82–89.

48. An excellent model for a new and intensive approach to Lutheran catechesis is *Welcome to Christ: A Lutheran Catechetical Guide* (Minneapolis: Augsburg Fortress, 1997). The actual rites are published as *Welcome to Christ: Lutheran Rites for the Catechumenate* (Minneapolis: Augsburg Fortress, 1997), and introductory essays as *Welcome to Christ: A Lutheran Introduction to the Catechumenate* (Minneapolis: Augsburg Fortress, 1997).

49. For a helpful model, see Ralph W. Quere, *Evangelical Witness: The Message, Medium, Mission, and Method of Evangelism* (Minneapolis: Augsburg Books, 1975), especially chapter 3: "An Evangel for Evangelists," 44–66.

50. For the meaning of and examples of Christian "practices," see Dorothy C. Bass and Miroslav Volf, eds., *Practicing Theology: Beliefs and Practices in Christian Life* (Grand Rapids: Eerdmans, 2002).

51. See Mark A. Olson, *The Evangelical Pastor: Pastoral Leadership for a Witnessing People* (Minneapolis: Augsburg Fortress, 1992).

52. See Robert Wuthnow, ed., *"I Come Away Stronger": How Small Groups are Shaping American Religion* (Grand Rapids: Eerdmans, 1994).

Study Guide

1. The focus of this book is on Lutherans in general and the Evangelical Lutheran Church in America in particular. But readers from other faith traditions are encouraged to reflect on how their own theological and confessional understandings are similar to or different from those raised in this book. The study questions should then be adjusted to address these similarities and differences.

INDEX OF TOPICS

absolution, 26, 83,120
Alpha, 2
anthropology, 33
    contemporary, 5, 18
    Lutheran, 5, 7, 133, 139, 146
Augsburg Confession, 10, 19, 20, 61, 63, 135, 137
"Babylonian Captivity," 32–51
Babylonian captivity (historic), 53
baptism, vii, 23, 26, 33–35, 39, 42, 44, 46, 61, 63,
    64, 71, 74, 78, 80, 81, 82, 89, 95, 96,
    113, 116, 117, 119, 126, 135
    adult, 47, 49, 146
    catechetical preparation for, 47, 137, 146
baptismal call, 34, 46, 81, 137
baptismal identity, 19, 82
Baptists, 4
Bible, 5, 7, 13, 14, 16, 18, 19, 23, 26, 30, 32, 33, 35,
    37, 38, 42–45, 47, 49, 51, 52–60, 61,
    63, 68, 74–81, 86, 90, 98, 99,101, 102,
    106, 121, 123, 124, 128–30
Black churches, 114, 121, 122, 144
Buddhism, 124
call, ix, 5, 12, 13, 17, 22, 26, 27, 29, 31, 34, 37, 41,
    44, 45, 49, 52, 62, 71, 73, 81, 84, 90,
    97, 136, 137. *See also* gift and call
    costly, 30, 31, 75, 76, 84, 94, 140
    to discipleship, vii, 20, 21, 22, 25, 26, 38, 40,
    47, 85
Calvinist, 7, 19, 33
catechesis and education, 33, 47, 75, 80–82, 89,
    96, 116, 128, 129
Christendom, ix, 6, 24, 27, 37, 64, 104, 111, 122
Christian, 22, 27, 28, 35, 38, 55
    community, 10, 32, 55, 63, 64, 71–73, 75,
    84, 101, 108
    exclusivism, 95, 97, 99

freedom, 13, 22, 44, 84, 89, 135, 146
    new life, 10, 11, 13, 30, 31, 44, 52, 61, 77,
    113
    triumphalism, 97, 105
church, 51, 55, 67, 90
    context dynamics, 67, 69, 77, 85, 86, 88, 89
    culture change, 16, 118, 119
    evangelizing. *See* evangelizing, church
    ever reforming, 21, 41, 89, 90, 137
    gathered, 62, 71, 74, 80
    gathered and sent, 72, 73, 74, 75, 87
    growth, 6, 20, 40, 56, 58, 59, 89, 90
    growth strategies, 2, 47, 48
    homogenous unit principle, 4, 42
    holy and human, 63
    identity, 10, 47
    inherently translatable, 65
    institutional program, 68
    invisible, 69
    in mission, 47
    multicultural, 70, 75
    overly contextualized, 67
    and personal-rights and political coalition
    church, 68
    relational, 63
    suburban family church, 68
    village-folk church, 67, 68
    welcoming, 76, 86, 89, 128
    witnessing, 128
clergy, 21, 34, 35, 43, 46, 47
clericalism, 21,34, 40, 43, 48, 49, 113, 115, 116,
    133, 136
comfort zones, vii, 71–91, 114, 115, 128, 143
Communion. *See* Lord's Supper
confession (of sin), 26, 83
contextualization, 7, 47, 65–67, 76, 86

conversion, 20, 33, 44, 103

covenant, vii, 15, 29, 53

cross, 5, 14, 26, 40, 43, 44, 52, 62, 77, 83, 85, 97,
102, 104–7, 109, 111, 112, 136, 146
of the risen Christ, 106, 107

crusading, 4, 100, 102, 104, 105

Devil, 16, 17, 22, 51, 63, 78

dialogue, 100, 102, 103, 110

discipleship, 6, 20, 21, 22, 25, 26, 30, 47, 55, 56,
62, 75, 76, 77, 80, 81, 84, 96, 107,111

discipline of community, 26

ecclesiology, 5, 9, 22, 28, 40, 46, 47, 73

ecumenism, 4, 21, 47

ekklesia, 55, 71, 90, 91, 143

ELCA, vii, ix, 3, 4, 5, 14, 26, 27, 65, 72, 73, 79, 86,
87, 93, 118, 127, 128, 137, 138
demographics, 72
evangelism initiative, 72
Evangelism Task Force, ix, 76
Mission Statement, 65
"Toward a Vision for Evangelism Report,"
87

election, 53, 54

engagement with conviction, 110, 111, 112

Enlightenment, 18

eschatology, 28, 60, 62, 64, 83, 105–7, 126,
and community, 61
and vision, 16

ethnic idolatry, 113, 118, 119, 133

evangelical, ix, 6
calling, x
identity, 4, 48, 37, 49, 50
and Lutheran, vii, 4, 26, 27, 34
missional church, 18, 35, 37
proclamation, vii, 4, 37, 39, 40, 42, 44, 45,
47, 73

Evangelicals, 4, 114, 120, 144

evangelism, vii, 3, 6, 7, 9, 22, 28, 32, 33, 38, 47,
52, 66, 71, 72, 73, 81, 82, 114, 115, 139
death of, 10, 113, 114, 116, 118, 119, 127,
132, 133, 137, 144, 146
paralysis of, 22
violent evangelization, 104, 105

Evangelism Explosion, 2

evangelist, 18, 34, 40, 47, 81, 115, 117, 123

evangelizing, 1, 5–9, 26, 27, 32–35, 38, 39, 41, 42,
44–49, 51, 52, 55, 56, 58, 62, 65, 66,
71, 75, 80, 88, 93–96, 102–4, 106, 109,
111–14, 121, 123, 129, 139
by baptized, 34, 116
biblical foundations for, 7, 8, 52–60
center of church's mission, 5, 33, 37, 38, 45,
47–50, 85, 87
church, vii, 3, 4, 6, 26, 37, 41, 44, 45, 48, 70,
102, 107, 109, 114, 135, 137, 146

church, gathers and scatters, 46, 62

church, obstacles to, vii, 18–21, 34, 36, 39,
41, 113, 144

congregations, 10, 46, 47, 78, 79–82, 84, 89

church culture, 8, 34, 44–47, 73,76–80, 86,
87, 89, 90, 114–24, 128–32, 141, 143

identity, 35, 37, 40, 47, 50, 55, 62, 71–73,
76, 85, 114, 127, 143
from Lutheran perspective, 3, 4, 7–9, 34,
35, 113, 114
Lutheran skepticism of, 1–3, 33
pragmatic, vii, 2–4, 6, 9, 12, 32, 44, 71, 72,
76, 87, 93, 103, 114, 115
resurrection of evangelizing church, 10, 113,
114, 116, 119, 127–130, 132, 141, 144
romanticized, 2, 3
Spirit-led, 58, 59, 66
strategic, 58, 59, 66
theological foundations for, ix, 4, 6, 8, 35,
44, 45, 61, 95, 100, 101, 144
Trinitarian foundations, 8, 124
verbal dimension of, 45, 60, 65, 79, 106–7,
126, 127

faith, 14, 19, 20, 22, 26, 39, 45, 52, 60, 62, 75, 90,
94, 95, 98, 101–2, 117, 134

for the sake of the World, vii, 8, 10, 13, 23, 51–73,
80, 82, 84–86, 89, 90, 137, 143

forgiveness, 2, 13,16, 20, 22, 26, 30, 42, 46, 53, 55,
62, 63, 76, 79, 82–84, 94, 96, 115, 123,
129, 133, 134

freedom, 12, 13, 22, 28, 29, 31, 54, 82, 84, 89,
135, 136
from sin for service, 20, 21, 28, 29, 84, 113,
135, 136

Freedom of a Christian, 21, 22

gift. *See* grace

gift and call, 8, 9, 10, 11–31, 36, 37, 44, 49, 52,
53, 56, 73, 76, 80–82, 84, 90, 114, 137,
140, 141, 146
to evangelizing, 37–40

global church, 21, 23, 122, 123, 144

globalization, 66

God
action of, 5, 19, 20, 27, 35, 76, 78, 87, 101,
122, 134
comes down in Jesus, 6, 11–13, 15, 21, 31,
39
hidden and revealed, 101
reconciling intent of, 72–75, 77
redemptive intent of, 52–56, 61, 64, 72
right and left hand of, 99, 101
solidarity with humanity, 105–7, 136

good works, 19, 20, 22–25, 137

gospel, 2–4, 6, 8–11, 13–15, 18–21, 23, 26, 29, 33,
34, 36, 38, 40, 42–45, 47, 51–54,

gospel (*continued*)
          56, 58–61, 63, 65, 66, 68, 69, 74, 83,
          89, 96, 100, 101, 103, 107, 109, 113,
          114, 120, 133, 134, 146
     crossing boundaries, 16, 56–59, 65
     and culture, 33, 59, 67
     inherently translatable, 65, 66
grace, vii, 5, 7, 10, 12, 19, 21, 22, 25, 26, 28, 30,
          31, 37–39, 41, 44, 47, 49, 60, 63, 73,
          75, 76, 79, 80, 83, 84, 86, 87, 90, 94,
          98–103, 110, 123, 129, 134, 137, 139
     cheap grace, 6, 25, 26, 31, 137
     costly grace, 25, 26
Great Commandment, 80
Great Commission, ix, 23, 80, 113
Heidelberg Disputation, 105, 106
hell, 94, 107
Hinduism, 124
Holocaust, 104
Holy Spirit, vii, 13, 16, 17, 20, 51, 52, 55, 56, 58,
          60–65, 69, 73–77, 83, 87, 103, 119,
          121, 123, 125, 126, 136, 137, 142, 146
human action, 5, 12, 13, 19, 20, 22, 40, 80, 121
imagination, 6, 9, 10, 16, 17, 35, 40, 41, 50, 61
incarnation, 39, 52, 65, 97
individualism, 18, 94
indulgences, 13
Islam, 95, 96, 104, 105, 123
Jesus
     alone, 98, 99, 134
     comes to people, 41, 44–47, 50, 134
     comes with a call, 12–13, 15, 20, 26–31, 40,
          137
     concretely present in Christian community,
          10, 38–40, 44, 45, 62, 64, 125
     concretely present but hidden, 39
     cosmic, 99
     encountering, 35, 36, 38–41, 63, 65, 129,
          135
     historic, 99
Jubilee, 36
Judaism, 123
justification, 3, 6, 9, 21, 33, 43, 83, 106
     and evangelizing, 21, 37
     and salvation by grace through faith, 2, 4,
          12, 19–21, 23, 31, 37, 68, 81, 113, 135
katallasso, 83
kingdom of God, 7, 15–17, 19, 37, 42, 43, 52, 54,
          55, 60, 64, 74, 81, 83, 87, 100, 111,
          126, 129, 135, 142
     already/not yet, 16, 17, 60, 64, 89, 101
     and church, 55
     as mystery, 54
     inaugurated by Christ, 17, 52, 54, 100
laity, 9, 23, 33, 34, 116

Large Catechism, 16
law, 23, 28, 66, 99, 134
     and gospel, 7, 19, 61, 85, 99–101, 113
LCMS, 46
liberalism, 18, 20
Lilly Endowment, ix, 7
"listen, discern, speak, and act," 73, 74, 76, 77–82,
          85, 87
Lord's Supper, 5, 26, 39, 43, 46, 49, 62, 63,
          113, 126, 137. *See also* Word and
          Sacrament
     Eucharistic evangelism, 47, 62
Lutheran
     centrality of Jesus Christ, 113, 114, 133,
          134, 146
     confessing, ix, 1, 3, 4, 25, 35, 44, 47, 129
     confessional tradition, ix, 3, 8, 9, 34, 37, 61,
          92, 113, 139, 142
     confessional tradition and evangelizing,
          60–65
     confessional tradition, captivity of, ix, 3
     confessions, 6, 20, 33
     decline, 4, 12, 14, 24, 25, 32, 35, 46, 72, 93,
          140
     dialectics, 7, 99, 100, 101
     evangelizing ineffectiveness, 4, 40, 42, 44,
          45, 72, 73, 92, 113, 132, 138
     exclusivism, 98, 99, 100
     heritage, 1, 3–7, 9, 10, 13, 14, 35, 37, 41, 47,
          49, 50, 114, 128, 131, 133
     historic documents, 6, 22
     hermeneutic, 9, 99
     inaction, 9, 12, 15, 19, 20, 23, 24
     inclusivism, 101
     lack of evangelical power, 1, 14, 21, 36, 73
     and northern European ethnicity, 3, 4, 12,
          18, 42, 48, 68, 79, 92, 118, 139
     theological pride, 19, 44
     theology, ix, 3, 6, 8, 19, 33, 35, 40, 44, 48,
          50, 93, 98, 101, 109, 113, 120, 134,
          137
Lutheran World Federation, 21, 35, 65, 77, 124
Luther's Works, 22
mainline decline, 36, 86, 93
martyria, 85
means of grace, 10, 39, 41, 44, 45, 46, 47, 48, 50,
          74, 80, 113, 115, 121, 135
meta-narrative, 108, 109, 118
metanoia, 15
ministry, ix, 5
     of the baptized, 14, 34, 46, 48, 49, 81, 116,
          123, 136, 146
     equipping baptized for, 33, 46, 47, 81, 82,
          89, 116, 123, 136
     ineffectiveness of, 36

ministry (*continued*)
    on the margins, 59, 90, 111
mission, xi, 5–7, 14, 17, 20, 21, 23, 24, 26–28,
        35, 41, 45–50, 55, 56, 58, 60, 66, 75,
        83, 102
    of the church, 8, 15, 26, 28, 36, 50, 55, 61,
        65, 70, 73–77, 87–91, 111, 126, 127,
        137
    and confession, 3, 4, 6, 34, 35, 37, 47
    to everyone everywhere, 1, 6, 23, 50, 52–57,
        60, 61, 65, 67, 73, 75
    of God (*Missio Dei*), x, 8, 15–17, 21, 28, 31,
        35–38, 44, 49–52, 55, 57, 61–65, 70,
        71, 73, 75–77, 81, 85–87, 89–91, 117,
        125, 126, 133, 136, 142
    in reverse, 46, 70
    lack of among Lutherans after Luther,
        22–24
    overseas, 6, 69
    societies, 115
    theology, 5, 6
    vision for, 36, 37, 42, 48, 76, 78, 80
missional, 35, 64
    church, 37, 44, 47, 49, 50, 73–75, 76, 80
    ecclesiology, 40, 46, 47, 50
    engagement, ix
    hermeneutic, 3, 9, 44, 60, 61, 90
    identity, vii, 27, 28, 31, 35, 37, 49, 55, 60,
        71, 90
modernity, 67, 108, 109
multicultural church, 49
mutual conversation and consolation, 10, 46, 53,
        63, 64, 73, 74, 126
neighbor, 14, 22, 30, 35, 49, 78, 81, 84, 103, 120,
        136
outreach, 6, 27
office of the Keys, 46, 63, 64
Orthodox (Eastern) theology, 124
orthodoxy, 22–24, 41, 110
particularity, 53, 65, 98, 102
pastoral ministry, 116
    discern gifts, 136
    to evangelize, 39, 42, 47, 113, 116, 121, 136
    See also ministry, equipping
Pentecost, 56, 74, 119
Pentecostals, 4, 114, 121, 144
perichoresis, 125
Pietism, 23, 115
Pietists, 23, 24, 41, 140
post-Christendom, 18, 27, 35, 37, 47
postmodernity, 8, 18, 27, 67, 93, 94, 107, 108,
        109, 110, 111, 117, 144
    bridges to, 67
    and centerless society, 108
    nihilism, 67

    and relativism, 12, 67
practical theology, 45
prayer, 5, 26, 27, 33, 44, 73–78, 80, 84, 85, 87,
        120, 123, 129
pre-Christian culture, 27
priesthood of believers, 14, 21, 23, 43, 46, 81, 82,
        123, 136
principalities and powers, 60, 63, 66, 83, 85, 106
privatization of faith, 12, 113, 115–118, 133
proclamation, 4, 5, 22, 29, 36, 41–44, 47, 58, 71,
        75, 80, 106, 107, 113, 122, 126. *See
        also* evangelical, proclamation
proselytism, 2, 95
realm of creation/realm of redemption, 99
reconciliation, 16, 34, 53, 61, 72, 73, 75, 77, 79,
        82–85, 87, 103, 110, 136, 143
redemption, 6, 51, 53, 54, 57, 61, 62, 64, 84, 87,
        100
reformers, later, 19, 22
reign of God. *See* kingdom of God
renewal, 44, 46, 48
repentance, 15, 26, 37, 54, 75, 96, 107, 113, 120,
        132
resurrection, 44, 62, 84, 89, 102, 105–107, 113,
        136, 146
revivalism, 6, 115
Roman Catholic, 19, 83, 114, 122, 144
salvation, 2, 4, 12, 13, 15, 19, 20, 22, 23, 25, 28,
        29, 31, 38, 39, 52, 54, 61, 97, 98, 100,
        103, 134. *See also* justification
sanctification, 2, 13, 20, 46, 62, 64, 137
"Saturday people," 106–7
self-organizing systems, 87–89
sending, ix, 15, 16, 29, 31, 46, 47, 49, 51, 52,
        62–65, 71–76, 85, 96, 97, 125–27, 129,
        136, 143
service, 13, 14, 21–23, 26–31, 50, 53, 54, 63, 64,
        75, 76, 78, 81, 82, 84, 85, 89
simul justus et peccator, 7, 85, 89, 101, 109, 133,
        134
simuls, 100–101, 102, 134, 135, 144, 146
simuls and solas, 8, 9, 89, 101, 102, 111
sin, 5, 12, 19, 22, 28, 30, 51, 53, 60–63, 83, 106,
        110, 113, 115, 120, 125, 135
Smalcald Articles, 10, 63, 126
Small Catechism, 65, 82
socio-economic class, 18, 40, 43, 93
solas, 98, 99, 101, 102, 134, 144, 146
sōtēria, 98
sōthenai, 98
speaking the faith, 128, 129, 130, 131, 137
spiritual disciplines, 5, 40
spirituality, 67, 110, 111, 117
theology
    confessional, ix

theology (*continued*)
    of the cross, 7, 8, 44, 104–7, 110, 111, 113,
        136, 144
    decision, 2, 33, 115, 120
    of embrace, 107
    of engagement, 100–101
    of glory, 43, 105, 106
    systematic, and evangelizing, 45
    transformation, 7, 14, 19, 22, 23, 42, 44, 60, 76,
        78, 79, 85, 88–90, 105, 130,
    trinity, x, 16, 51, 71, 73, 75, 117, 118, 124–28,
        132, 133, 137, 144
    as communion, 124–26
    church communing with, 125, 130, 136
    drawing creation into divine communion,
        136
    foundation for evangelizing, 8, 124
Trinitarian missiology, 124
two-kingdoms doctrine, 7, 113
United States of America, 3–5, 9, 14, 21, 26, 27,
    34, 36, 40, 66, 69, 86, 92, 94, 108, 113
    and civil rights movement, 69
    glory and success orientation of, 5, 43, 44,
        68
    as increasingly non-churched, 27, 44, 93,
        107, 108
    as increasingly secular, 4, 86, 93
    as mission context, 26, 27, 36, 85, 86
    as multiscriptural society, 98
    and plurality, vii, 2, 4, 5, 18, 35, 44, 66, 79,
        86, 93–100, 102, 103, 108, 109, 111,
        112, 144

post-Christendom, 18
    and slavery, 69
    spiritual hunger in, 12, 26, 27
universality, 53, 65, 96, 102, 122
"unreached," 103
vocation, 14, 46, 61, 64, 81
Wesleyan, 33
witness, ix, 13, 14, 16, 17, 21, 26, 27, 29–31, 45,
    53, 56, 60, 73, 75, 76, 80–83, 85, 90,
    95, 96, 98, 102, 103, 120–23, 131
    of congregation, 72, 74, 85, 87, 90, 91, 110,
        111, 128
word, 3, 22, 42, 48, 58, 65, 81, 97, 98, 99, 113,
    121, 126, 135, 136
    as captive, 42–44, 45
Word and Sacrament, 8–10, 20, 37, 40, 41, 49, 61,
    62–64, 73, 76, 77, 79, 81, 83, 101, 111,
    115, 116, 126, 129, 135, 136
    captivity of, 40–44, 141
    as inherently missional, 8, 61, 62
Word, Sacrament, and community, 7–11, 35–47,
    49, 50, 73, 74, 87, 88, 113, 115, 116,
    129, 135, 136, 141, 146
    as foundation for mission, 49
    human dimension of, 39
worship, 5, 16, 21, 36, 55, 62, 65, 74–76, 87–89,
    126, 128, 129, 135
    evangelizing and, 29, 135, 146

INDEX OF NAMES

Ariarajah, Wesley, 144
Augustine, 126
Barth, Karl, 124
Bliese, Richard, ix, xi, 8, 79; editor, author ch. 3,
    co-author ch. 1
Bonhoeffer, Dietrich, vii, 6, 25, 40, 41, 137, 140,
    140, 141
Bowen, John, 144
Briese, Russell, 81, 82, 114, 147
Bullock, M. Wyvetta, xi, 8; author ch. 5
Bush, George W., 104
D'Aviano, Marco, 104
Douglas, Frederick, 122
Finney, Charles, 18
Franke, August H., 23
Fryer, Kelly, xi, 8, 143; author ch. 2
Funck, John, 19
Gibson, Mel, 107, 109
Graham, Billy, 18
Guder, Darrell, 139, 143
Hanson, Mark, vii, 14, 128; author foreword
Hunter, George, 127, 146
Jenkins, Philip, 122
John of Damascus, 125
Kallenberg, Brad, 144
Keillor, Garrison, 92
King, Martin Luther, Jr., 122
Kierkegaard, Søren, 24, 25, 41, 140
Kolb, Robert, 114, 141
Krauth, Charles, 3
Lindbeck, George, 110
Linn, Jan, 127, 147
Luther, Martin, 5, 6, 7, 10, 12, 13, 14, 16, 17, 19,
    21, 22, 24, 35, 41, 43, 44, 45, 46, 63,
    64, 65, 70, 71, 75, 81, 82, 105, 106,
    113, 121, 135, 139, 140, 140, 141, 142

Mead, Sidney, 115
Moody, D. L., 18
Nessan, Craig, xi-xii, 8, 9, 144; author ch. 7,
    epilogue
Noll, Mark, 1, 7
Olson, Mark, 146
John Paul II, Pope, 104
Paul IV, Pope, 122
Potok, Chaim, 94
Rajashekar, J. Paul, xii, 8; author ch. 6
Rahner, Gunter, 32, 35
Scherer, James, 35, 81
Schlottoff, Bernd, 32
Schmalzie, Bob, 78
Schmucker, Samuel, 3
Schreiter, Robert, 78
Spener, Phillip J., 23
Stache, Kristine, xii
Stromberg, Peter, 127
Thomsen, Mark, 144
Tiede, David, x; author preface
Truth, Sojourner, 122
Tumsa, Gudina, 161
Van Gelder, Craig, ix, xii, 8, 139; editor, author
    ch. 4, co-author ch.1
Wheatley, Margaret, 88
Zizioulas, John, 124

Bible Names
Abraham, 53
Adam, 15
Andrew, 38
David, 53
Cornelius, 59, 69
Dorcas, 58

Elisha, 84
Isaiah, 30
James, 38
Jeremiah, 15, 53
John, 17, 38
Lazarus, 38
Levi, 38
Martha, 15, 77
Mary, 17, 77
Mary (mother of Jesus), 38
Moses, 53, 106
Naaman, 84
Nebuchadnezzar, 53
Noah, 53
Paul, 28, 29, 30, 57, 58, 59, 60, 91, 105

Peter, 17, 30, 59, 69, 75, 97, 139
Phillip, 90
Priscilla, 17
Samaritan woman, vii
Sarah, 15
Stephen, 17
Suffering Servant, 54
Syrophoenician woman, 38
Thomas, 38, 97

FICTIONAL CHARACTERS
Kirk, James, 108
Picard, Jean-Luc, 108